Dr. Radium
and the Gizmos
of Boola Boola!

The Dr. Radium Collection Volume One

By Scott Saavedra

Amaze Ink • An Imprint of SLG Publishing
San Jose, CA

Some material previously published in *GAKK, CHOKE, BLURG! It's Science with Dr. Radium* (collecting *It's Science with Dr. Radium Special* and *Dr. Radium and the Gizmos of Boola Boola*) and *Slave Labor Stories* #1.

ISBN 0-943151-92-9

Published by Amaze Ink, an imprint of
SLG Publishing, PO Box 26427, San Jose, CA 95159-6427
www.slavelabor.com

SLG President & Publisher: Dan Vado
Editor-In Chief: Jennifer de Guzman Belew
Director of Sales: Deb Moskyok

1st Printing, July 2004

Printed in Canada

ov rly complet contents page

Take a quick tour of Dr. Radium's World of Tomorrow in, um, "Dr. Radium's World of Tomorrow," over on page 5. A blob and a robot star in "The Substance" on page 12. Over on pages 20 and 26 are stories that, at first glance, appear to be parodies of Dr. Suess books and old horror comics of the fifties, respectively. In fact, the stories were an opportunity to write nonsense poetry and draw monsters, as I enjoy both activities. I have no idea why I've never done a monster poetry comic. A story, a "gag" page, and another story can be found on pages 33,42 and 43. "Do Scientists Dream of Electric Sheep?" was no doubt inspired by a significant period of insomnia and can be found on page 47. It originally appeared in SLAVE LABOR STORIES #1, a short-lived anthology comic. "Flee, Puny Humans!" began life about ten years ago as a proposed tenth anniversary of Dr. Radium comic book. I opted instead to celebrate Dr. Radium's tenth anniversary by not finishing the story. For this book I've dusted off the old art, rewrote the story, and added new pages (the new/old mix is 50/50). I've forgotten something... Oh, yeah. It begins on page 53. And finally, we have "Dr. Radium and the Gizmos of Boola Boola" on page 65. It's the longest Dr. Radium story I've ever written. I'm sure it has many other worthy attributes but you'll have to discover them for yourselves. Just because you've bought my book (you did buy it, didn't you?) doesn't mean I'm going to do all the work for you.

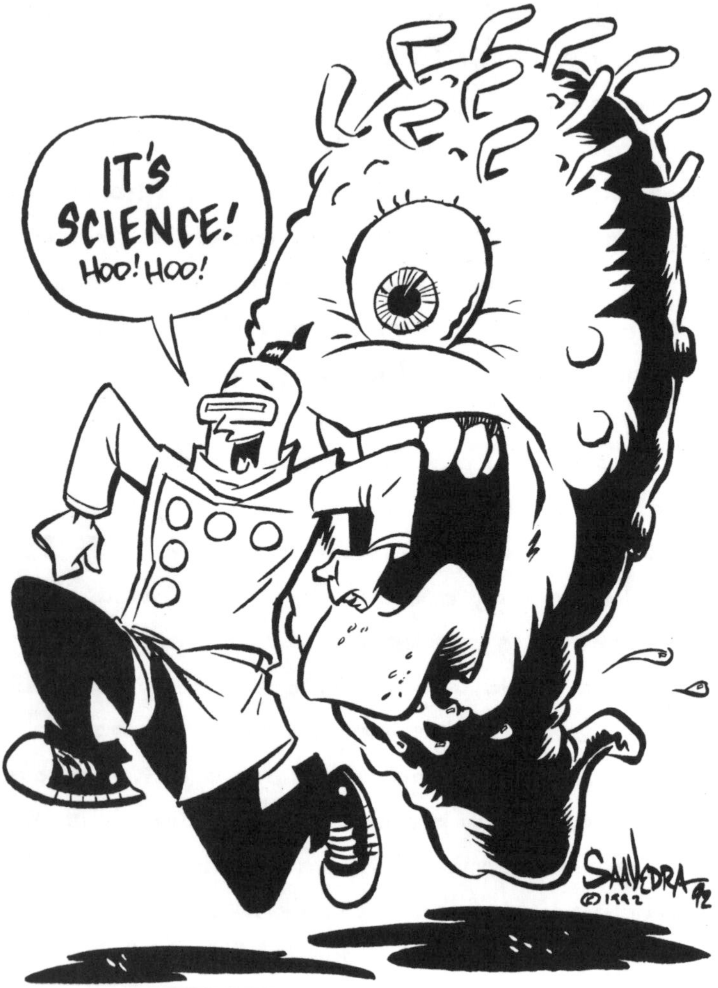
IT'S SCIENCE!
HOO! HOO!
SAAVEDRA 92
©1992

DR. RADIUM'S WORLD OF TOMORROW

(HUBBA-HUBBA, DING-DING!)

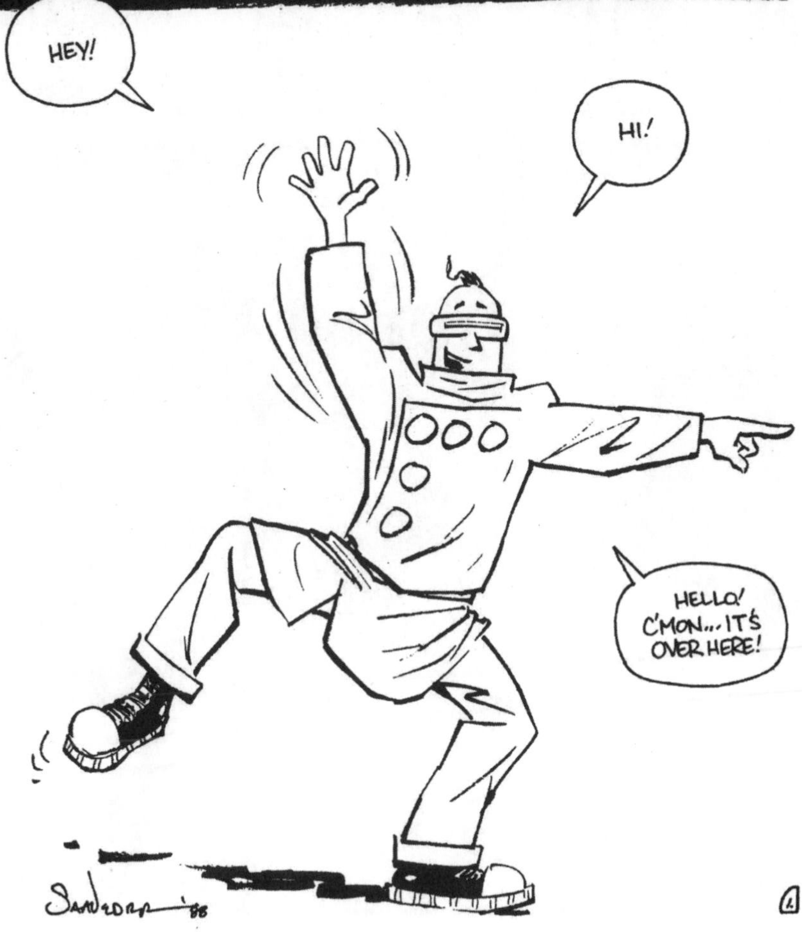
HEY!
HI!
HELLO! C'MON... IT'S OVER HERE!

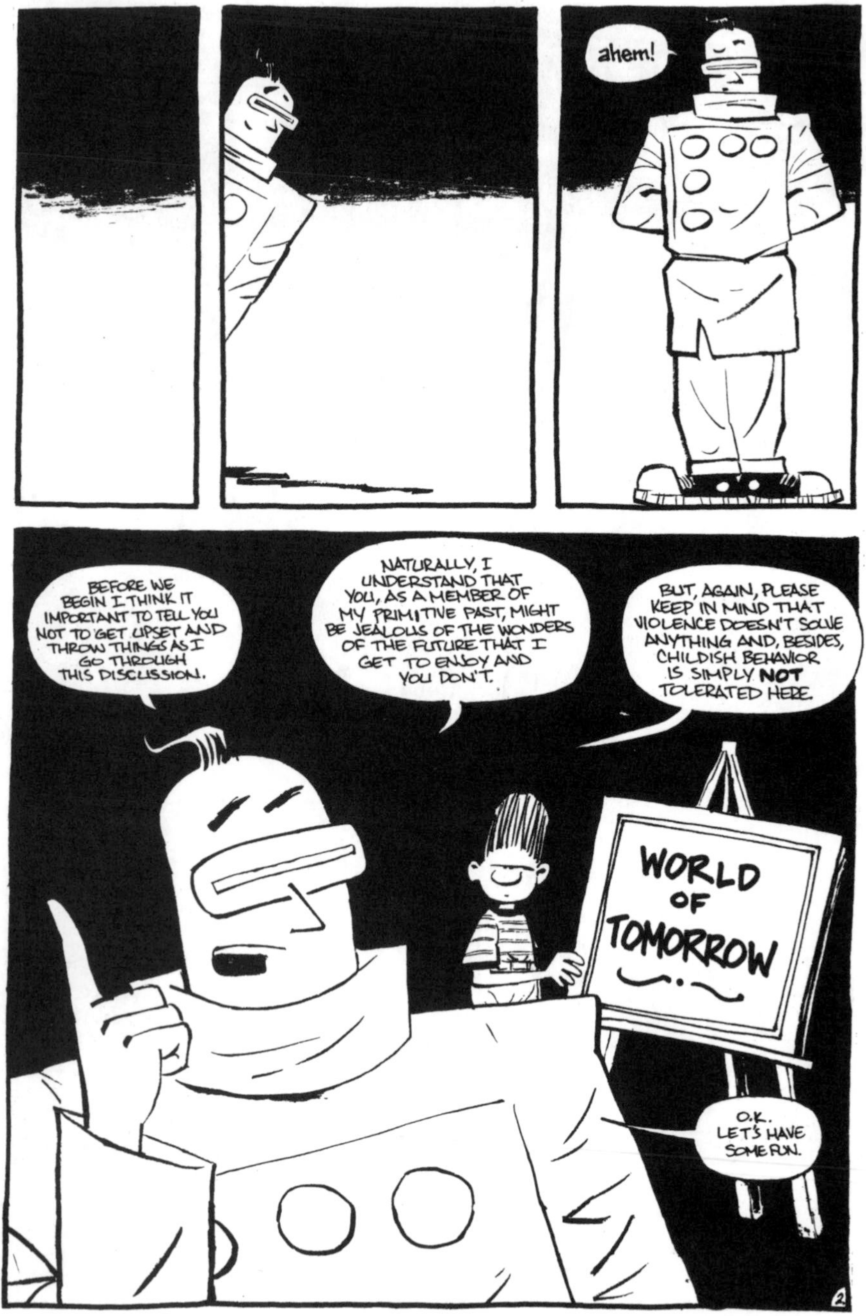
ahem!
BEFORE WE BEGIN I THINK IT IMPORTANT TO TELL YOU NOT TO GET UPSET AND THROW THINGS AS I GO THROUGH THIS DISCUSSION.
NATURALLY, I UNDERSTAND THAT YOU, AS A MEMBER OF MY PRIMITIVE PAST, MIGHT BE JEALOUS OF THE WONDERS OF THE FUTURE THAT I GET TO ENJOY AND YOU DON'T.
BUT, AGAIN, PLEASE KEEP IN MIND THAT VIOLENCE DOESN'T SOLVE ANYTHING AND, BESIDES, CHILDISH BEHAVIOR IS SIMPLY **NOT** TOLERATED HERE.
WORLD OF TOMORROW
O.K. LET'S HAVE SOME FUN.
2

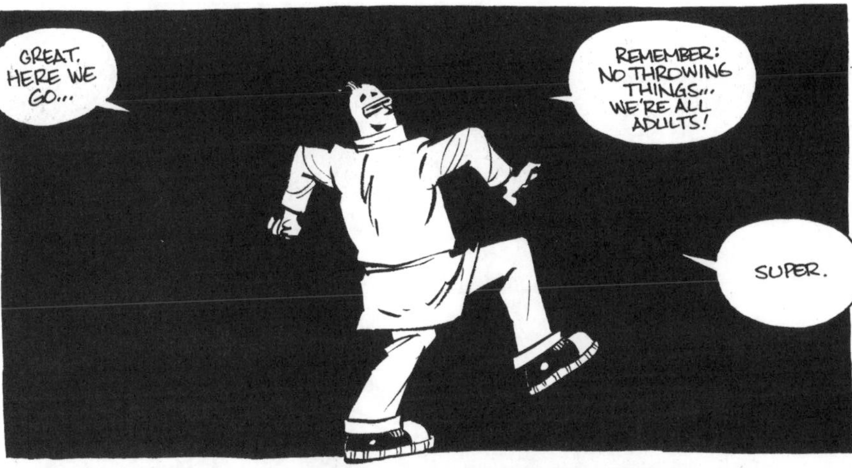
GREAT. HERE WE GO...
REMEMBER: NO THROWING THINGS... WE'RE ALL ADULTS!
SUPER.

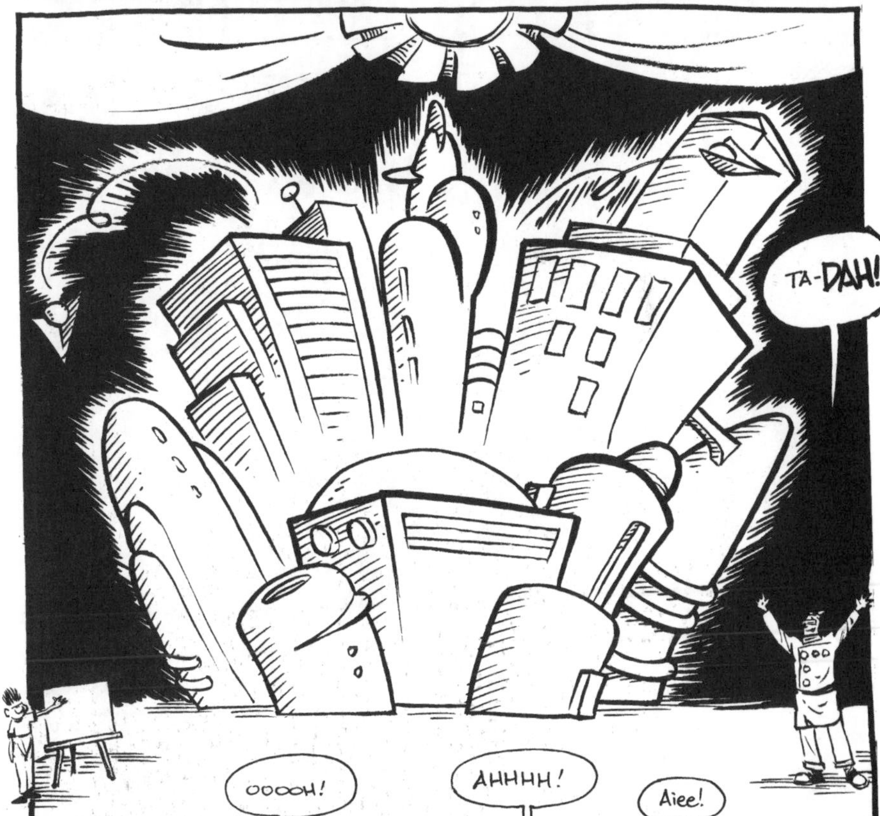
TA-DAH!
OOOOH!
AHHHH!
Aiee!

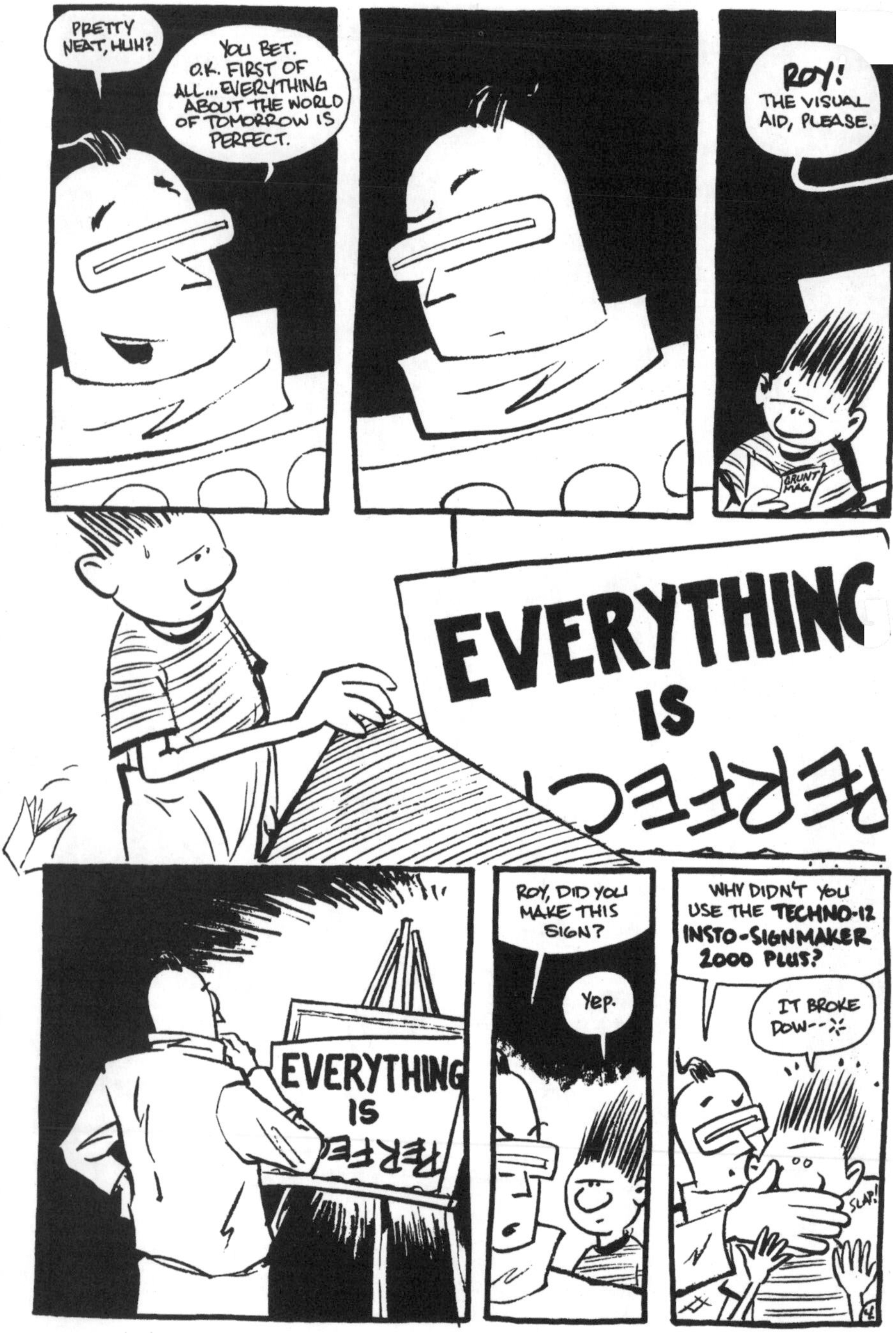
PRETTY NEAT, HUH?
YOU BET. O.K. FIRST OF ALL... EVERYTHING ABOUT THE WORLD OF TOMORROW IS PERFECT.
ROY! THE VISUAL AID, PLEASE.
GRUNT MAG
EVERYTHING IS PERFECT
EVERYTHING IS
ROY, DID YOU MAKE THIS SIGN?
Yep.
WHY DIDN'T YOU USE THE TECHNO-12 INSTO-SIGNMAKER 2000 PLUS?
IT BROKE DOW--
SLAP!

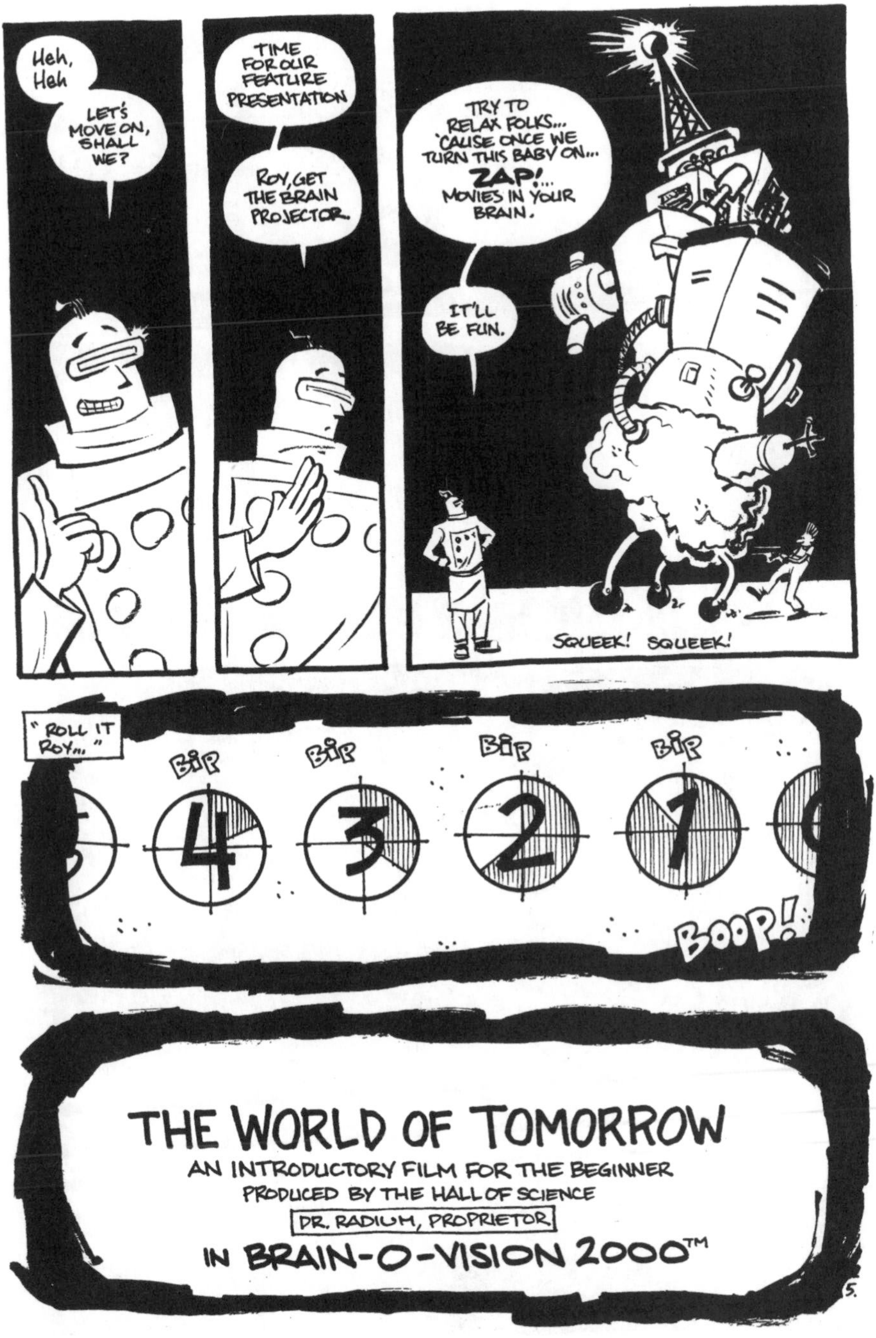
Heh, Heh
LET'S MOVE ON, SHALL WE?
TIME FOR OUR FEATURE PRESENTATION
ROY, GET THE BRAIN PROJECTOR.
TRY TO RELAX FOLKS... 'CAUSE ONCE WE TURN THIS BABY ON... ZAP!... MOVIES IN YOUR BRAIN.
IT'LL BE FUN.
SQUEEK! SQUEEK!
"ROLL IT ROY..."
BIP
BIP
BIP
BIP
4
3
2
1
BOOP!
THE WORLD OF TOMORROW
AN INTRODUCTORY FILM FOR THE BEGINNER
PRODUCED BY THE HALL OF SCIENCE
DR. RADIUM, PROPRIETOR
IN BRAIN-O-VISION 2000™
5.

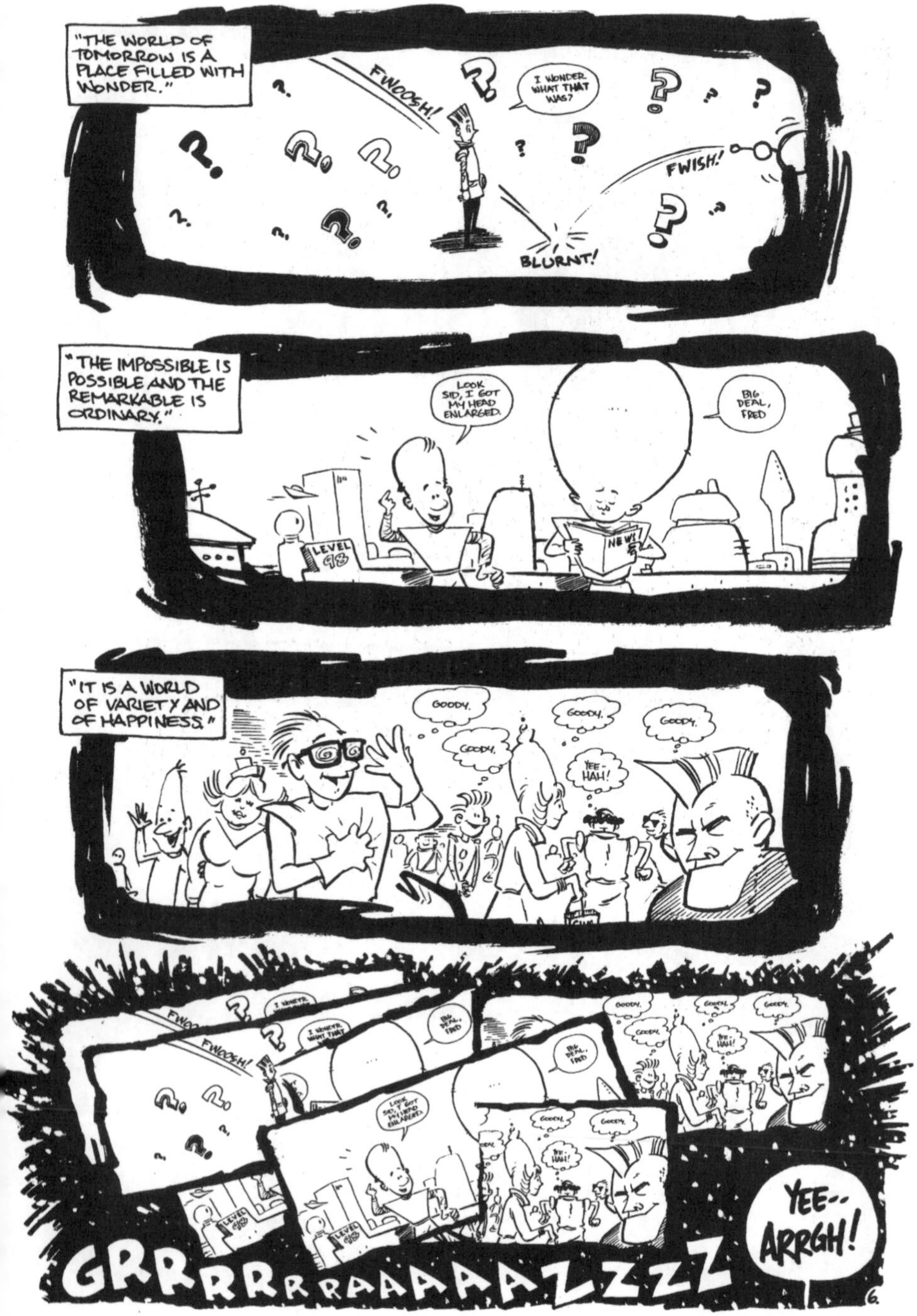
"THE WORLD OF TOMORROW IS A PLACE FILLED WITH WONDER."
FWOOSH!
I WONDER WHAT THAT WAS?
FWISH!
BLURNT!
"THE IMPOSSIBLE IS POSSIBLE AND THE REMARKABLE IS ORDINARY."
LOOK SID, I GOT MY HEAD ENLARGED.
...
BIG DEAL, FRED
LEVEL 98
NEWS
"IT IS A WORLD OF VARIETY AND OF HAPPINESS."
GOODY.
GOODY.
GOODY.
GOODY.
YEE-HAH!
GRRRRRAAAAAZZZZZ
YEE-- ARRGH!
6.

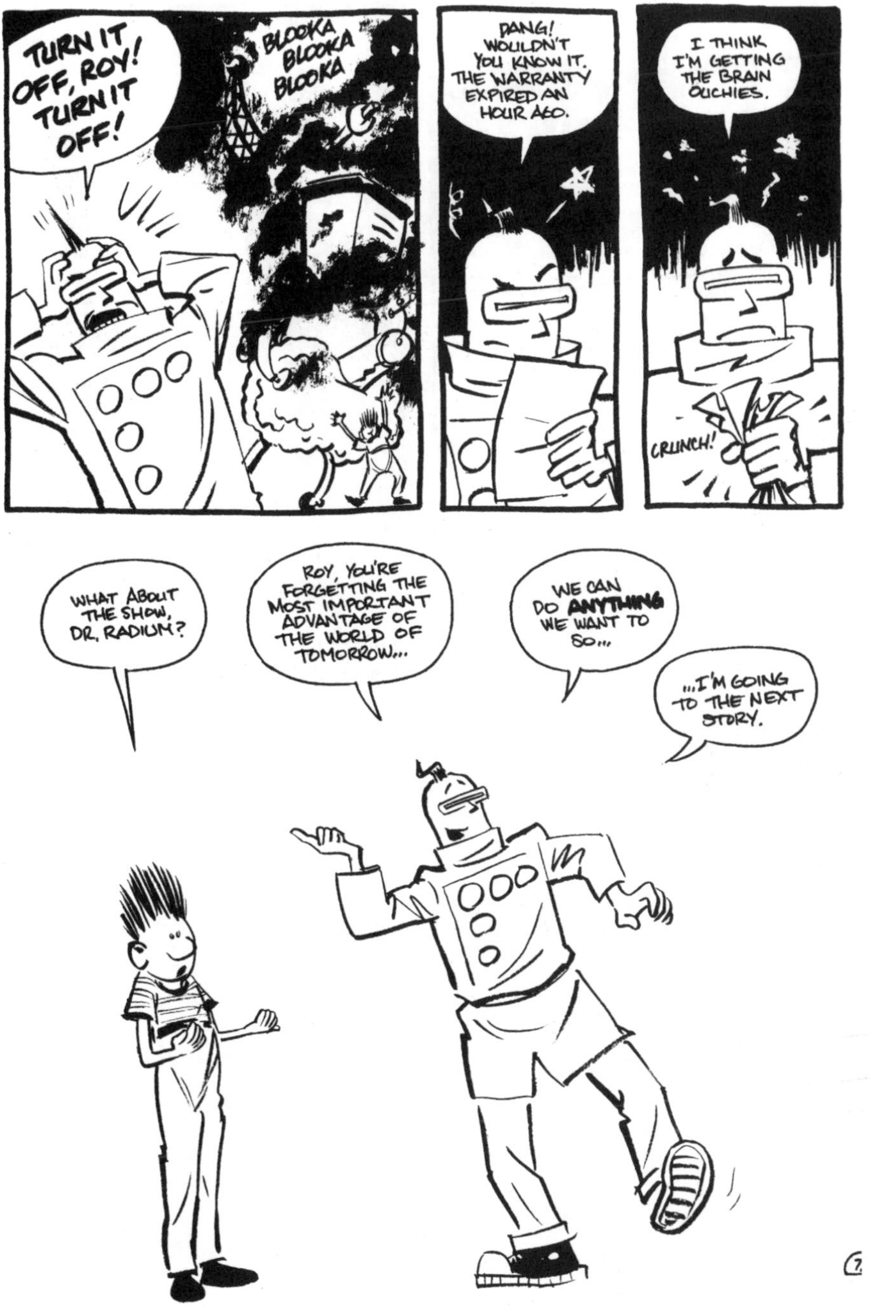
TURN IT OFF, ROY! TURN IT OFF!
BLOOKA BLOOKA BLOOKA
DANG! WOULDN'T YOU KNOW IT. THE WARRANTY EXPIRED AN HOUR AGO.
I THINK I'M GETTING THE BRAIN OUCHIES.
CRUNCH!
WHAT ABOUT THE SHOW, DR. RADIUM?
ROY, YOU'RE FORGETTING THE MOST IMPORTANT ADVANTAGE OF THE WORLD OF TOMORROW...
WE CAN DO ANYTHING WE WANT TO SO...
...I'M GOING TO THE NEXT STORY.

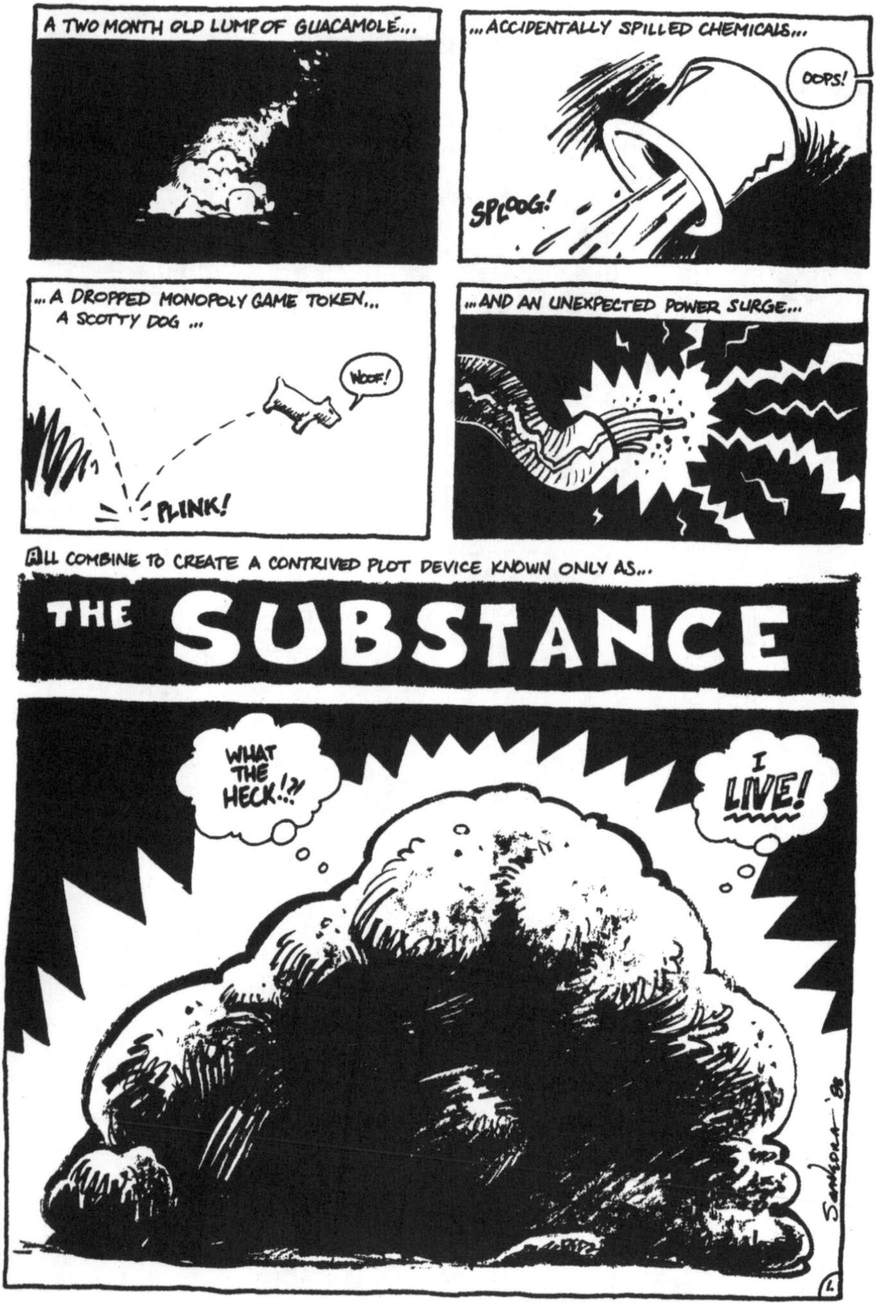
A TWO MONTH OLD LUMP OF GUACAMOLÉ...
...ACCIDENTALLY SPILLED CHEMICALS...
OOPS!
SPLOOG!
...A DROPPED MONOPOLY GAME TOKEN... A SCOTTY DOG ...
WOOF!
PLINK!
...AND AN UNEXPECTED POWER SURGE...
ALL COMBINE TO CREATE A CONTRIVED PLOT DEVICE KNOWN ONLY AS...
THE SUBSTANCE
WHAT THE HECK!?!
I LIVE!

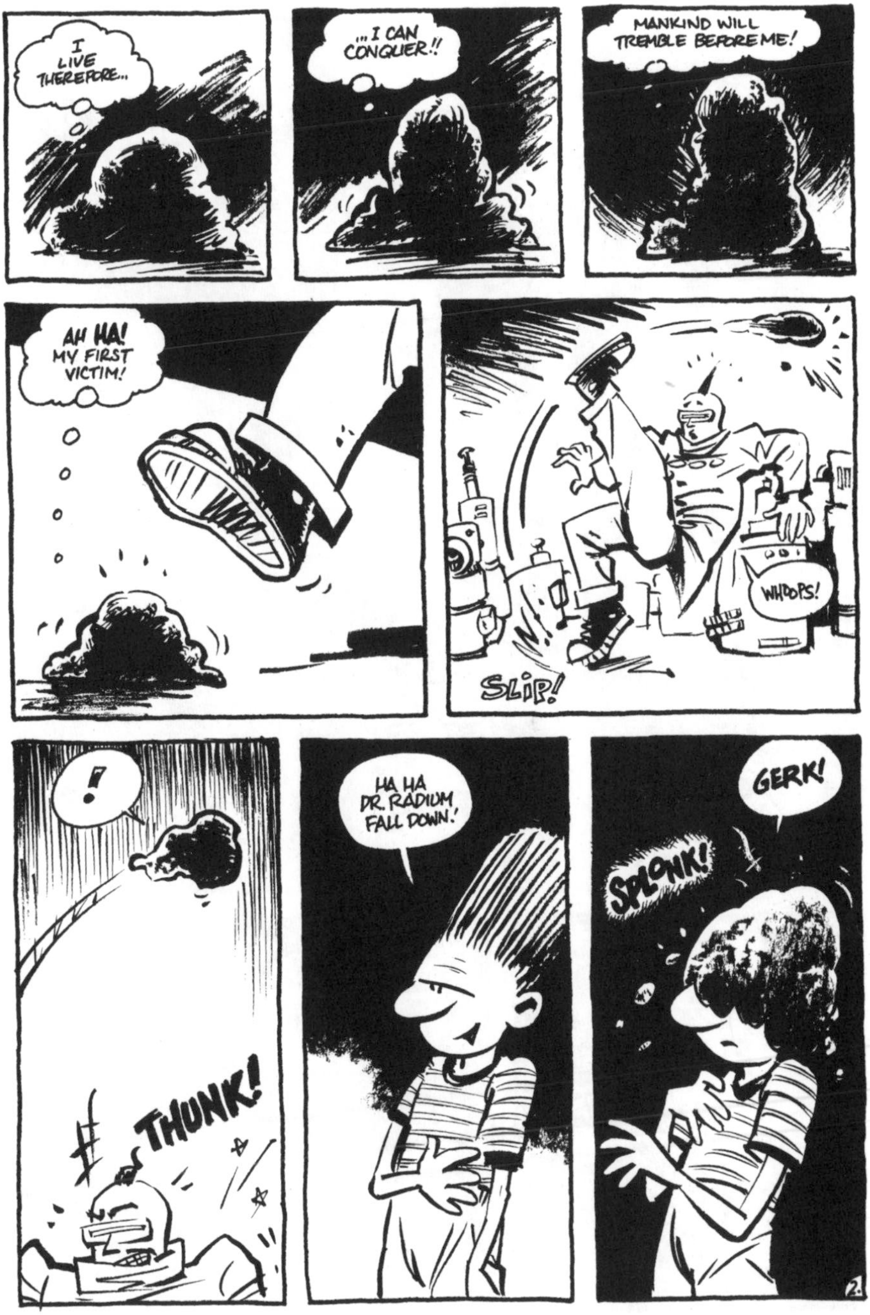

I LIVE THEREFORE...
...I CAN CONQUER!!
MANKIND WILL TREMBLE BEFORE ME!
AH HA! MY FIRST VICTIM!
WHOOPS!
SLIP!
!
THUNK!
HA HA DR. RADIUM FALL DOWN!
GERK!
SPLONK!
2.

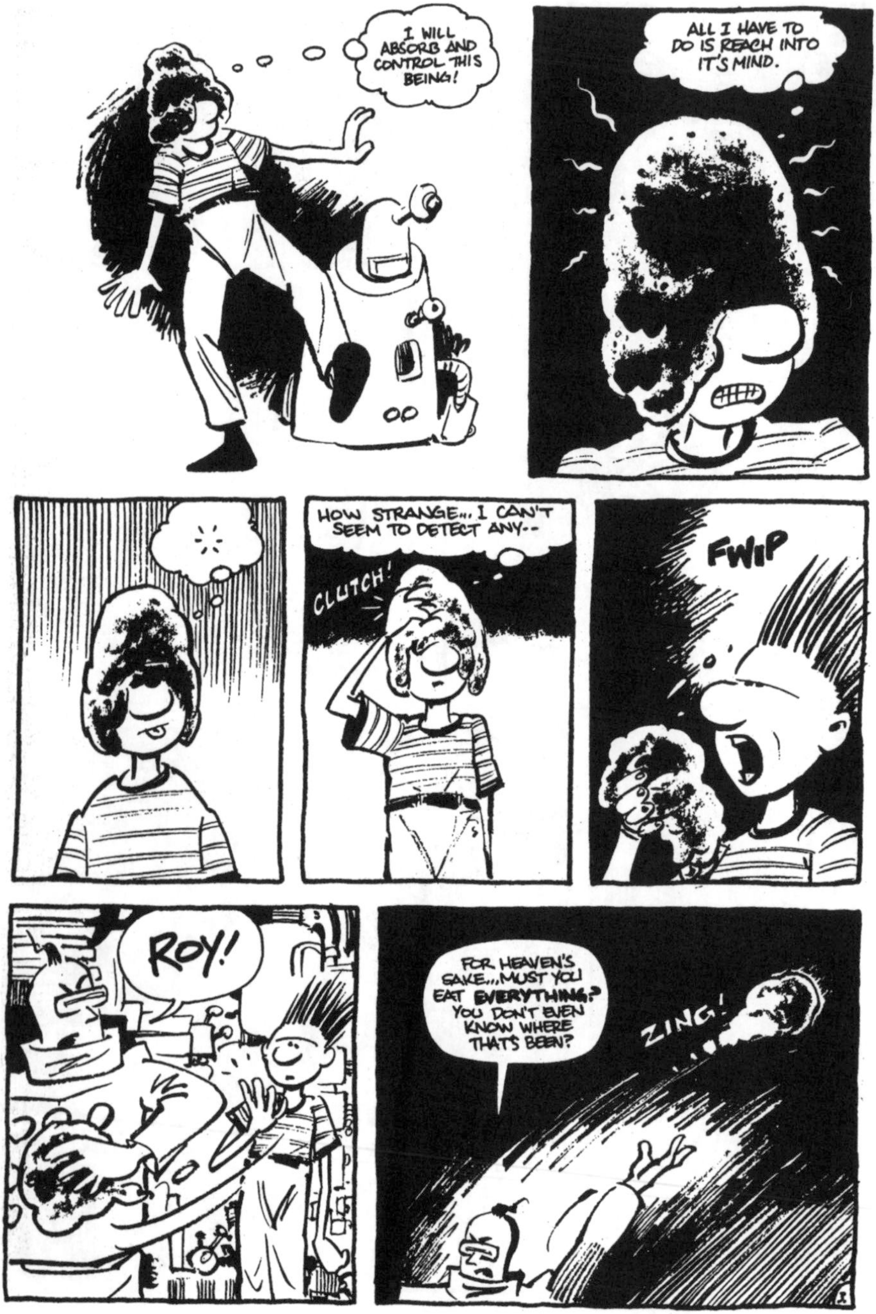
I WILL ABSORB AND CONTROL THIS BEING!
ALL I HAVE TO DO IS REACH INTO IT'S MIND.
HOW STRANGE... I CAN'T SEEM TO DETECT ANY--
CLUTCH!
FWIP
ROY!
FOR HEAVEN'S SAKE... MUST YOU EAT EVERYTHING? YOU DON'T EVEN KNOW WHERE THAT'S BEEN?
ZING!

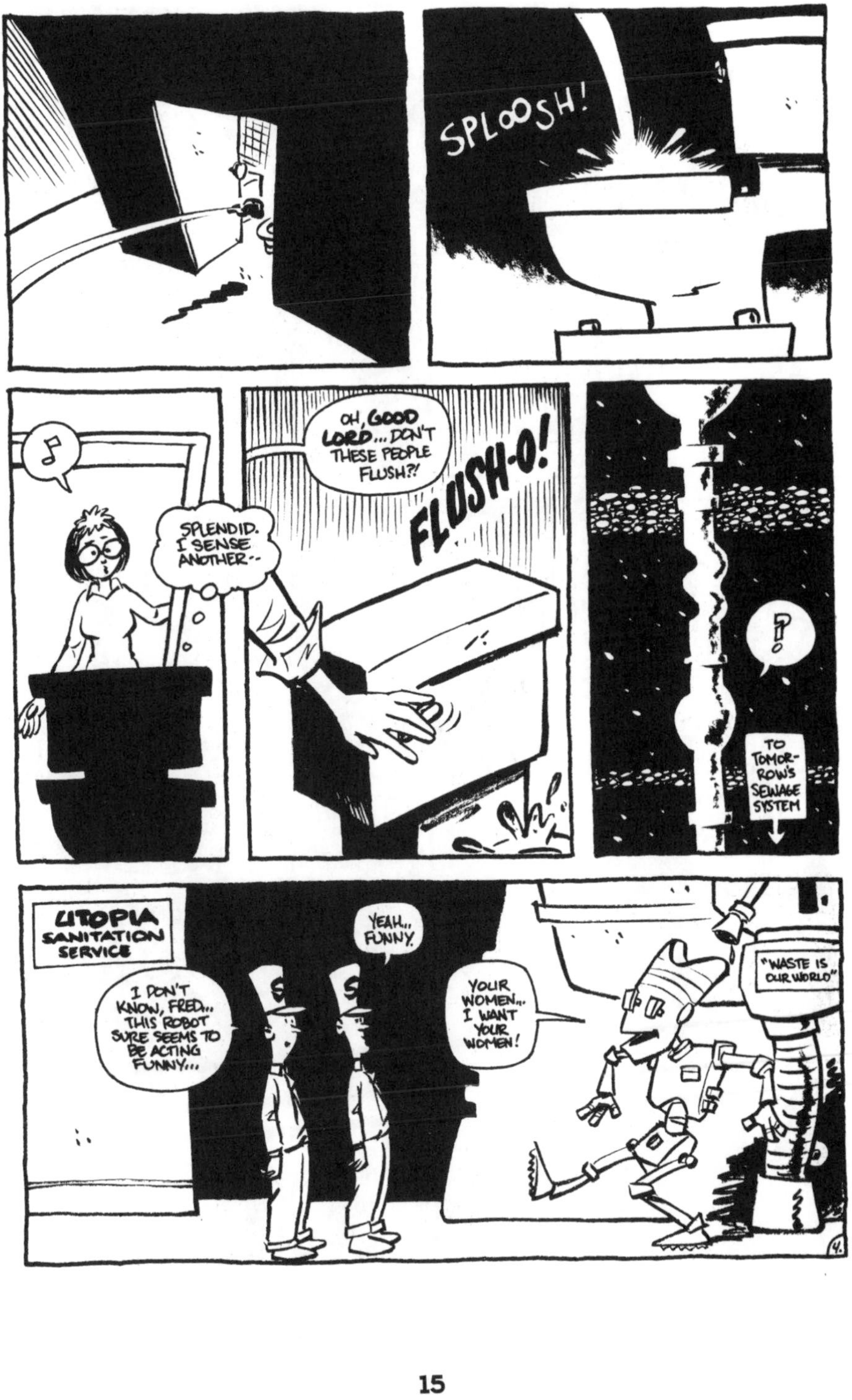
SPLOOSH!
♪
SPLENDID. I SENSE ANOTHER--
OH, GOOD LORD... DON'T THESE PEOPLE FLUSH?!
FLUSH-O!
?
TO TOMOR-ROW'S SEWAGE SYSTEM
UTOPIA SANITATION SERVICE
YEAH... FUNNY.
I DON'T KNOW, FRED... THIS ROBOT SURE SEEMS TO BE ACTING FUNNY...
YOUR WOMEN... I WANT YOUR WOMEN!
"WASTE IS OUR WORLD"
4.

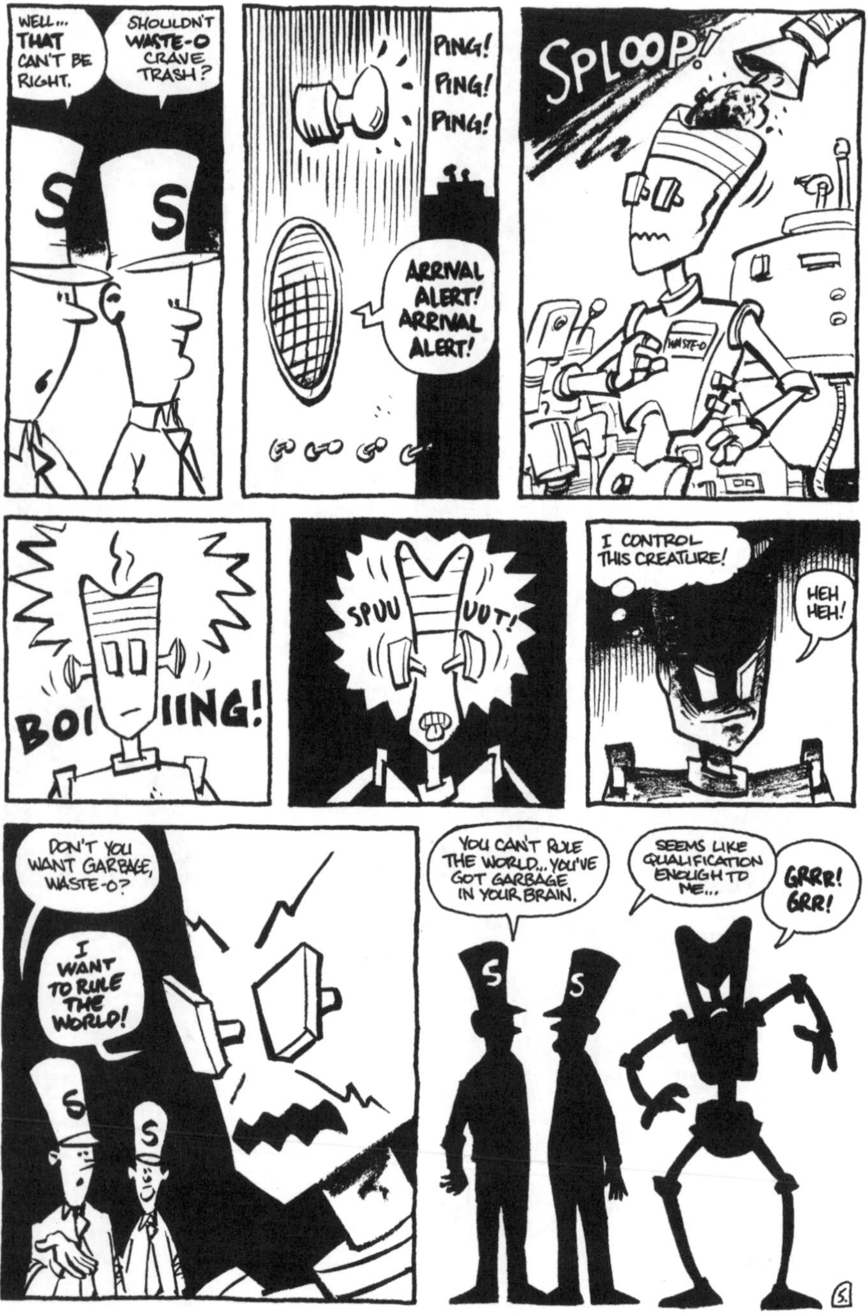
WELL... THAT CAN'T BE RIGHT.
SHOULDN'T WASTE-O CRAVE TRASH?
PING! PING! PING!
ARRIVAL ALERT! ARRIVAL ALERT!
SPLOOP!
WASTE-O
BOI IING!
SPUU UUT!
I CONTROL THIS CREATURE!
HEH HEH!
DON'T YOU WANT GARBAGE, WASTE-O?
I WANT TO RULE THE WORLD!
YOU CAN'T RULE THE WORLD... YOU'VE GOT GARBAGE IN YOUR BRAIN.
SEEMS LIKE QUALIFICATION ENOUGH TO ME...
GRRR! GRR!

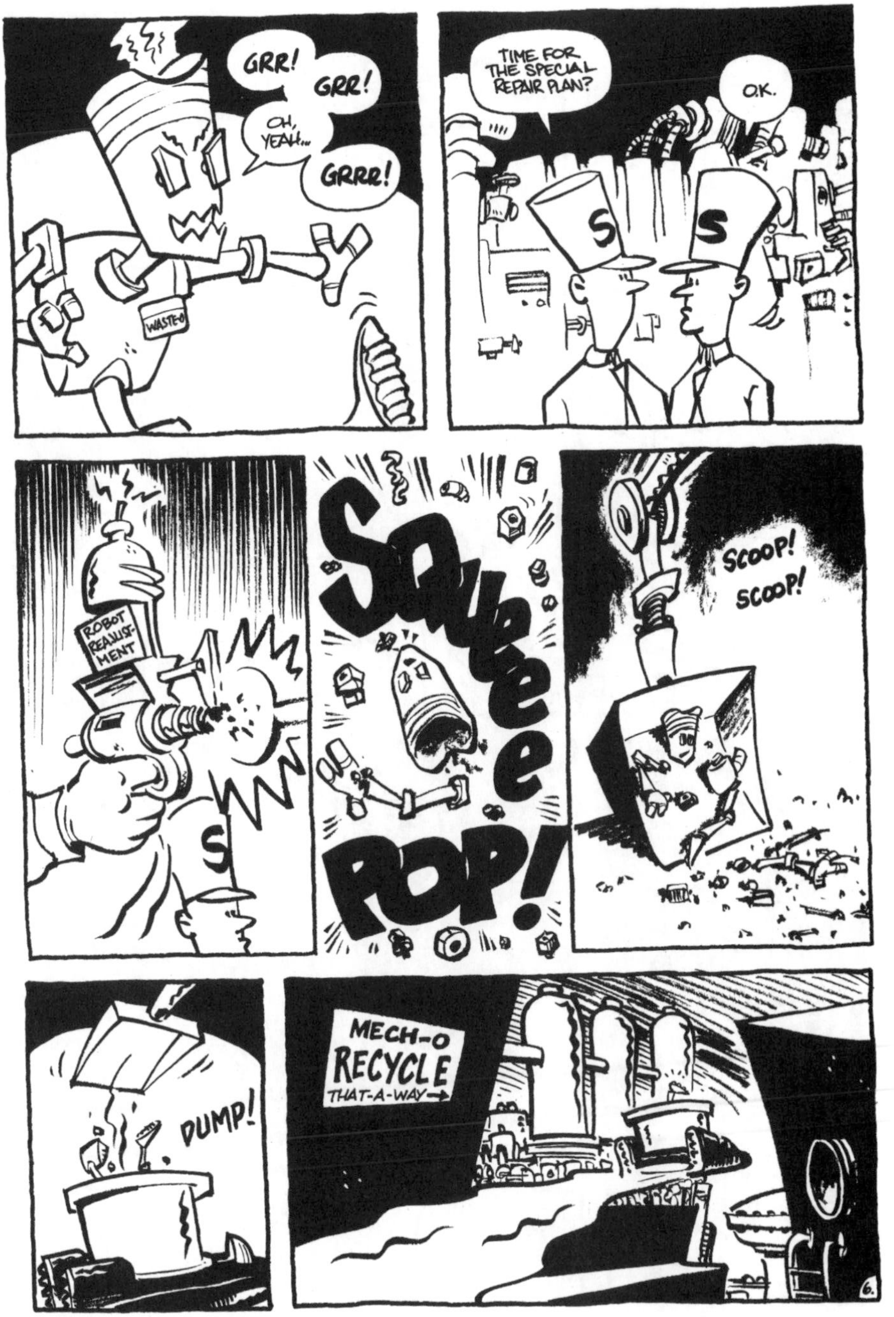
GRR!
GRR!
OH, YEAH...
GRRR!
WASTE-O
TIME FOR THE SPECIAL REPAIR PLAN?
O.K.
ROBOT READJUST-MENT
SQUEEEE
POP!
SCOOP!
SCOOP!
DUMP!
MECH-O RECYCLE THAT-A-WAY→
6.

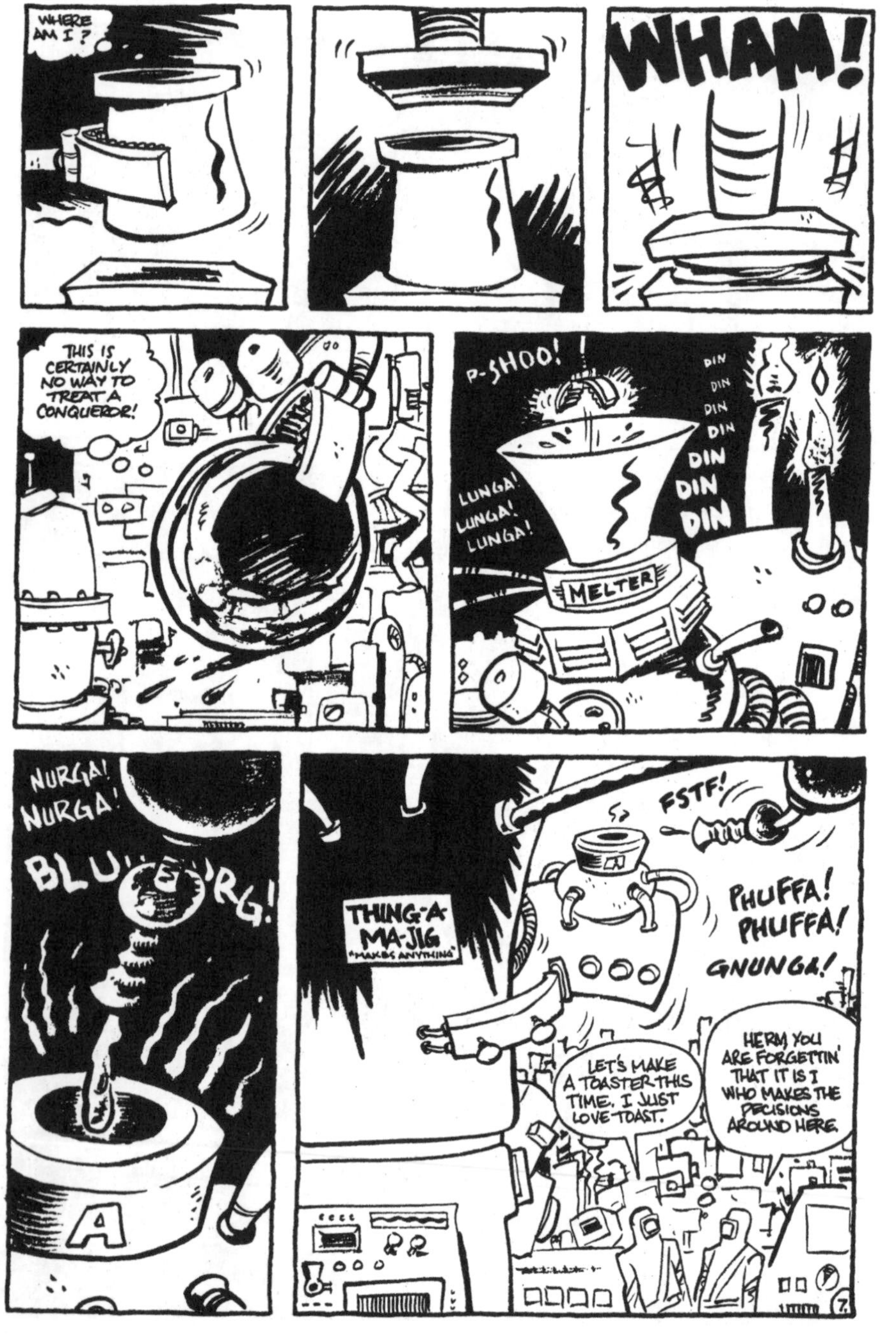
WHERE AM I?
WHAM!
THIS IS CERTAINLY NO WAY TO TREAT A CONQUEROR!
P-SHOO!
DIN DIN DIN DIN DIN DIN DIN
LUNGA! LUNGA! LUNGA!
MELTER
NURGA! NURGA!
BLUBURG!
A
THING-A-MA-JIG "MAKES ANYTHING"
FSTF!
PHUFFA! PHUFFA!
GNUNGA!
LET'S MAKE A TOASTER THIS TIME. I JUST LOVE TOAST.
HERM, YOU ARE FORGETTIN' THAT IT IS I WHO MAKES THE DECISIONS AROUND HERE.
7.

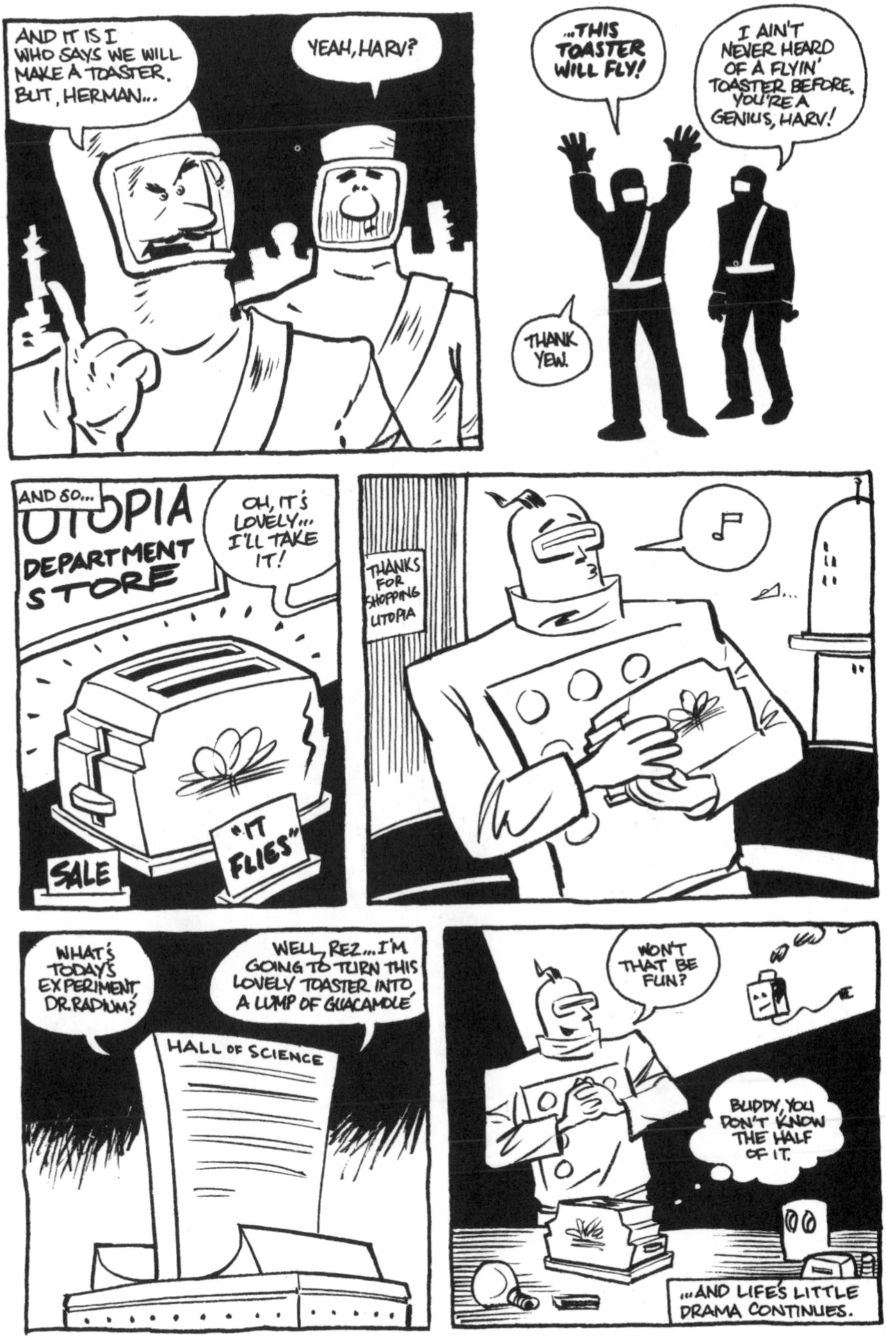
AND IT IS I WHO SAYS WE WILL MAKE A TOASTER. BUT, HERMAN...
YEAH, HARV?
...THIS TOASTER WILL FLY!
I AIN'T NEVER HEARD OF A FLYIN' TOASTER BEFORE. YOU'RE A GENIUS, HARV!
THANK YEW.
AND SO...
UTOPIA DEPARTMENT STORE
OH, IT'S LOVELY... I'LL TAKE IT!
SALE
"IT FLIES"
THANKS FOR SHOPPING UTOPIA
WHAT'S TODAY'S EXPERIMENT, DR. RADIUM?
WELL, REZ...I'M GOING TO TURN THIS LOVELY TOASTER INTO A LUMP OF GUACAMOLE
HALL OF SCIENCE
WON'T THAT BE FUN?
BUDDY, YOU DON'T KNOW THE HALF OF IT.
...AND LIFE'S LITTLE DRAMA CONTINUES.

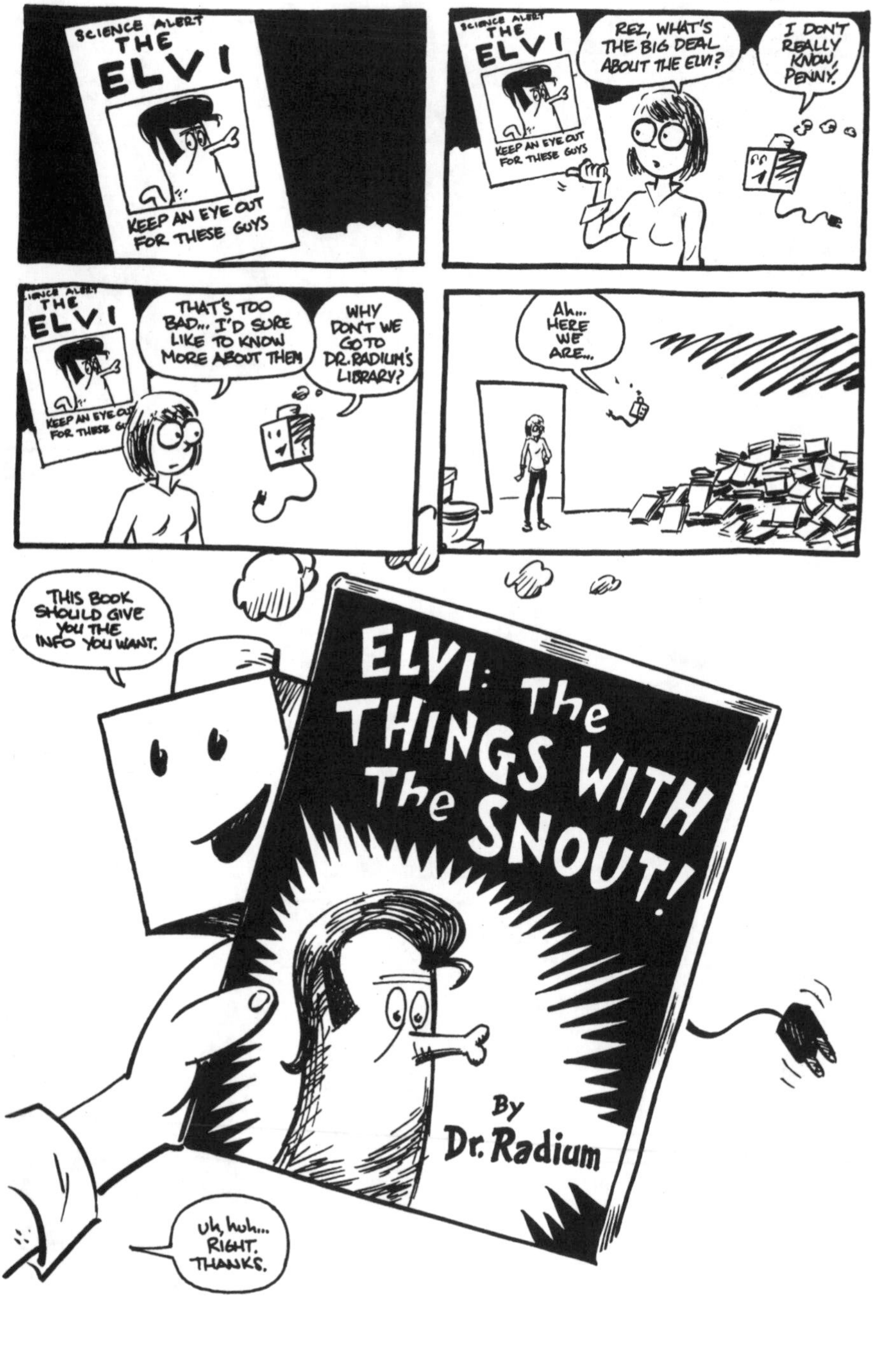
SCIENCE ALERT
THE ELVI
KEEP AN EYE OUT FOR THESE GUYS
REZ, WHAT'S THE BIG DEAL ABOUT THE ELVI?
I DON'T REALLY KNOW, PENNY.
THAT'S TOO BAD... I'D SURE LIKE TO KNOW MORE ABOUT THEM
WHY DON'T WE GO TO DR. RADIUM'S LIBRARY?
Ah... HERE WE ARE...
THIS BOOK SHOULD GIVE YOU THE INFO YOU WANT.
ELVI: The THINGS WITH The SNOUT!
By Dr. Radium
uh, huh... RIGHT. THANKS.

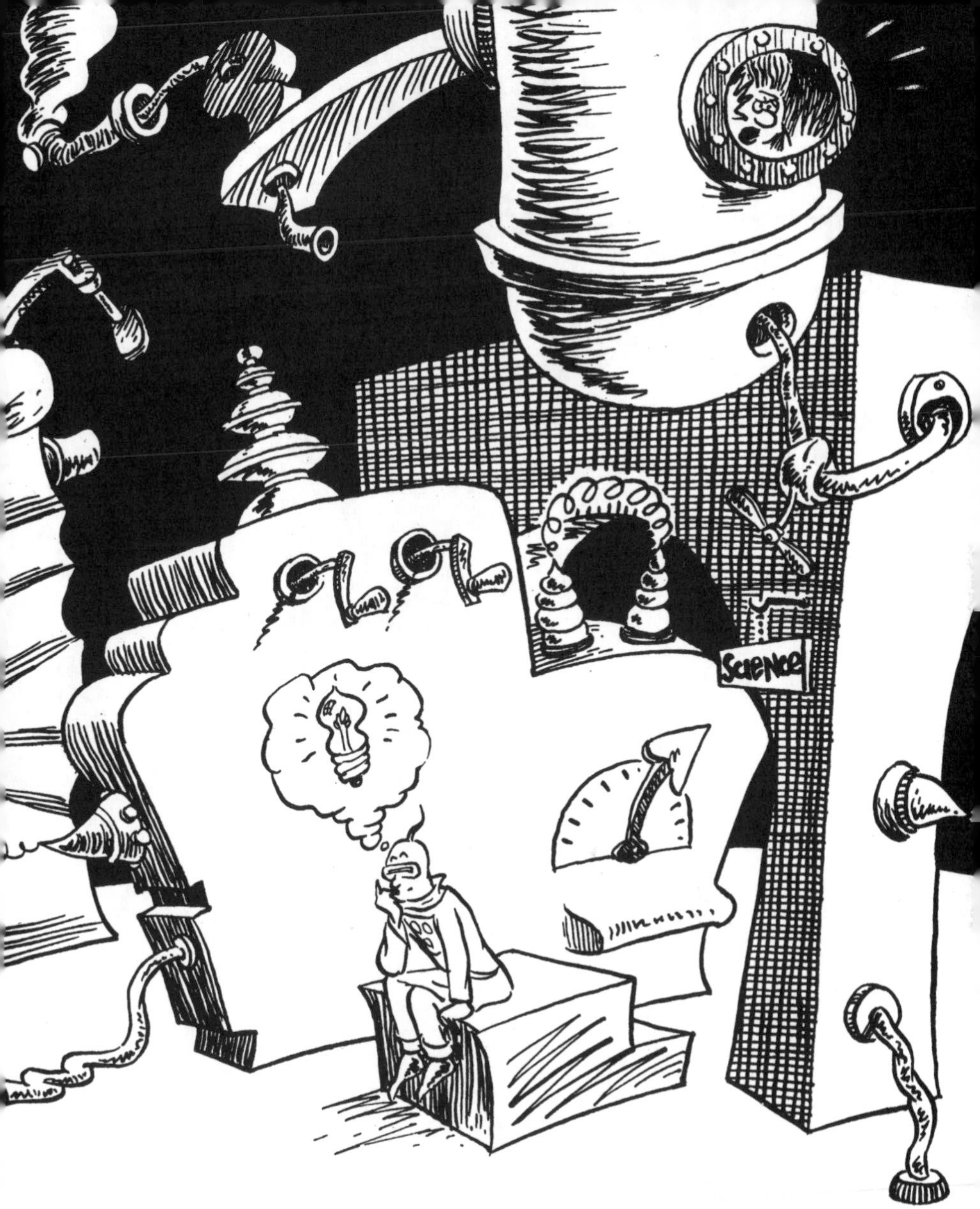
SCIENCE

One day during tomorrow he sat some and thought
This man, Dr. Radium, about the fight he has fought.
Against the icky-yuck Elvi who are always about.
They are strange and are silly, those things with the snout.

Who are they?
What are they?
From whence have they come?
From far away, long away, just past
the sun.

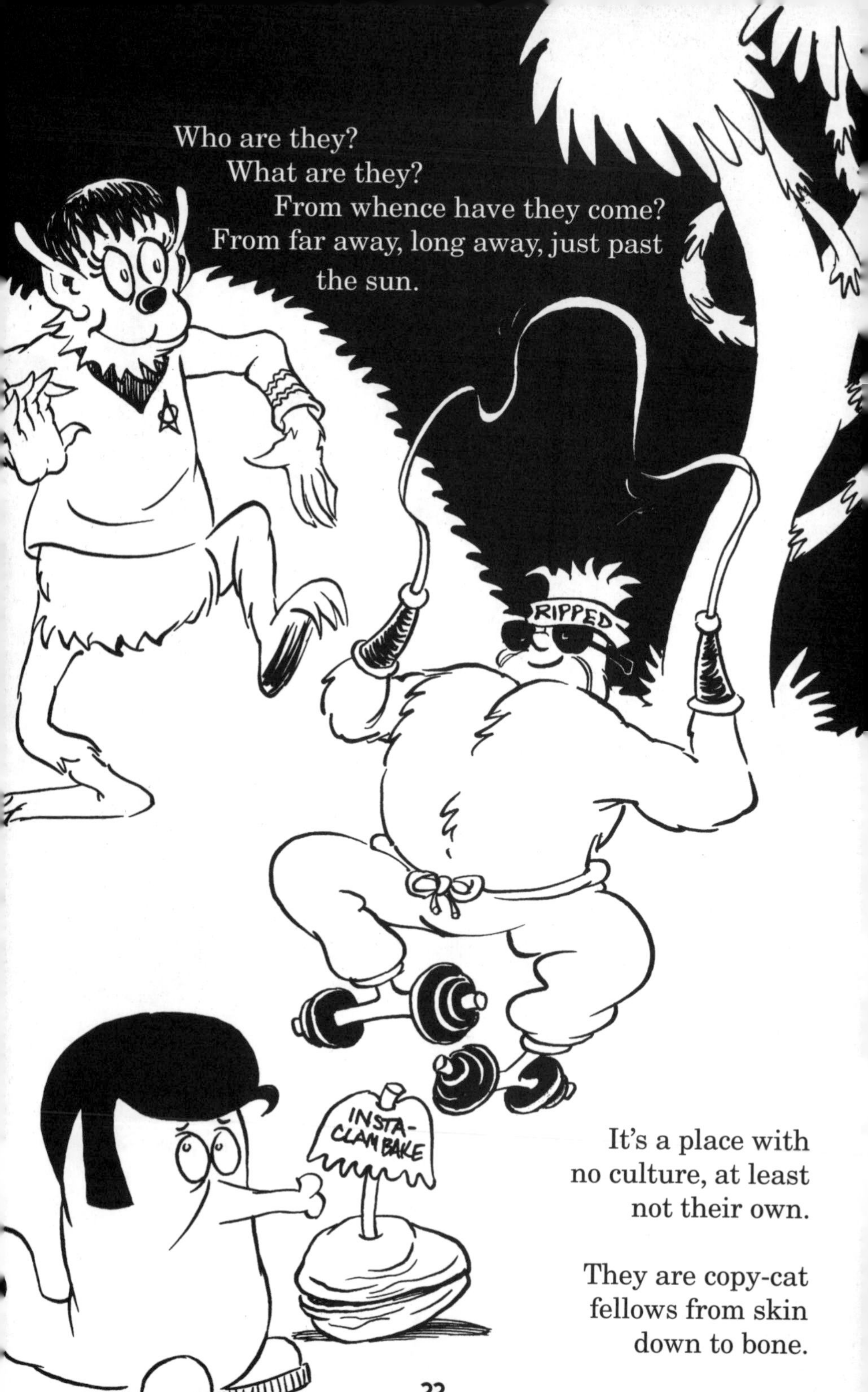
RIPPED
INSTA-
CLAM BAKE

It's a place with
no culture, at least
not their own.

They are copy-cat
fellows from skin
down to bone.

They came in a ship that somebody lent. The landing was hard, the tip got quite bent.

They left their craft nervous and in single file. Soon I would meet these things I revile.

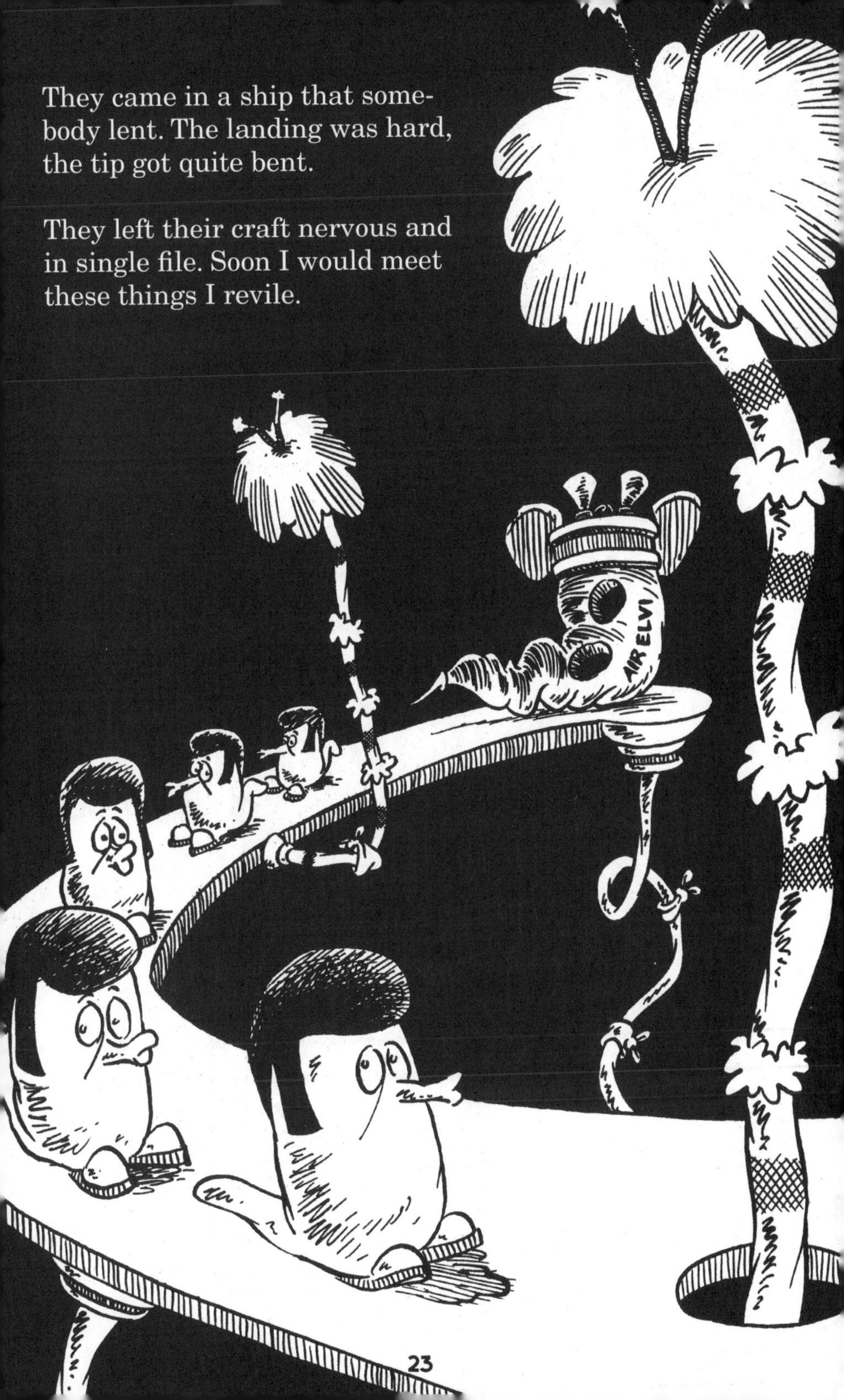
AIR ELVI

Here again, there again despite slight myopia
They poked around, snooped around, all over utopia.

Bored with tomorrow and with no way back
The Elvi soon found me and began their attack.

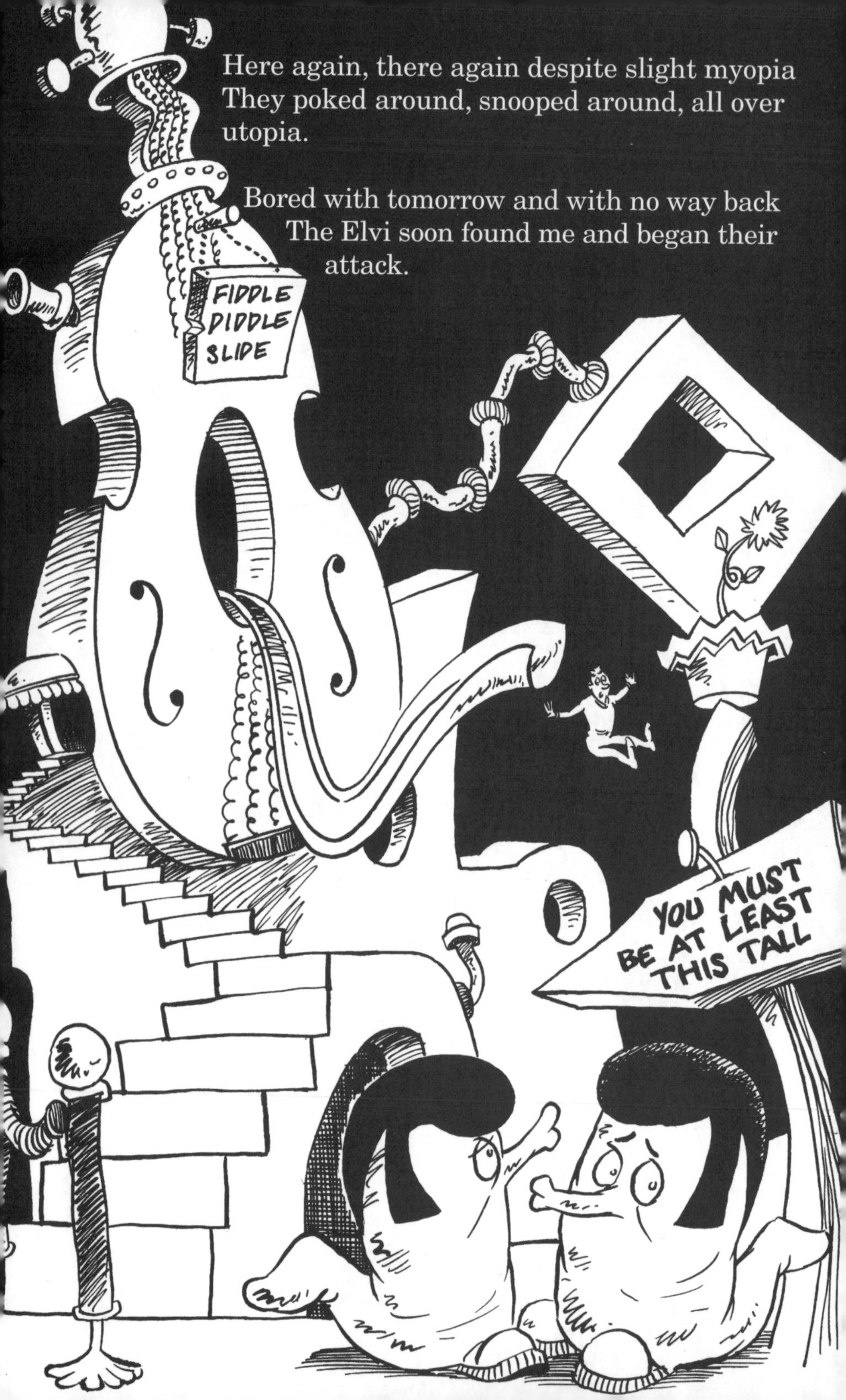
FIDDLE DIDDLE SLIDE
YOU MUST BE AT LEAST THIS TALL

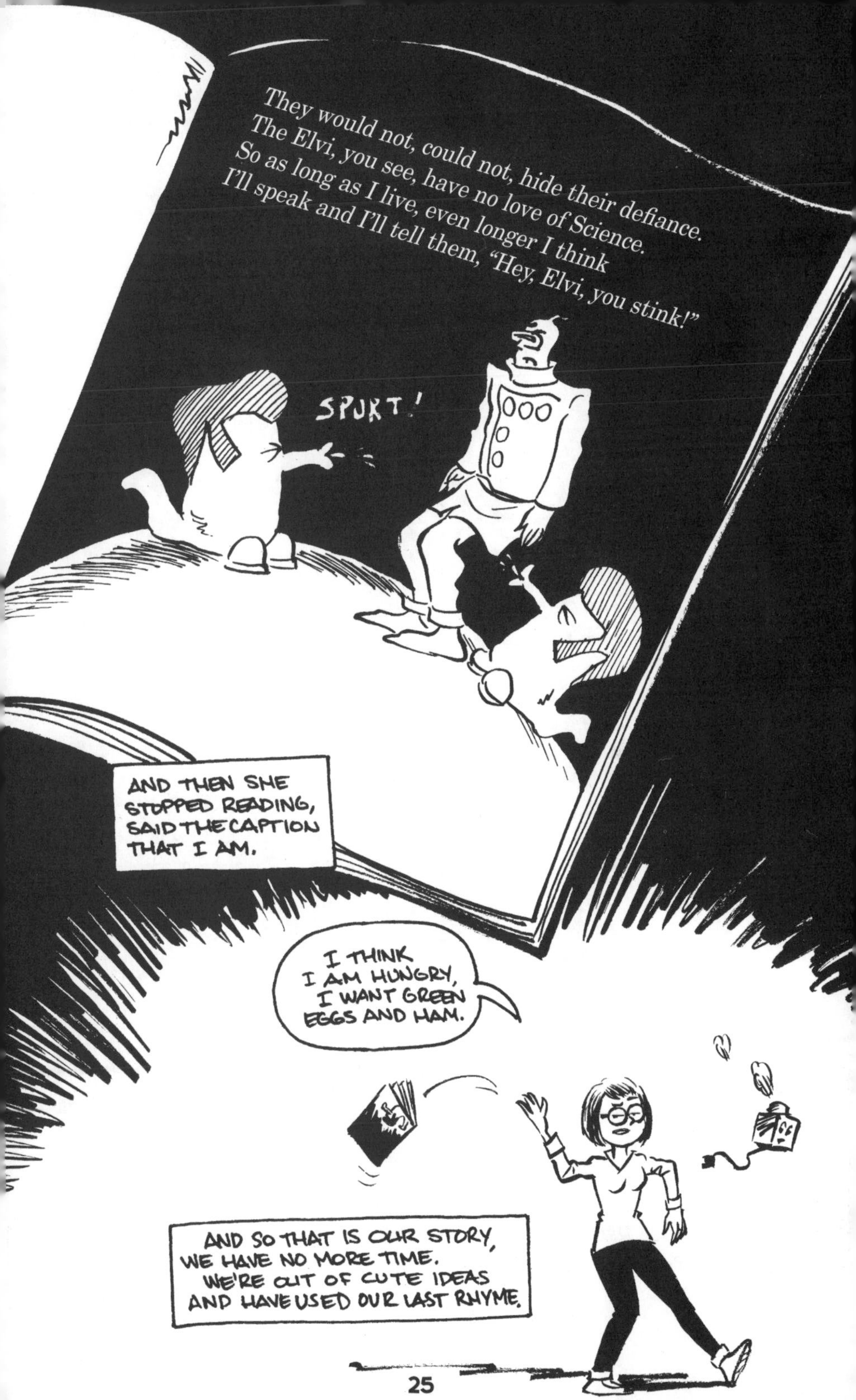
They would not, could not, hide their defiance.
The Elvi, you see, have no love of Science.
So as long as I live, even longer I think
I'll speak and I'll tell them, "Hey, Elvi, you stink!"
SPURT!
AND THEN SHE STOPPED READING, SAID THE CAPTION THAT I AM.
I THINK I AM HUNGRY, I WANT GREEN EGGS AND HAM.
AND SO THAT IS OUR STORY, WE HAVE NO MORE TIME. WE'RE OUT OF CUTE IDEAS AND HAVE USED OUR LAST RHYME.

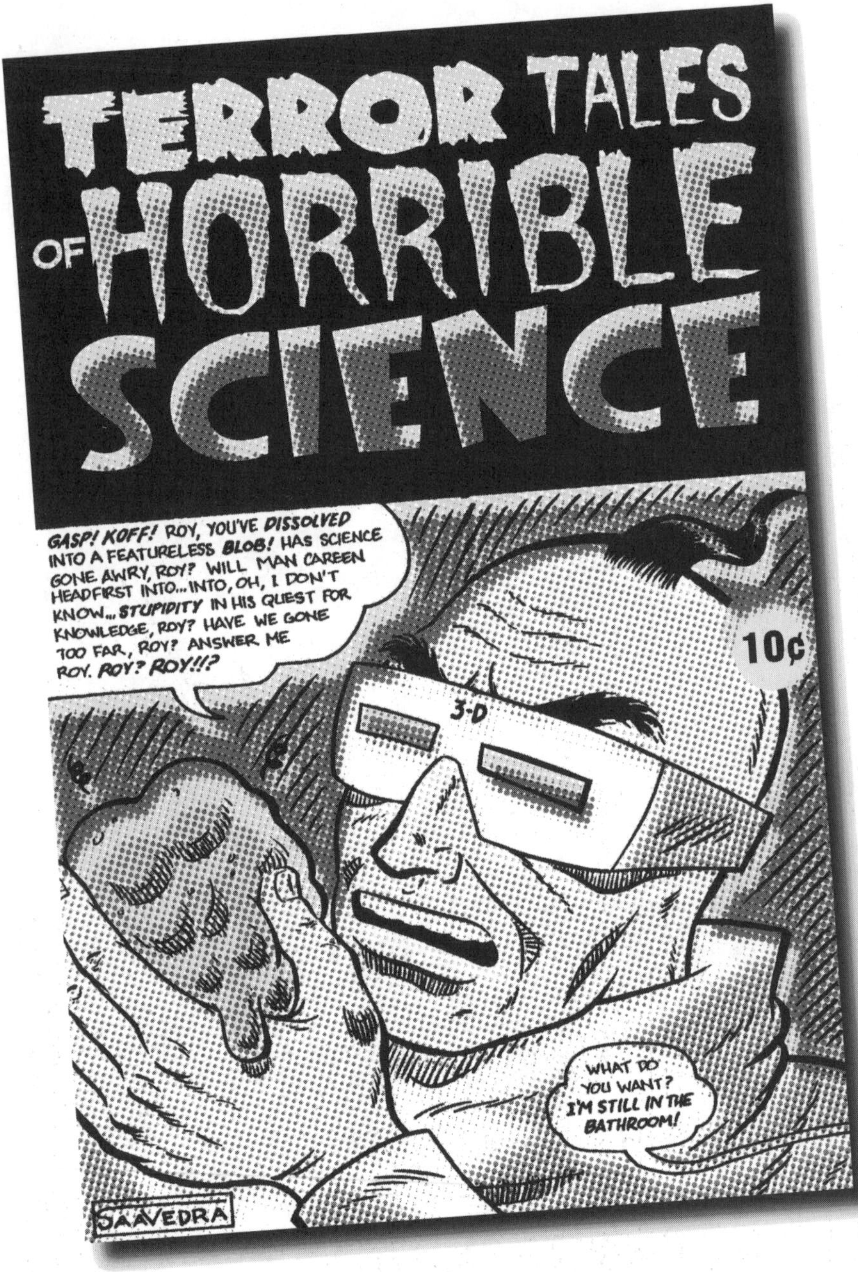
TERROR TALES OF HORRIBLE SCIENCE
GASP! KOFF! ROY, YOU'VE DISSOLVED INTO A FEATURELESS BLOB! HAS SCIENCE GONE AWRY, ROY? WILL MAN CAREEN HEADFIRST INTO...INTO, OH, I DON'T KNOW... STUPIDITY IN HIS QUEST FOR KNOWLEDGE, ROY? HAVE WE GONE TOO FAR, ROY? ANSWER ME ROY. ROY? ROY!!?
10¢
3-D
WHAT DO YOU WANT? I'M STILL IN THE BATHROOM!
SAAVEDRA

Here's a great old story reprinted from TERROR TALES OF HORRIBLE SCIENCE #19 (formerly DR. RADIUM'S TALES OF ATOMIC SCIENCE AND PRETTY PICTURE PUZZLES). Printed Periodical Publishing Co., May 1952

HO! HO! IT'S ME KIDDIES, THE 'OL SCIENTIST WITH ANOTHER FRIGHT-FILLED TALE OF SPOOKY..SCIENCE AND WHAT CAN BE MORE SCIENTIFIC THAN A STORY ABOUT A SICK LITTLE BOY AND HIS MAGIC COMIC BOOK! GOLLY, I GET LITTLE GOOSEY BUMPS JUST THINKING ABOUT IT, BRR! I CALL THIS ONE...OH...
THE LITTLE BOY'S COMIC BOOK!
POX COMICS
BLOODY GHOUL
10¢
COMICS AND STORIES
SLOBBER!
DROOL!
THIS ISSUE:
"SHIP OF GHOULS"
"THE TROUBLE WITH GHOULS"
CUTE LITTLE BOBBY WILKINS HAS A RARE, FATAL BLOOD DISEASE. HE CAN'T RUN AND PLAY WITH THE OTHER CUTE LITTLE BOYS. HE DOES, HOWEVER, GET TO STAY IN BED ALL DAY READING WHOLESOME COMIC BOOKS!
KOFF
ONE DAY, HIS WEIRD UNCLE BASIL BROUGHT HIM A NEW COMIC BOOK TO READ...
HEY, JANGLY DUDE!
GHOUL
HELLO, UNCLE BASIL.
KOFF
...A MAGIC COMIC BOOK!
KOFF
BLOOD

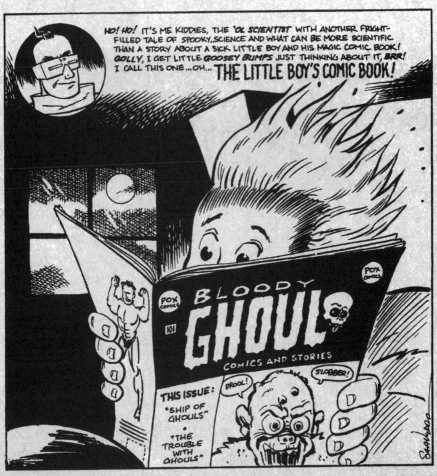

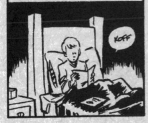

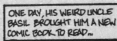

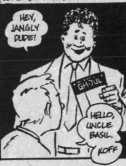

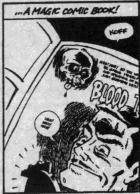

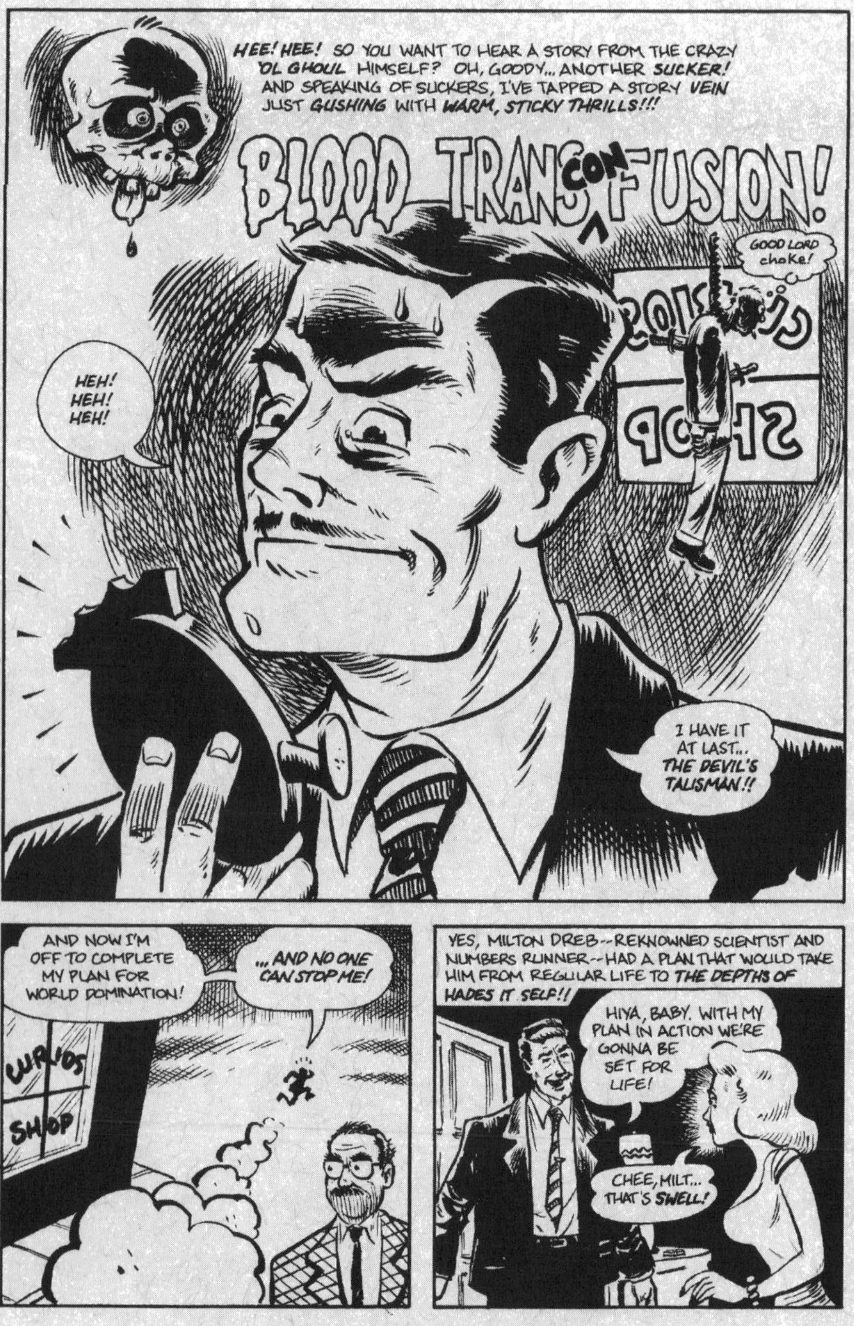
HEE! HEE! SO YOU WANT TO HEAR A STORY FROM THE CRAZY 'OL GHOUL HIMSELF? OH, GOODY... ANOTHER SUCKER! AND SPEAKING OF SUCKERS, I'VE TAPPED A STORY VEIN JUST GUSHING WITH WARM, STICKY THRILLS!!!
BLOOD TRANS-CON-FUSION!
GOOD LORD choke!
HEH! HEH! HEH!
I HAVE IT AT LAST... THE DEVIL'S TALISMAN!!
AND NOW I'M OFF TO COMPLETE MY PLAN FOR WORLD DOMINATION!
...AND NO ONE CAN STOP ME!
SHOP
YES, MILTON DREB--REKNOWNED SCIENTIST AND NUMBERS RUNNER--HAD A PLAN THAT WOULD TAKE HIM FROM REGULAR LIFE TO THE DEPTHS OF HADES IT SELF!!
HIYA, BABY. WITH MY PLAN IN ACTION WE'RE GONNA BE SET FOR LIFE!
CHEE, MILT... THAT'S SWELL!

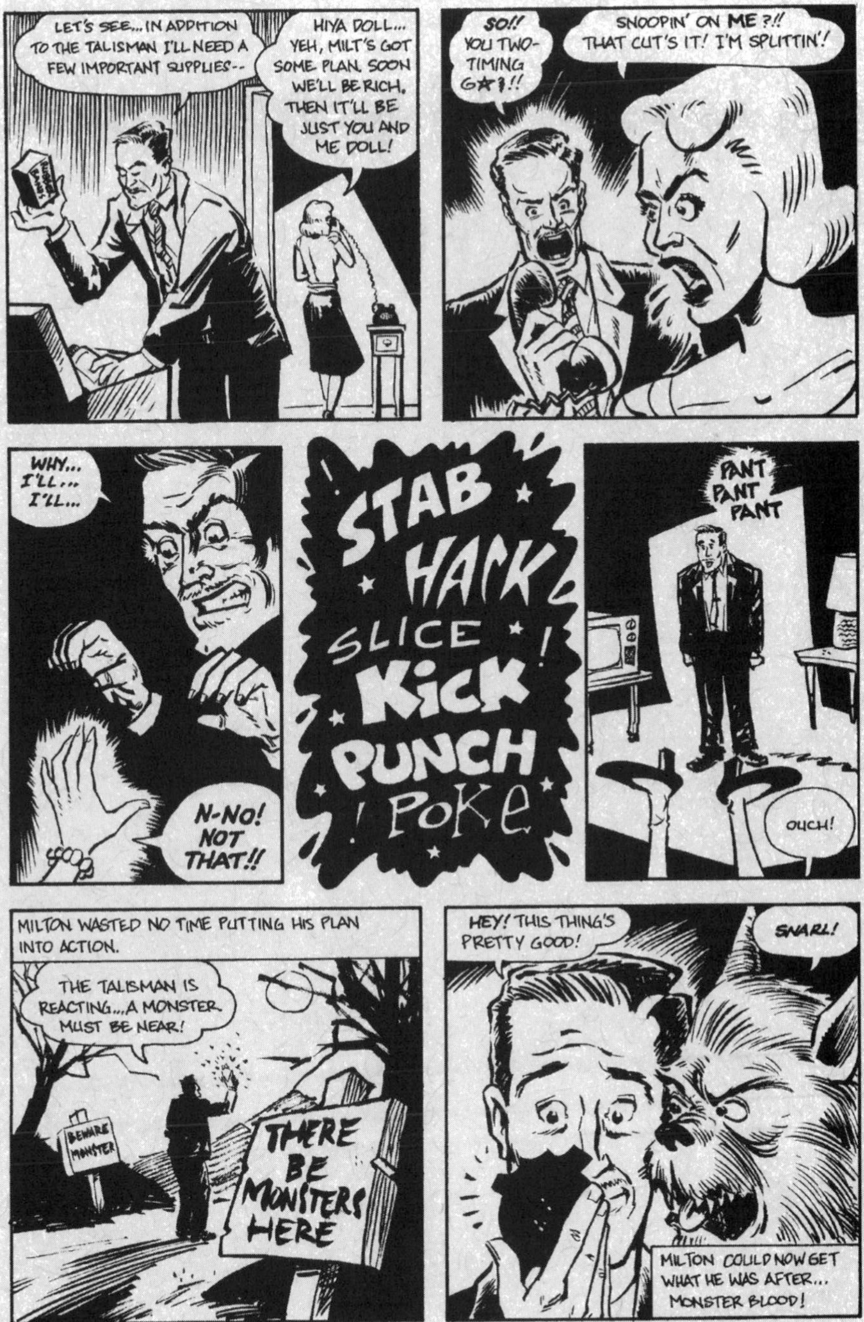
LET'S SEE... IN ADDITION TO THE TALISMAN I'LL NEED A FEW IMPORTANT SUPPLIES--
RUBBER BANDS
HIYA DOLL... YEH, MILT'S GOT SOME PLAN. SOON WE'LL BE RICH. THEN IT'LL BE JUST YOU AND ME DOLL!
SO!! YOU TWO-TIMING G☆?!!
SNOOPIN' ON ME?!! THAT CUT'S IT! I'M SPLITTIN'!
WHY... I'LL... I'LL...
N-NO! NOT THAT!!
STAB
HACK
SLICE
!
KICK
PUNCH
! POKE
PANT PANT PANT
OUCH!
MILTON WASTED NO TIME PUTTING HIS PLAN INTO ACTION.
THE TALISMAN IS REACTING... A MONSTER MUST BE NEAR!
BEWARE MONSTER
THERE BE MONSTERS HERE
HEY! THIS THING'S PRETTY GOOD!
SNARL!
MILTON COULD NOW GET WHAT HE WAS AFTER... MONSTER BLOOD!

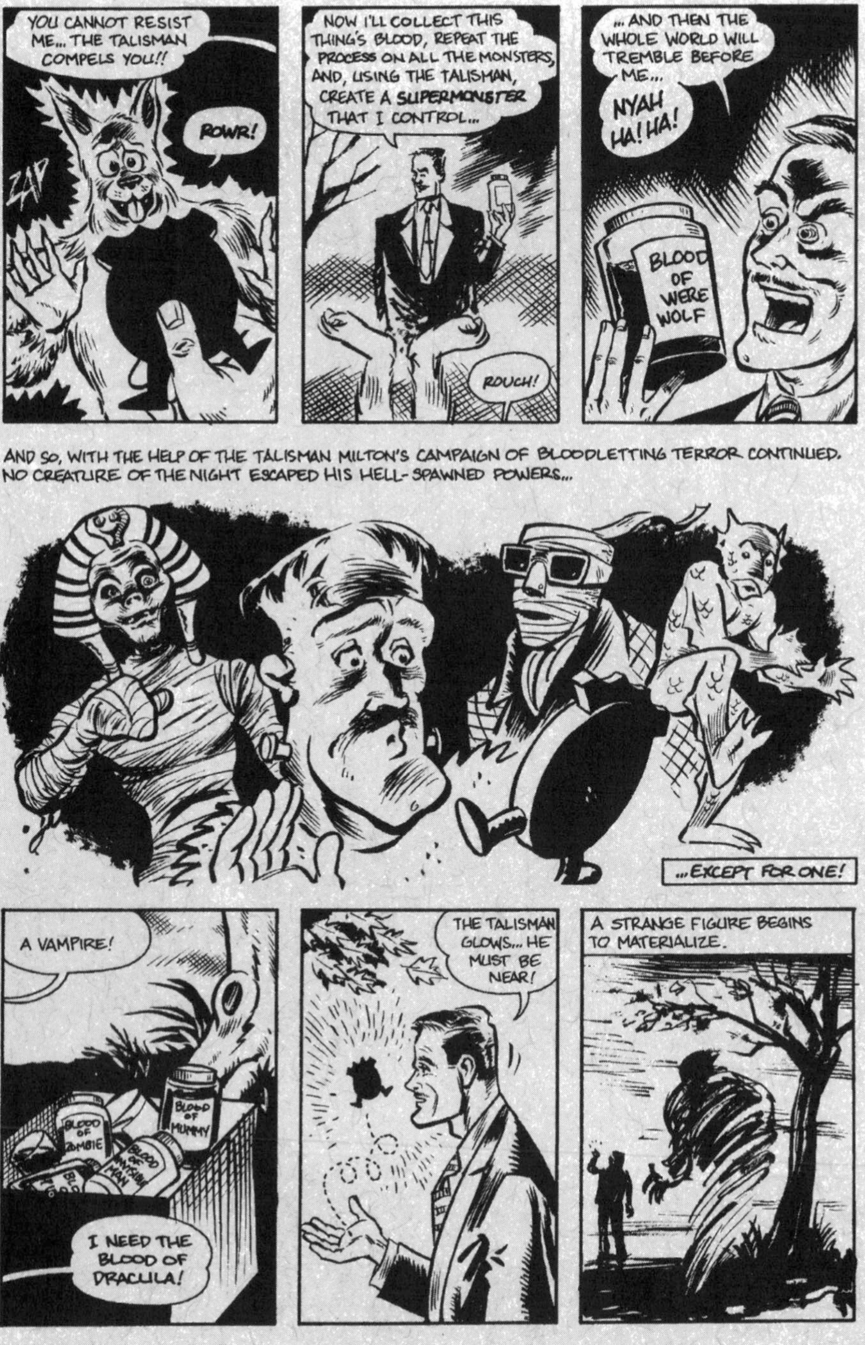
YOU CANNOT RESIST ME... THE TALISMAN COMPELS YOU!!
ZAP
ROWR!
NOW I'LL COLLECT THIS THING'S BLOOD, REPEAT THE PROCESS ON ALL THE MONSTERS, AND, USING THE TALISMAN, CREATE A SUPERMONSTER THAT I CONTROL...
ROUCH!
... AND THEN THE WHOLE WORLD WILL TREMBLE BEFORE ME...
NYAH HA! HA!
BLOOD OF WERE WOLF
AND SO, WITH THE HELP OF THE TALISMAN MILTON'S CAMPAIGN OF BLOODLETTING TERROR CONTINUED. NO CREATURE OF THE NIGHT ESCAPED HIS HELL-SPAWNED POWERS...
...EXCEPT FOR ONE!
A VAMPIRE!
BLOOD OF MUMMY
BLOOD OF ZOMBIE
I NEED THE BLOOD OF DRACULA!
THE TALISMAN GLOWS... HE MUST BE NEAR!
A STRANGE FIGURE BEGINS TO MATERIALIZE.

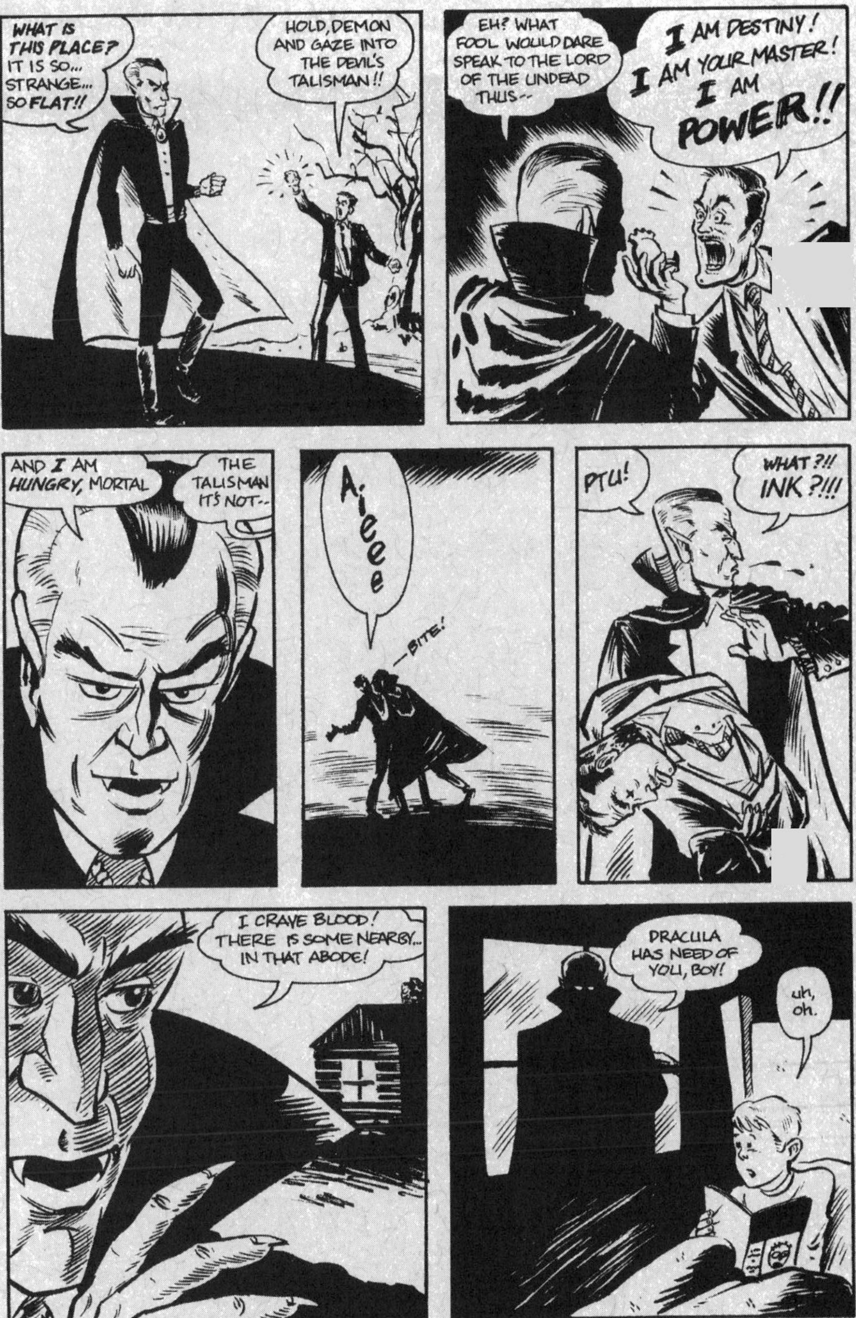
WHAT IS THIS PLACE? IT IS SO... STRANGE... SO FLAT!!
HOLD, DEMON AND GAZE INTO THE DEVIL'S TALISMAN!!
EH? WHAT FOOL WOULD DARE SPEAK TO THE LORD OF THE UNDEAD THUS--
I AM DESTINY! I AM YOUR MASTER! I AM POWER!!
AND I AM HUNGRY, MORTAL
THE TALISMAN IT'S NOT--
Aieee
--BITE!
PTU!
WHAT?!! INK?!!!
I CRAVE BLOOD! THERE IS SOME NEARBY... IN THAT ABODE!
DRACULA HAS NEED OF YOU, BOY!
uh, oh.

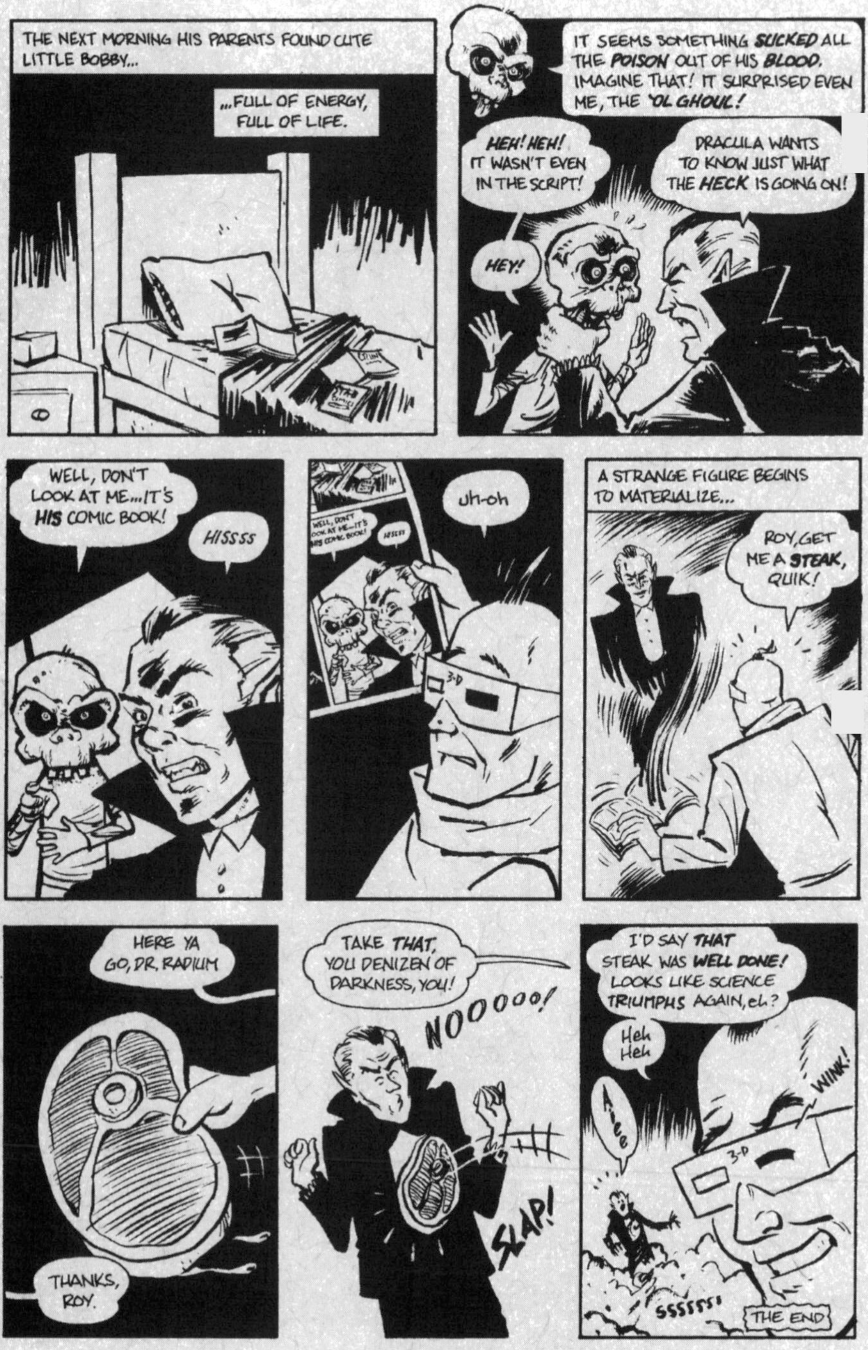
THE NEXT MORNING HIS PARENTS FOUND CUTE LITTLE BOBBY...
...FULL OF ENERGY, FULL OF LIFE.
IT SEEMS SOMETHING SUCKED ALL THE POISON OUT OF HIS BLOOD. IMAGINE THAT! IT SURPRISED EVEN ME, THE 'OL GHOUL!
HEH! HEH! IT WASN'T EVEN IN THE SCRIPT!
DRACULA WANTS TO KNOW JUST WHAT THE HECK IS GOING ON!
HEY!
WELL, DON'T LOOK AT ME...IT'S HIS COMIC BOOK!
HISSSS
uh-oh
3-D
A STRANGE FIGURE BEGINS TO MATERIALIZE...
ROY, GET ME A STEAK, QUIK!
HERE YA GO, DR. RADIUM
THANKS, ROY.
TAKE THAT, YOU DENIZEN OF DARKNESS, YOU!
NOOOOOO!
SLAP!
I'D SAY THAT STEAK WAS WELL DONE! LOOKS LIKE SCIENCE TRIUMPHS AGAIN, eh?
Heh Heh
WINK!
Aiee
3-D
SSSSSS
THE END

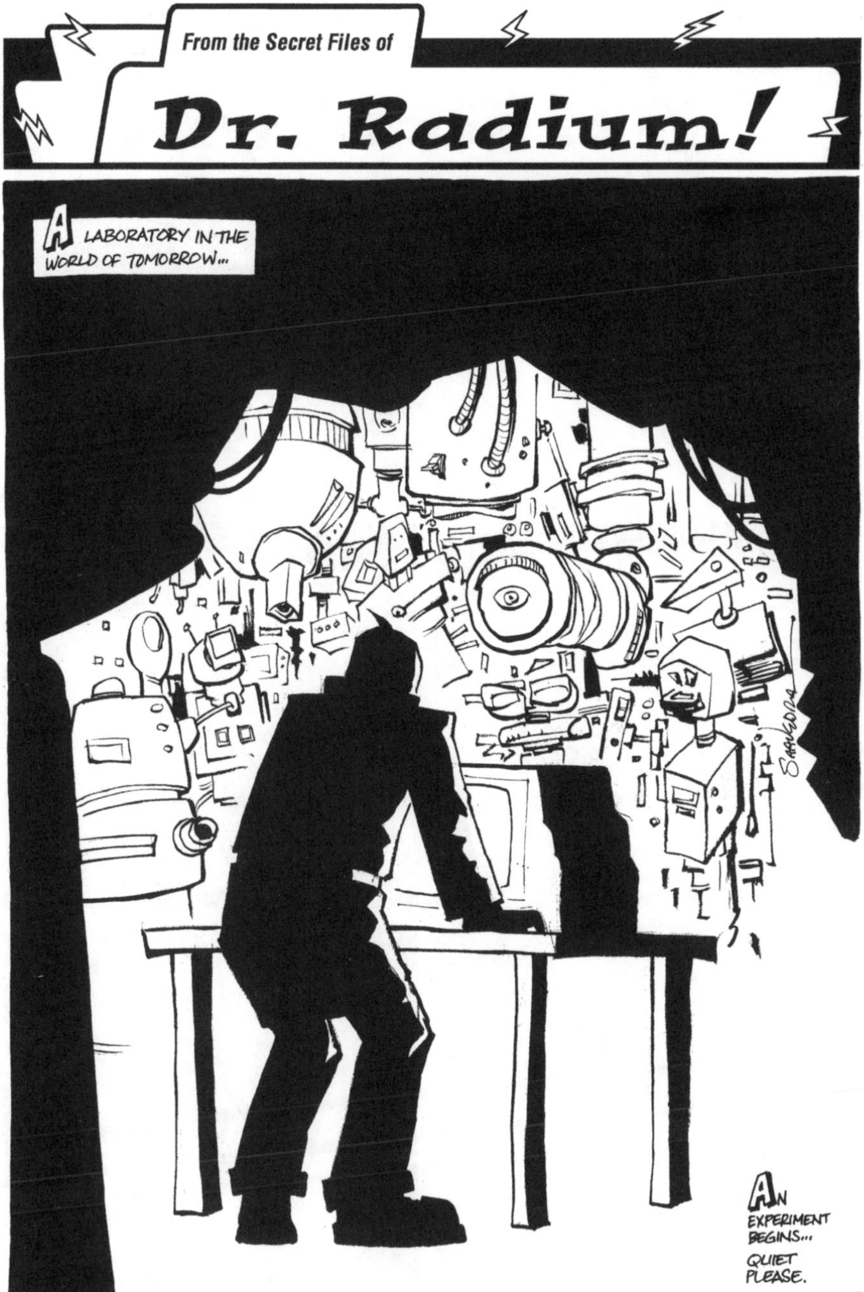
From the Secret Files of
Dr. Radium!
A LABORATORY IN THE WORLD OF TOMORROW...
AN EXPERIMENT BEGINS...
QUIET PLEASE.

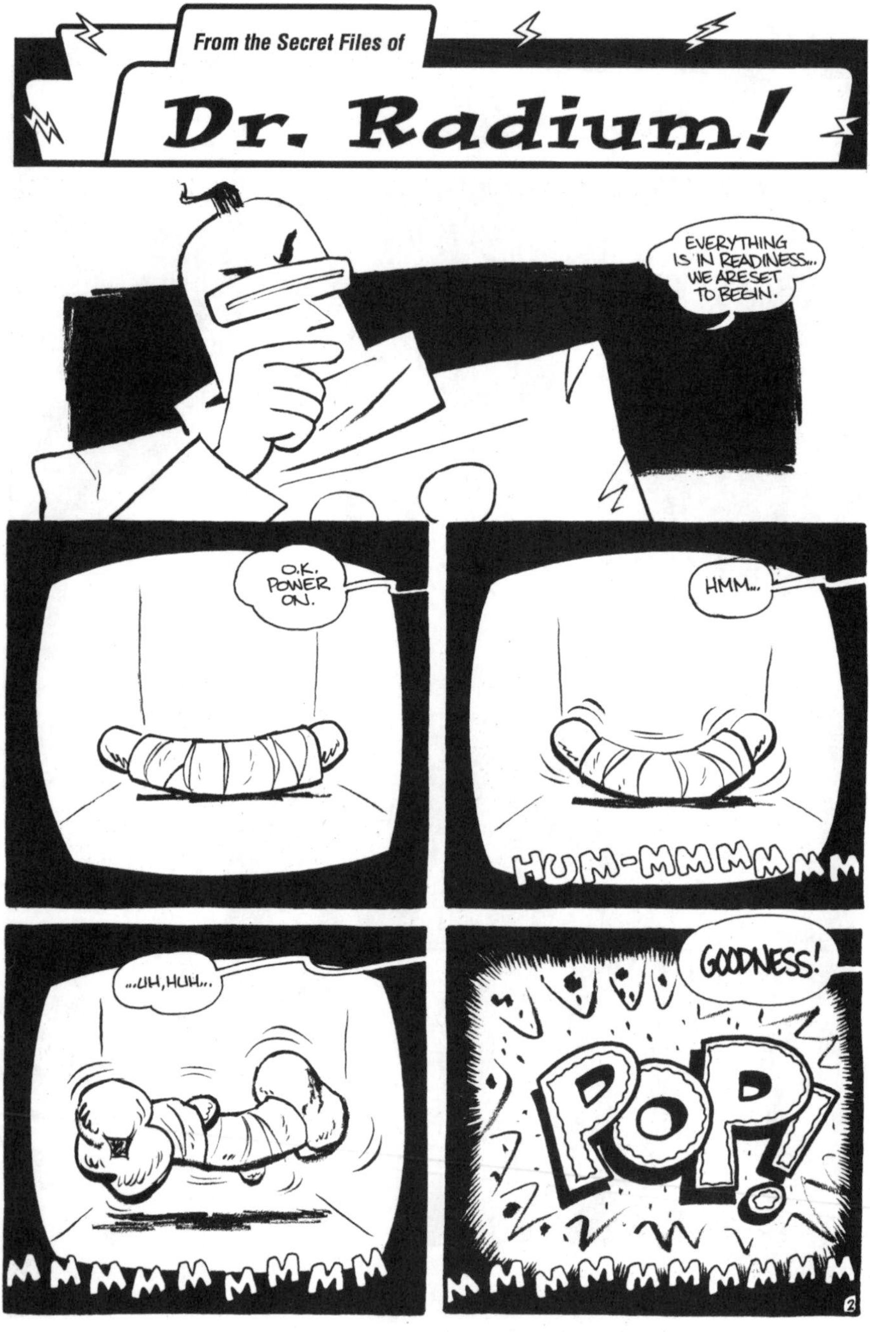
From the Secret Files of
Dr. Radium!
EVERYTHING IS IN READINESS... WE ARE SET TO BEGIN.
O.K. POWER ON.
HMM...
HUM-MMMMMMMM
...UH, HUH...
MMMMMMMMMMM
GOODNESS!
POP!
MMMMMMMMMMMMM
2

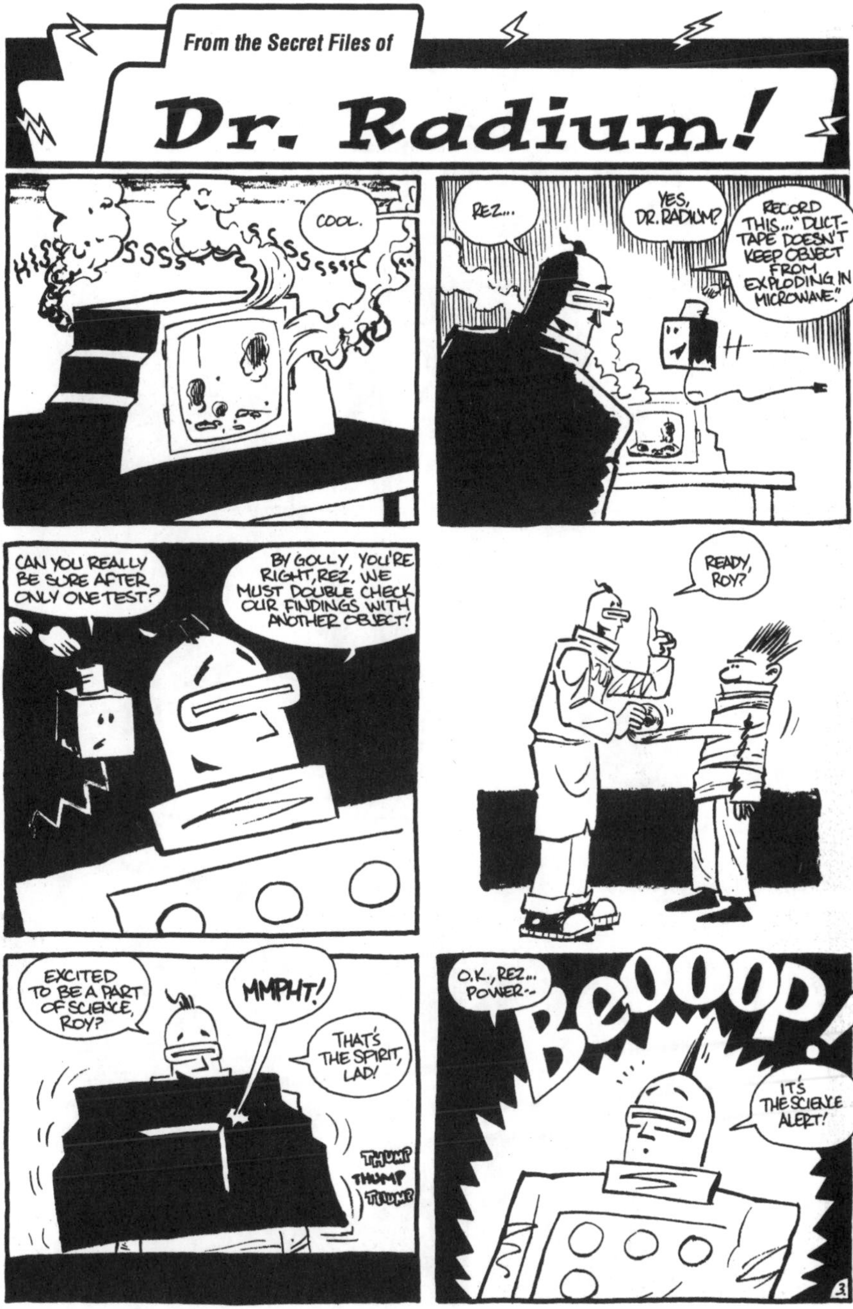
From the Secret Files of
Dr. Radium!
HISSSSSSSSSSSS
COOL.
REZ...
YES, DR. RADIUM?
RECORD THIS..."DUCT-TAPE DOESN'T KEEP OBJECT FROM EXPLODING IN MICROWAVE."
CAN YOU REALLY BE SURE AFTER ONLY ONE TEST?
BY GOLLY, YOU'RE RIGHT, REZ. WE MUST DOUBLE CHECK OUR FINDINGS WITH ANOTHER OBJECT!
READY, ROY?
EXCITED TO BE A PART OF SCIENCE, ROY?
MMPHT!
THAT'S THE SPIRIT, LAD!
THUMP THUMP THUMP
O.K., REZ... POWER-
BeOOOP!
IT'S THE SCIENCE ALERT!
3

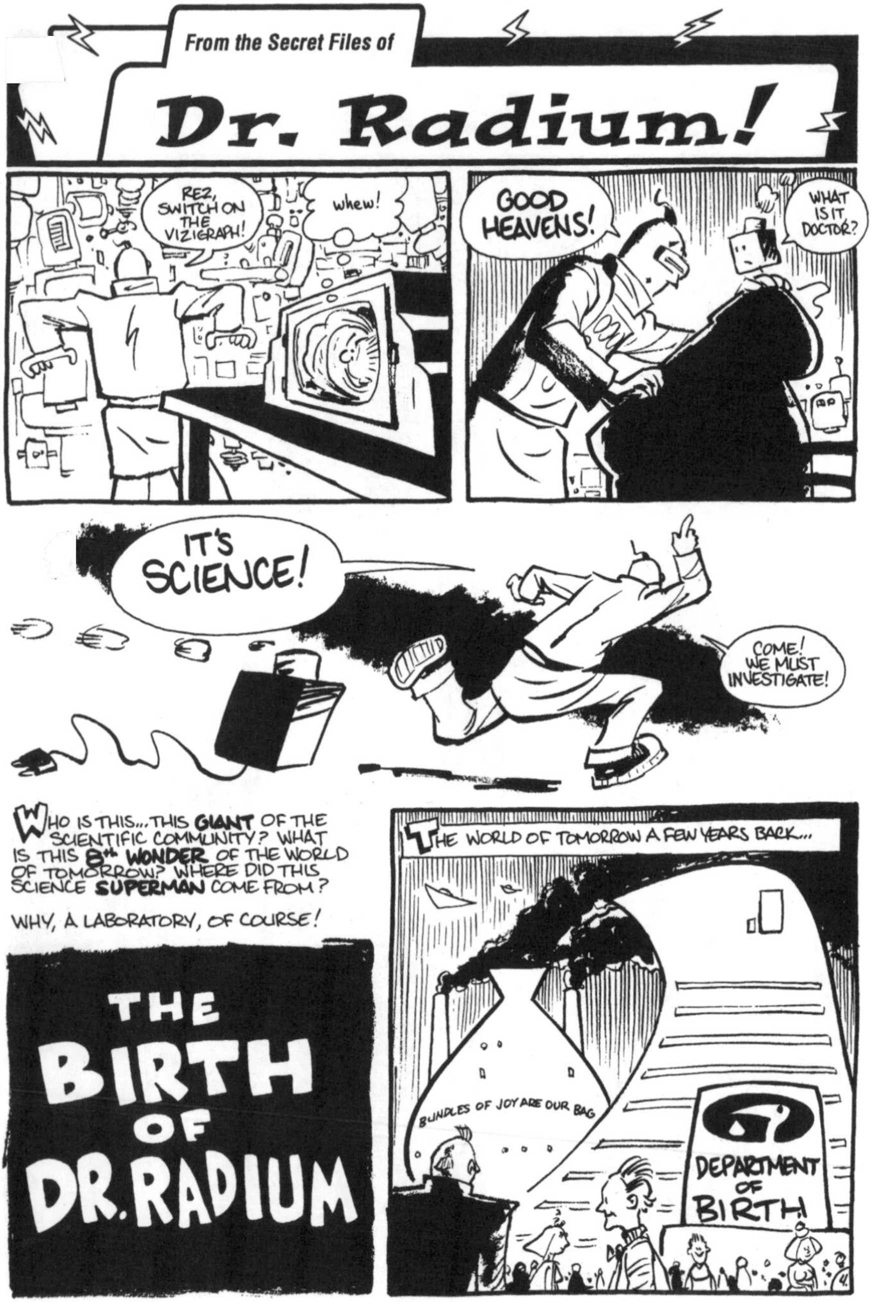
From the Secret Files of
Dr. Radium!
REZ, SWITCH ON THE VIZIGRAPH!
whew!
GOOD HEAVENS!
WHAT IS IT DOCTOR?
IT'S SCIENCE!
COME! WE MUST INVESTIGATE!
WHO IS THIS... THIS GIANT OF THE SCIENTIFIC COMMUNITY? WHAT IS THIS 8th WONDER OF THE WORLD OF TOMORROW? WHERE DID THIS SCIENCE SUPERMAN COME FROM?
WHY, A LABORATORY, OF COURSE!
THE BIRTH OF DR. RADIUM
THE WORLD OF TOMORROW A FEW YEARS BACK...
BUNDLES OF JOY ARE OUR BAG
DEPARTMENT OF BIRTH

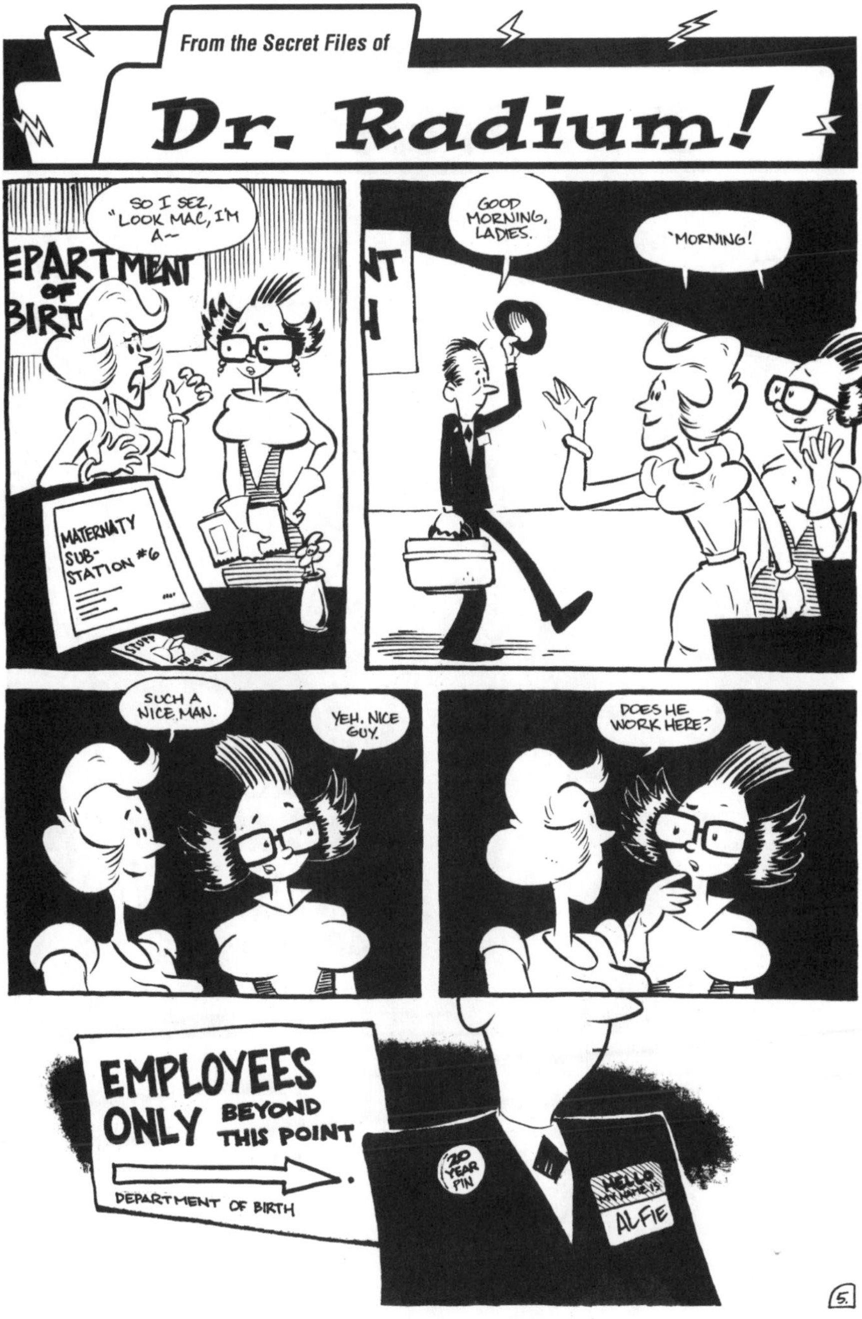

From the Secret Files of
Dr. Radium!
SO I SEZ, "LOOK MAC, I'M A–
EPARTMENT OF BIRT
MATERNATY SUB-STATION #6
GOOD MORNING, LADIES.
'MORNING!
SUCH A NICE MAN.
YEH. NICE GUY.
DOES HE WORK HERE?
EMPLOYEES ONLY BEYOND THIS POINT
DEPARTMENT OF BIRTH
20 YEAR PIN
HELLO MY NAME IS
ALFIE
5.

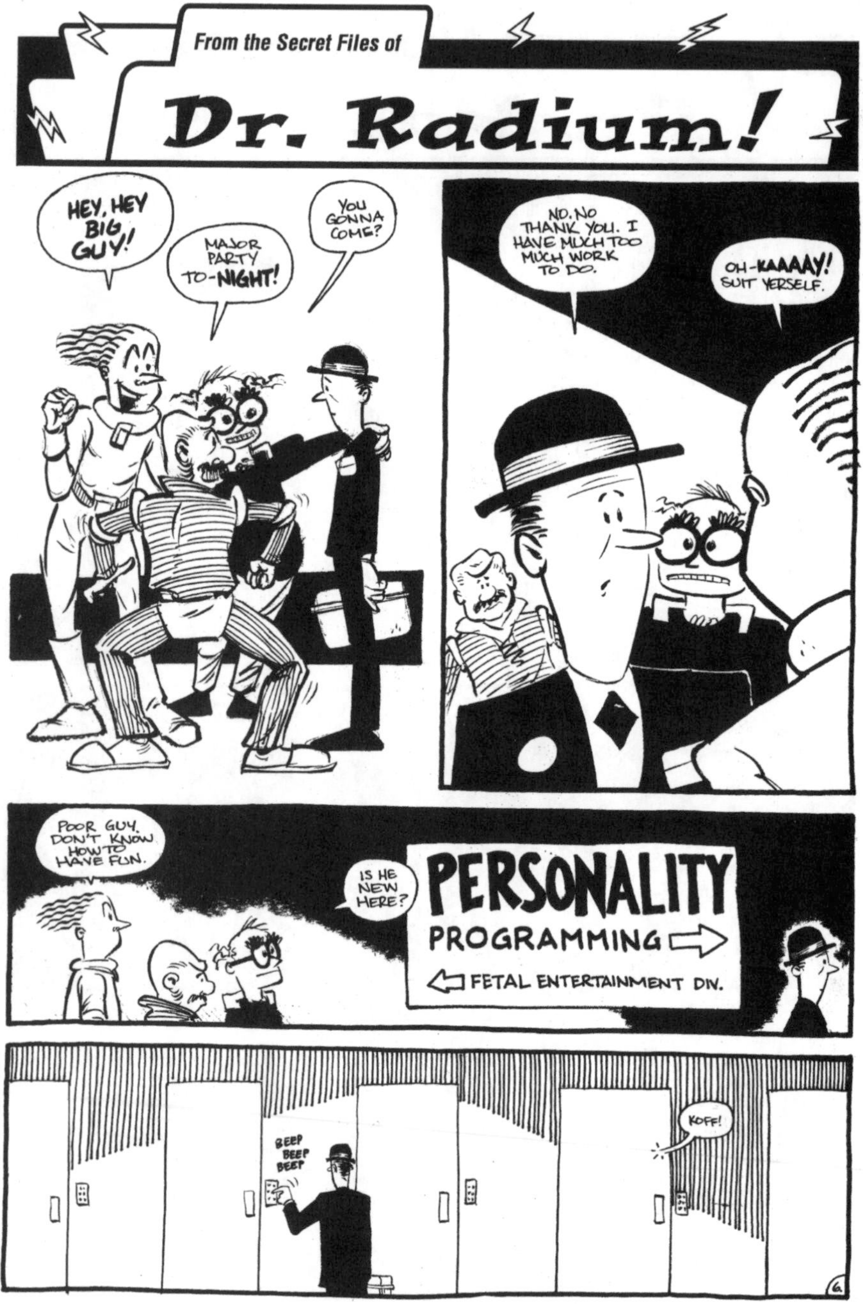
From the Secret Files of
Dr. Radium!
HEY, HEY BIG GUY!
MAJOR PARTY TO-NIGHT!
YOU GONNA COME?
NO, NO THANK YOU. I HAVE MUCH TOO MUCH WORK TO DO.
OH-KAAAAY! SUIT YERSELF.
POOR GUY. DON'T KNOW HOW TO HAVE FUN.
IS HE NEW HERE?
PERSONALITY
PROGRAMMING
FETAL ENTERTAINMENT DIV.
BEEP BEEP BEEP
KOFF!

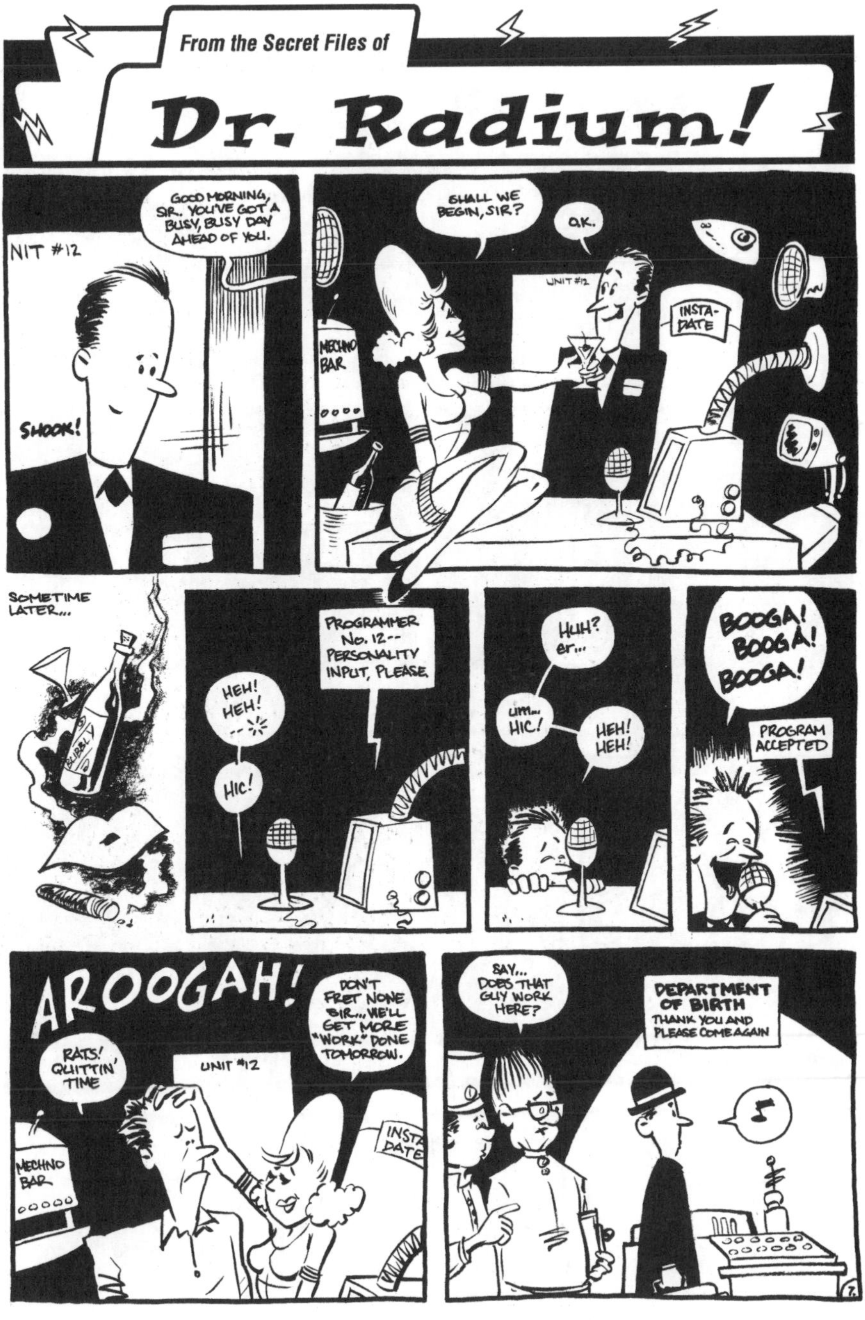
From the Secret Files of
Dr. Radium!
GOOD MORNING, SIR. YOU'VE GOT A BUSY, BUSY DAY AHEAD OF YOU.
NIT #12
SHOOK!
SHALL WE BEGIN, SIR?
O.K.
UNIT #12
MECHNO BAR
INSTA-DATE
SOMETIME LATER...
BUBBLY
PROGRAMMER No. 12-- PERSONALITY INPUT, PLEASE.
HEH! HEH!
HIC!
HUH? er...
UM... HIC!
HEH! HEH!
BOOGA! BOOGA! BOOGA!
PROGRAM ACCEPTED
AROOGAH!
RATS! QUITTIN' TIME
UNIT #12
DON'T FRET NONE SIR... WE'LL GET MORE "WORK" DONE TOMORROW.
MECHNO BAR
INSTA DATE
SAY... DOES THAT GUY WORK HERE?
DEPARTMENT OF BIRTH
THANK YOU AND PLEASE COME AGAIN

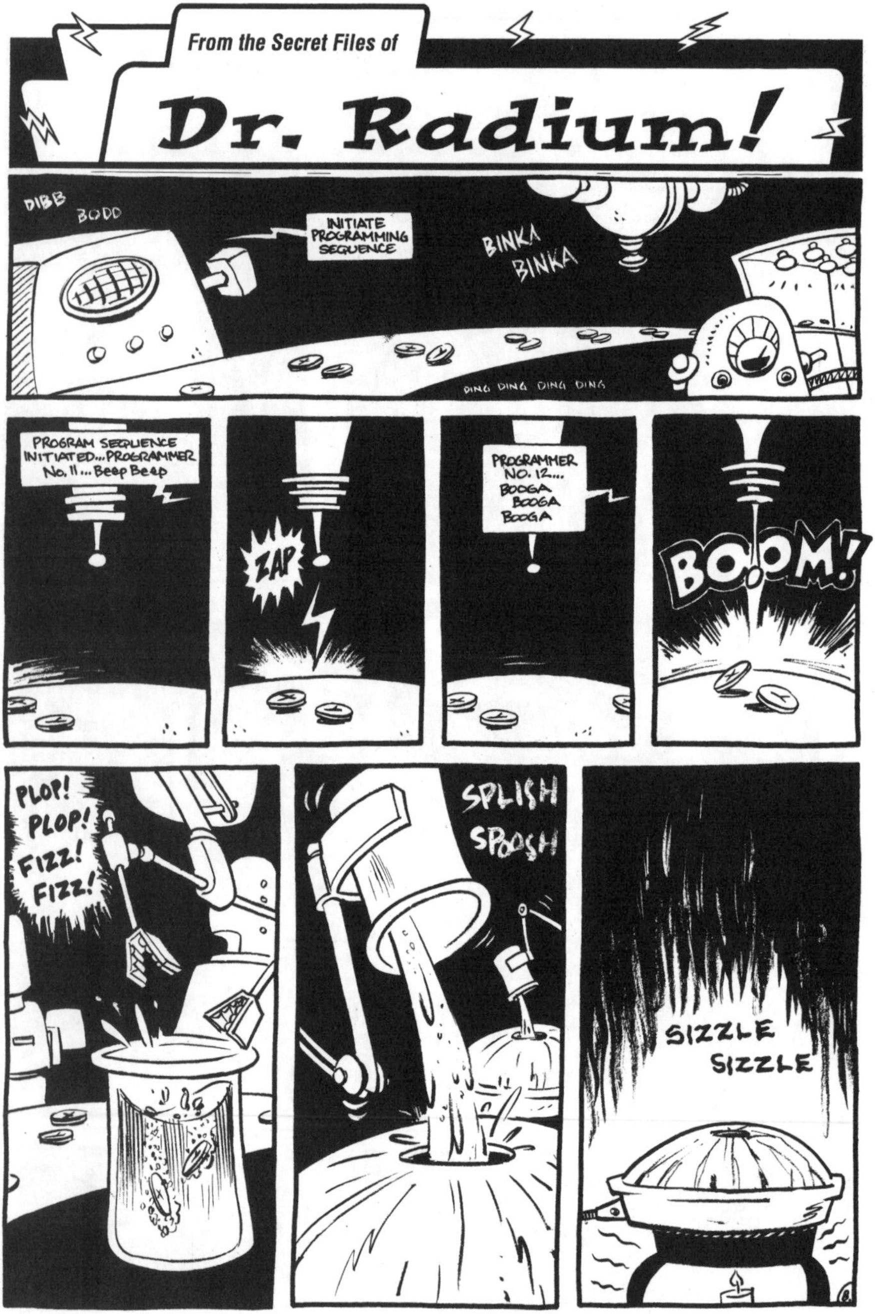
From the Secret Files of
Dr. Radium!
DIBB
BODD
INITIATE PROGRAMMING SEQUENCE
BINKA BINKA
DING DING DING DING
PROGRAM SEQUENCE INITIATED... PROGRAMMER No. 11... Beep Beep
ZAP
PROGRAMMER NO. 12... BOOGA BOOGA BOOGA
BOOM!
PLOP! PLOP! FIZZ! FIZZ!
SPLISH SPOOSH
SIZZLE SIZZLE

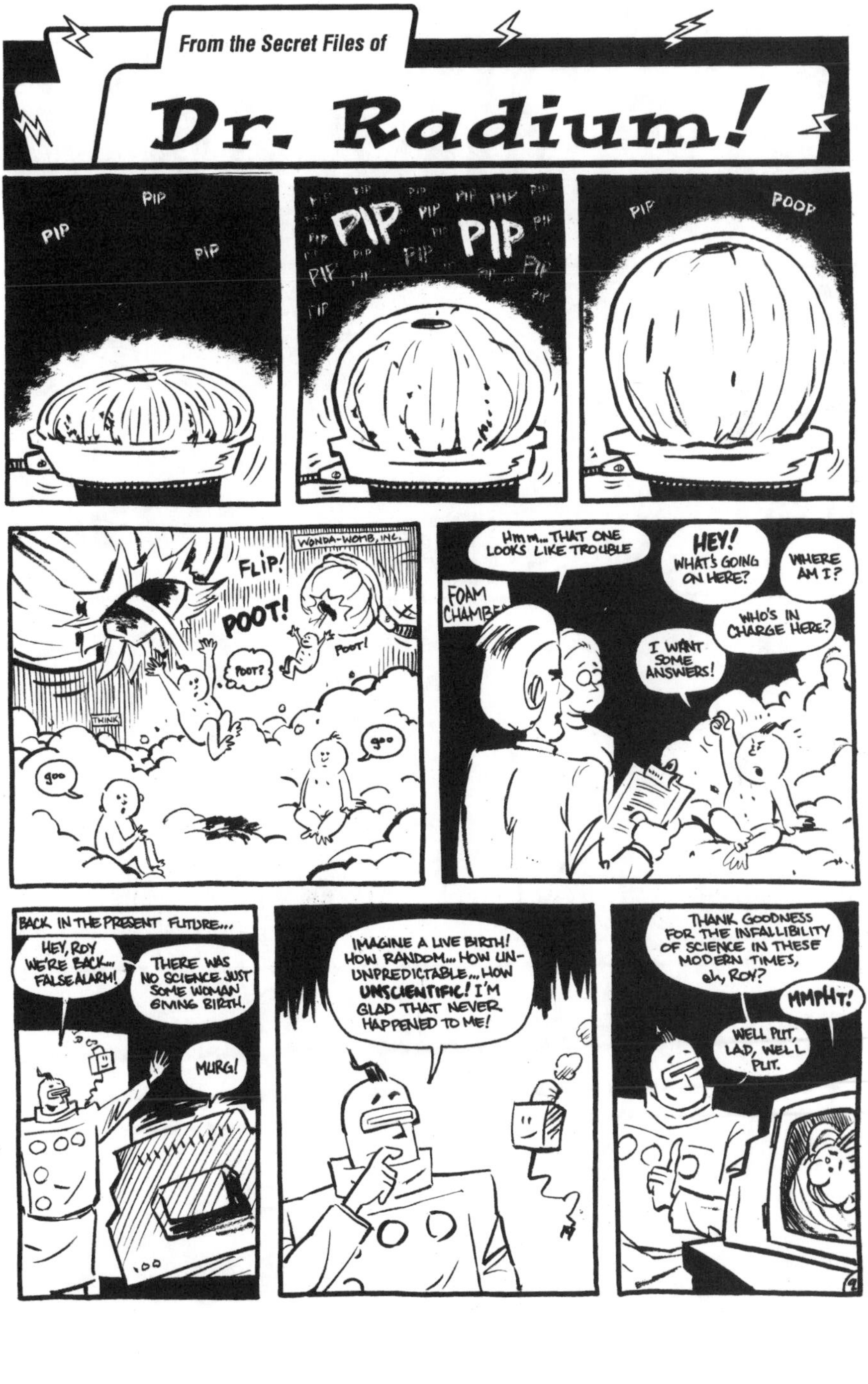
From the Secret Files of
Dr. Radium!
PIP
PIP
PIP
PIP
PIP
PIP
PIP
POOP
WONDA-WOMB, INC.
FLIP!
POOT!
POOT?
POOT!
THINK
goo
goo
HMM... THAT ONE LOOKS LIKE TROUBLE
FOAM CHAMBE
HEY! WHAT'S GOING ON HERE?
WHERE AM I?
WHO'S IN CHARGE HERE?
I WANT SOME ANSWERS!
BACK IN THE PRESENT FUTURE...
HEY, ROY WE'RE BACK... FALSE ALARM!
THERE WAS NO SCIENCE JUST SOME WOMAN GIVING BIRTH.
MURG!
IMAGINE A LIVE BIRTH! HOW RANDOM... HOW UN-UNPREDICTABLE... HOW UNSCIENTIFIC! I'M GLAD THAT NEVER HAPPENED TO ME!
THANK GOODNESS FOR THE INFALLIBILITY OF SCIENCE IN THESE MODERN TIMES, eh, ROY?
MMPHT!
WELL PUT, LAD, WELL PUT.

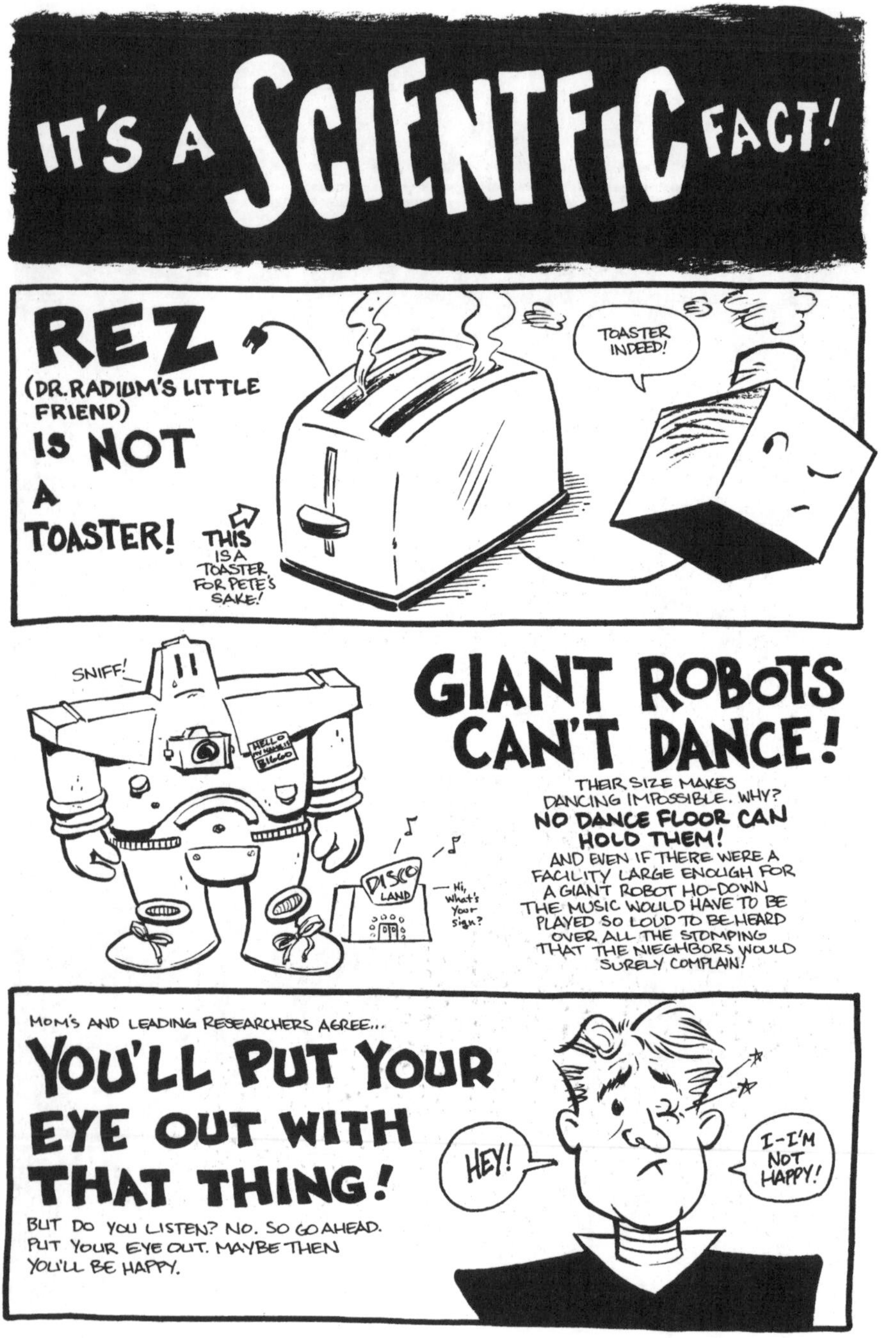
IT'S A SCIENTFIC FACT!
REZ (DR. RADIUM'S LITTLE FRIEND) IS NOT A TOASTER!
THIS IS A TOASTER FOR PETE'S SAKE!
TOASTER INDEED!
SNIFF!
HELLO MY NAME IS BIGGO
DISCO LAND
Hi, What's Your Sign?
GIANT ROBOTS CAN'T DANCE!
THEIR SIZE MAKES DANCING IMPOSSIBLE. WHY? NO DANCE FLOOR CAN HOLD THEM! AND EVEN IF THERE WERE A FACILITY LARGE ENOUGH FOR A GIANT ROBOT HO-DOWN THE MUSIC WOULD HAVE TO BE PLAYED SO LOUD TO BE HEARD OVER ALL THE STOMPING THAT THE NIEGHBORS WOULD SURELY COMPLAIN!
MOM'S AND LEADING RESEARCHERS AGREE...
YOU'LL PUT YOUR EYE OUT WITH THAT THING!
BUT DO YOU LISTEN? NO. SO GO AHEAD. PUT YOUR EYE OUT. MAYBE THEN YOU'LL BE HAPPY.
HEY!
I-I'M NOT HAPPY!

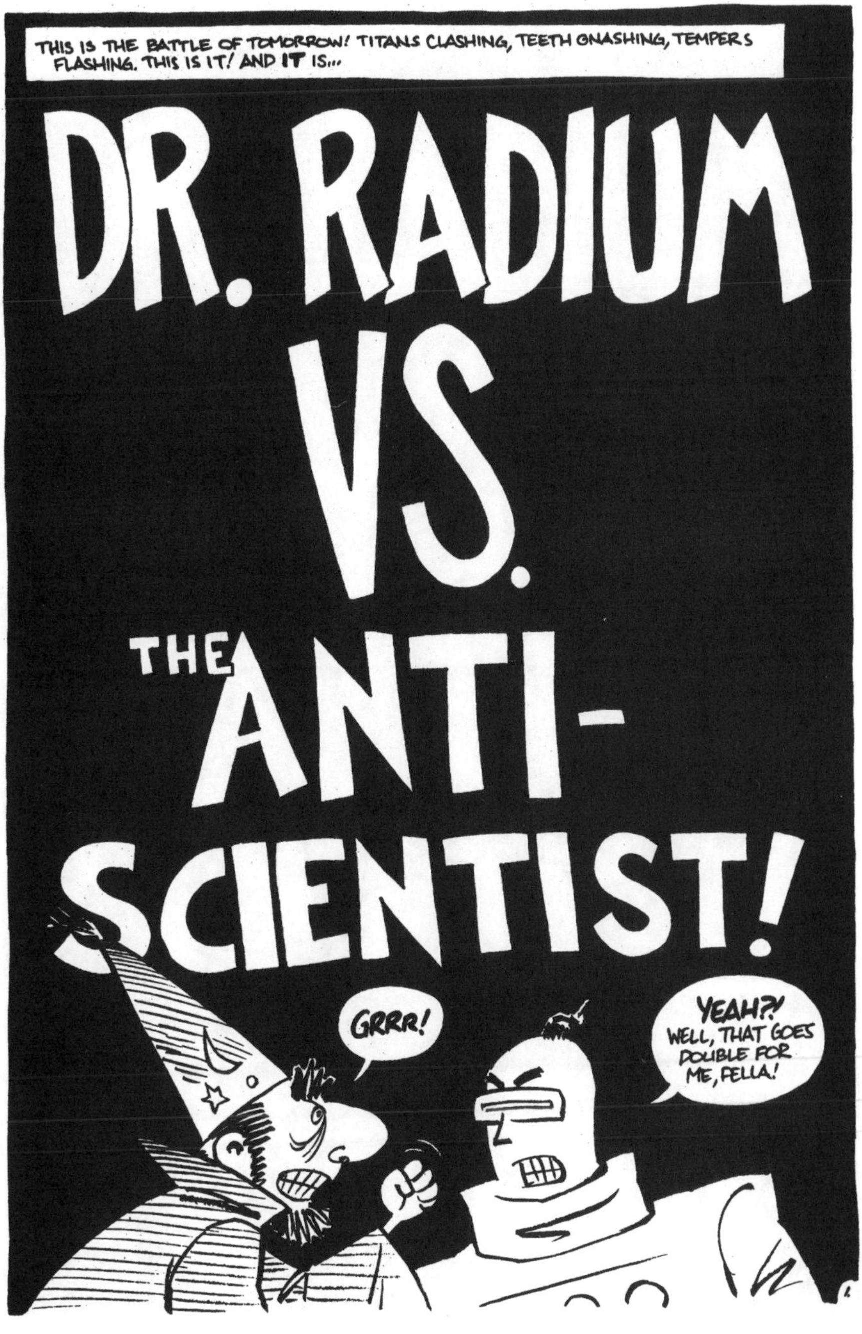
THIS IS THE BATTLE OF TOMORROW! TITANS CLASHING, TEETH GNASHING, TEMPERS FLASHING. THIS IS IT! AND IT IS...
DR. RADIUM VS. THE ANTI-SCIENTIST!
GRRR!
YEAH?! WELL, THAT GOES DOUBLE FOR ME, FELLA!

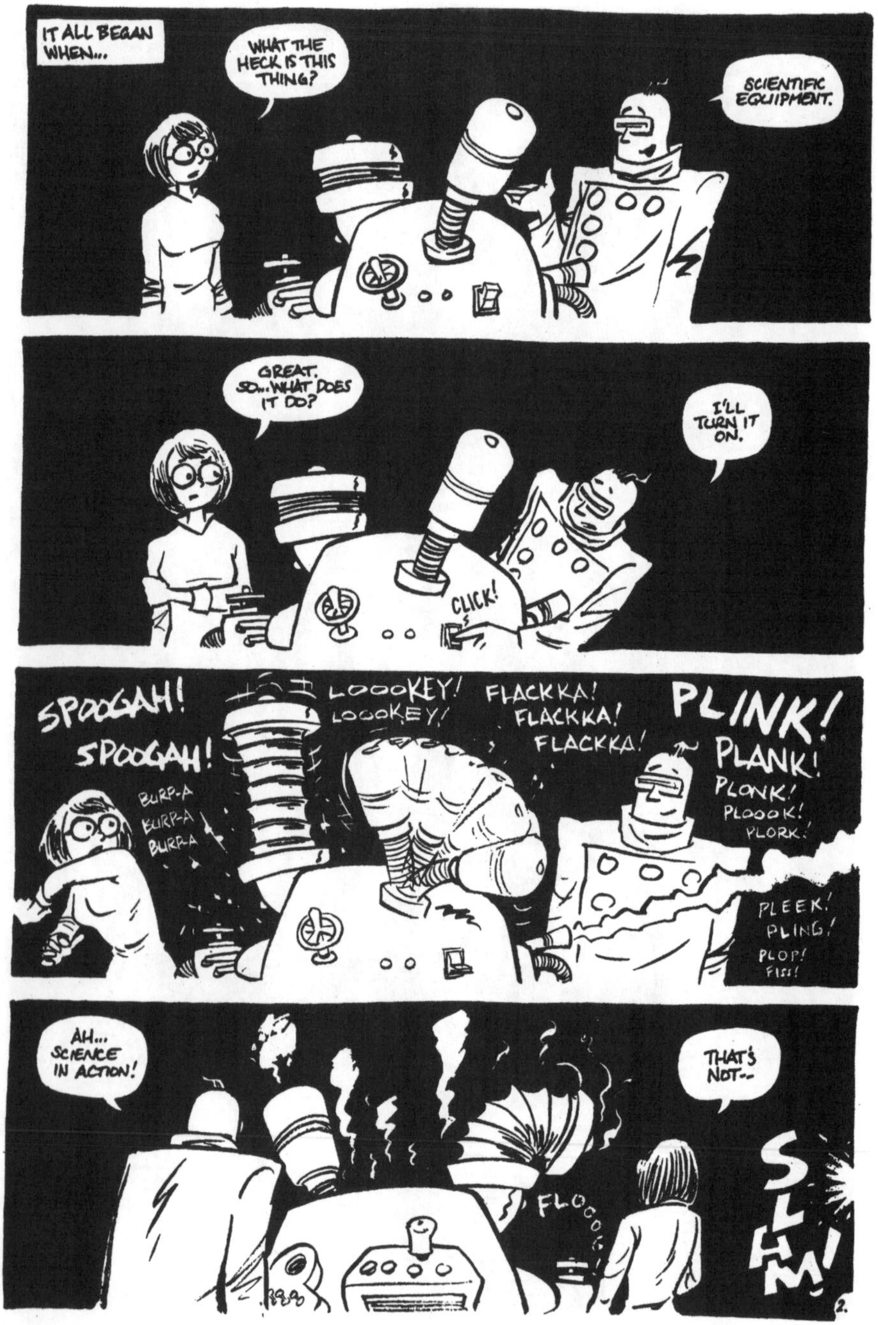
IT ALL BEGAN WHEN...
WHAT THE HECK IS THIS THING?
SCIENTIFIC EQUIPMENT.
GREAT. SO...WHAT DOES IT DO?
I'LL TURN IT ON.
CLICK!
SPOOGAH! SPOOGAH!
BURP-A BURP-A BURP-A
LOOOKEY! LOOOKEY!
FLACKKA! FLACKKA! FLACKKA!
PLINK! PLANK! PLONK! PLOOOK! PLORK!
PLEEK! PLING! PLOP! FISS!
AH... SCIENCE IN ACTION!
THAT'S NOT--
FLOOOG
SLAM!
2.

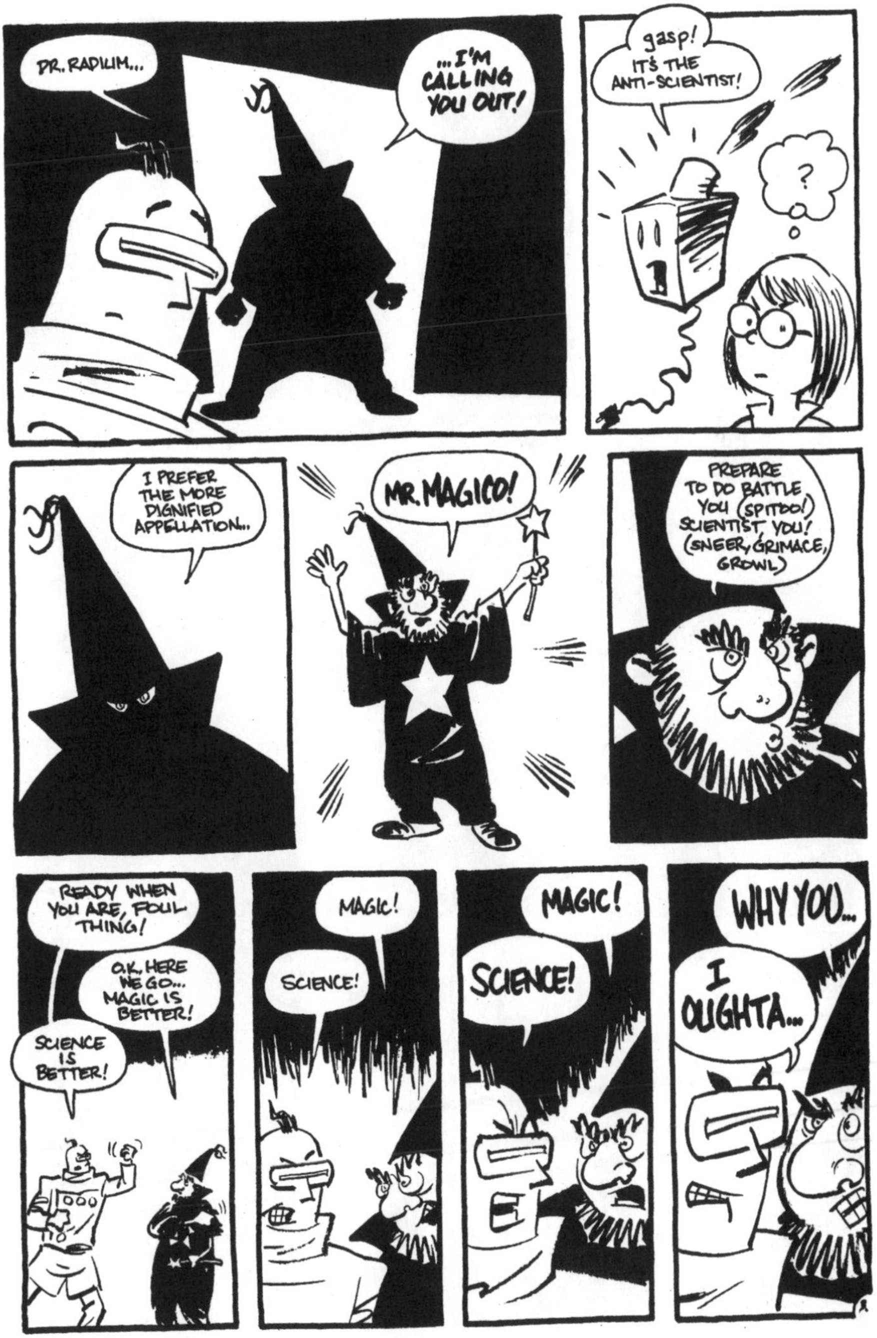

DR. RADIUM...
...I'M CALLING YOU OUT!
gasp! IT'S THE ANTI-SCIENTIST!
?
I PREFER THE MORE DIGNIFIED APPELLATION...
MR. MAGICO!
PREPARE TO DO BATTLE YOU (SPITOO!) SCIENTIST, YOU! (SNEER, GRIMACE, GROWL)
READY WHEN YOU ARE, FOUL THING!
O.K. HERE WE GO... MAGIC IS BETTER!
SCIENCE IS BETTER!
MAGIC!
SCIENCE!
MAGIC!
SCIENCE!
WHY YOU...
I OUGHTA...

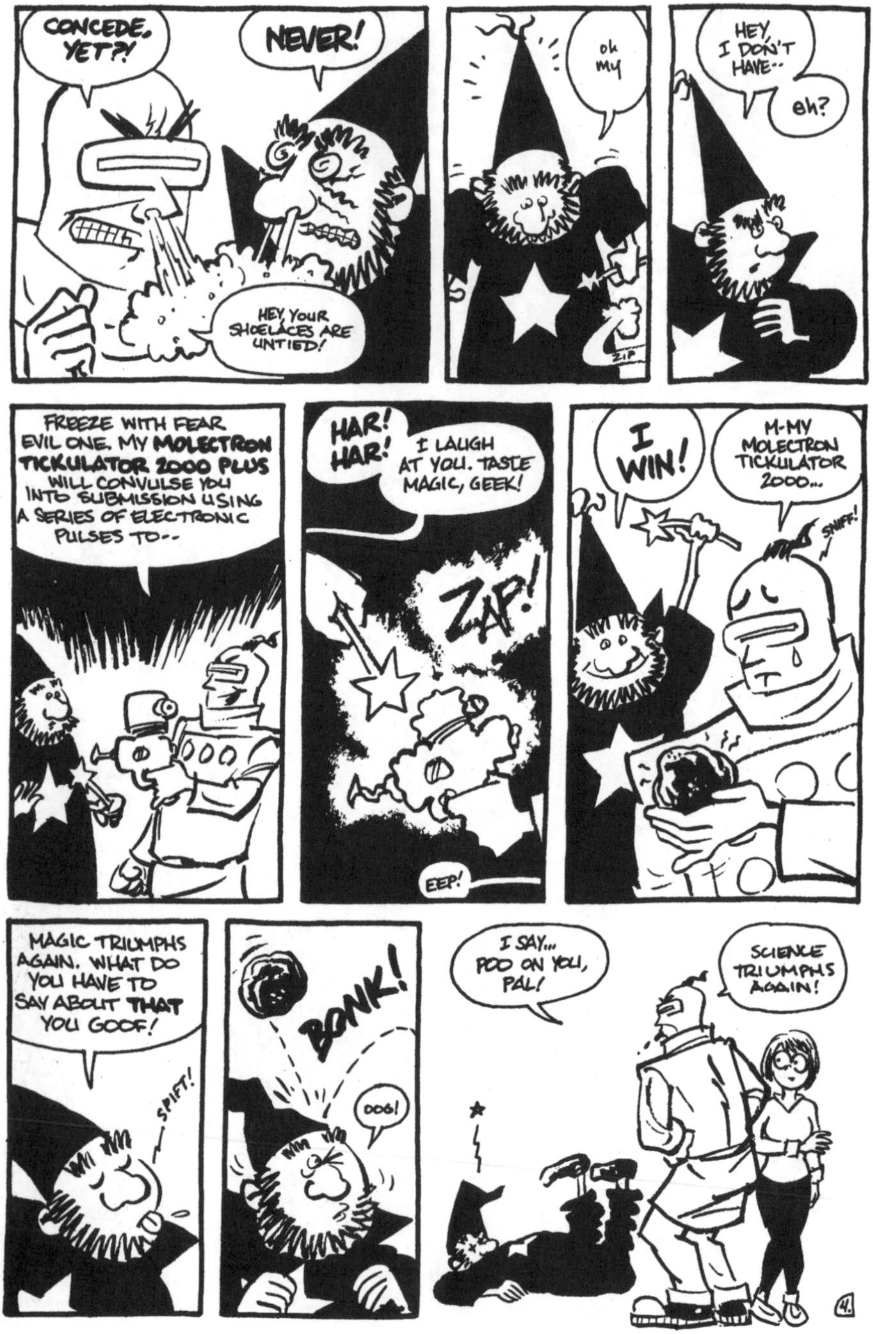
CONCEDE, YET?!
NEVER!
HEY, YOUR SHOELACES ARE UNTIED!
oh my
ZIP
HEY, I DON'T HAVE--
eh?
FREEZE WITH FEAR EVIL ONE. MY MOLECTRON TICKULATOR 2000 PLUS WILL CONVULSE YOU INTO SUBMISSION USING A SERIES OF ELECTRONIC PULSES TO--
HAR! HAR!
I LAUGH AT YOU. TASTE MAGIC, GEEK!
ZAP!
EEP!
I WIN!
M-MY MOLECTRON TICKULATOR 2000...
SNIFF!
MAGIC TRIUMPHS AGAIN. WHAT DO YOU HAVE TO SAY ABOUT THAT YOU GOOF!
SPIFT!
BONK!
OOG!
I SAY... POO ON YOU, PAL!
SCIENCE TRIUMPHS AGAIN!

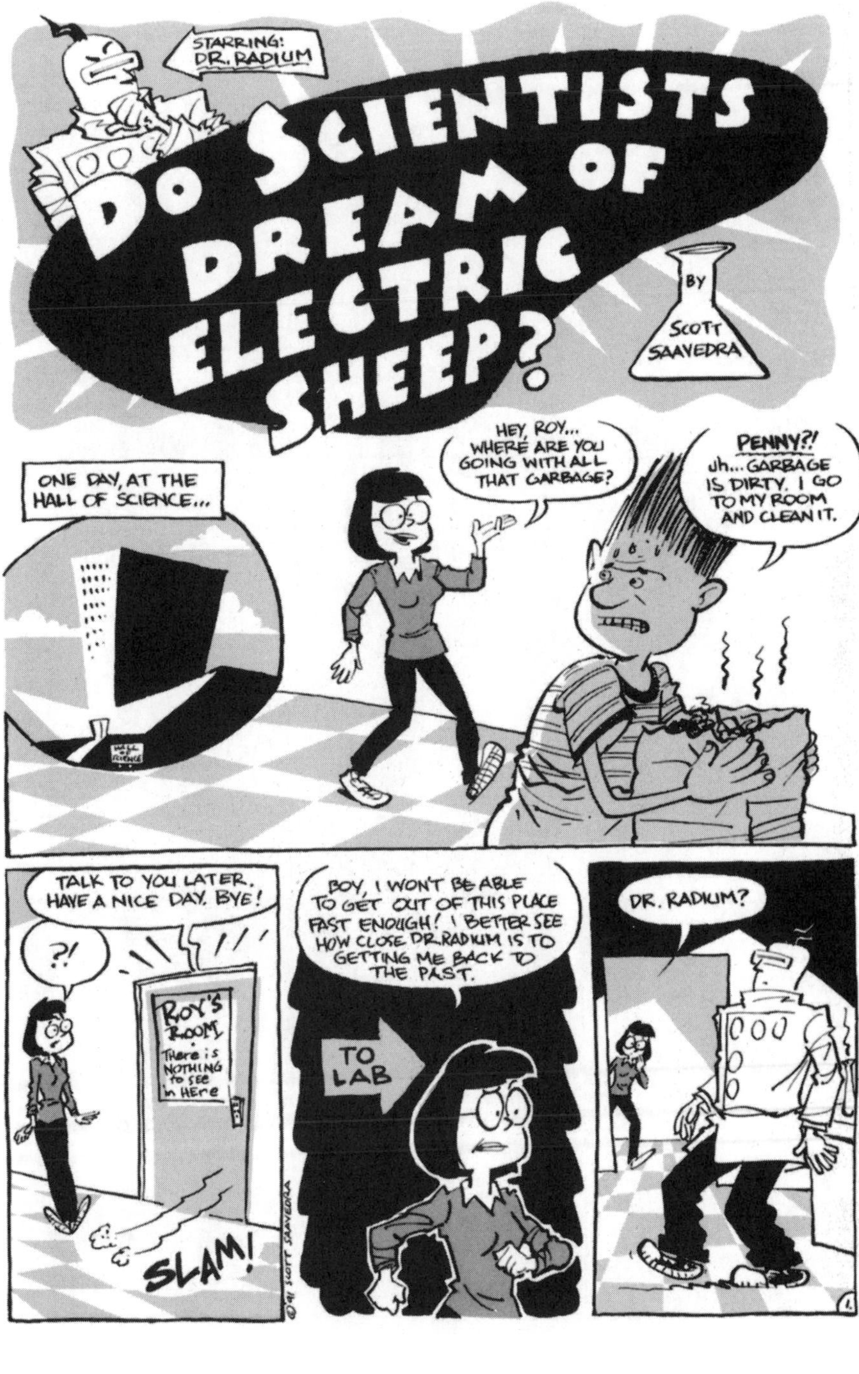
STARRING: DR. RADIUM
DO SCIENTISTS DREAM OF ELECTRIC SHEEP?
BY SCOTT SAAVEDRA
ONE DAY, AT THE HALL OF SCIENCE...
HALL OF SCIENCE
HEY, ROY... WHERE ARE YOU GOING WITH ALL THAT GARBAGE?
PENNY?! uh... GARBAGE IS DIRTY. I GO TO MY ROOM AND CLEAN IT.
TALK TO YOU LATER. HAVE A NICE DAY. BYE!
?!
ROY'S ROOM • There is NOTHING to see in HERE
SLAM!
© '91 SCOTT SAAVEDRA
BOY, I WON'T BE ABLE TO GET OUT OF THIS PLACE FAST ENOUGH! I BETTER SEE HOW CLOSE DR. RADIUM IS TO GETTING ME BACK TO THE PAST.
TO LAB
DR. RADIUM?
1.

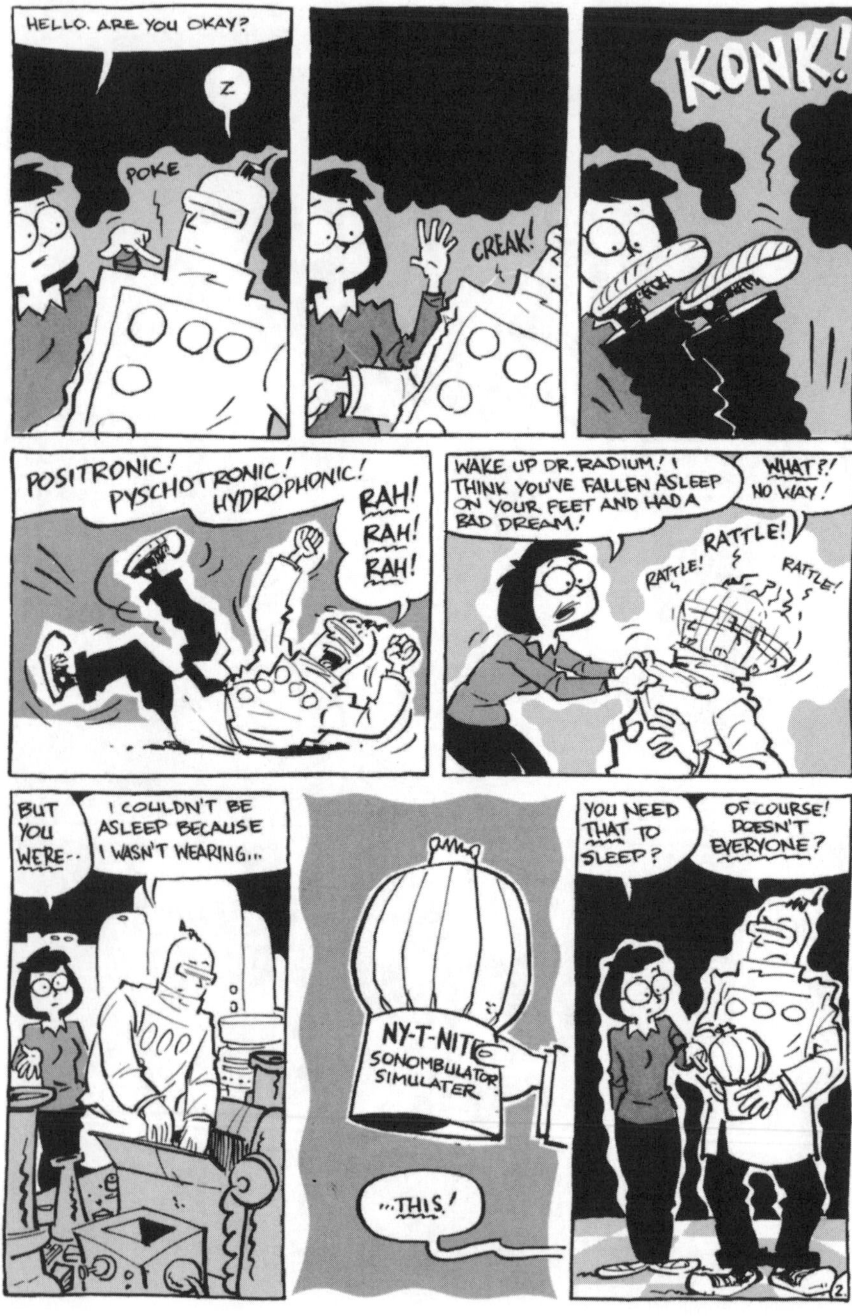
HELLO. ARE YOU OKAY?
Z
POKE
CREAK!
KONK!
POSITRONIC! PYSCHOTRONIC! HYDROPHONIC!
RAH! RAH! RAH!
WAKE UP DR. RADIUM! I THINK YOU'VE FALLEN ASLEEP ON YOUR FEET AND HAD A BAD DREAM!
WHAT?! NO WAY!
RATTLE! RATTLE! RATTLE!
BUT YOU WERE--
I COULDN'T BE ASLEEP BECAUSE I WASN'T WEARING...
NY-T-NITE SONOMBULATOR SIMULATER
...THIS!
YOU NEED THAT TO SLEEP?
OF COURSE! DOESN'T EVERYONE?
2.

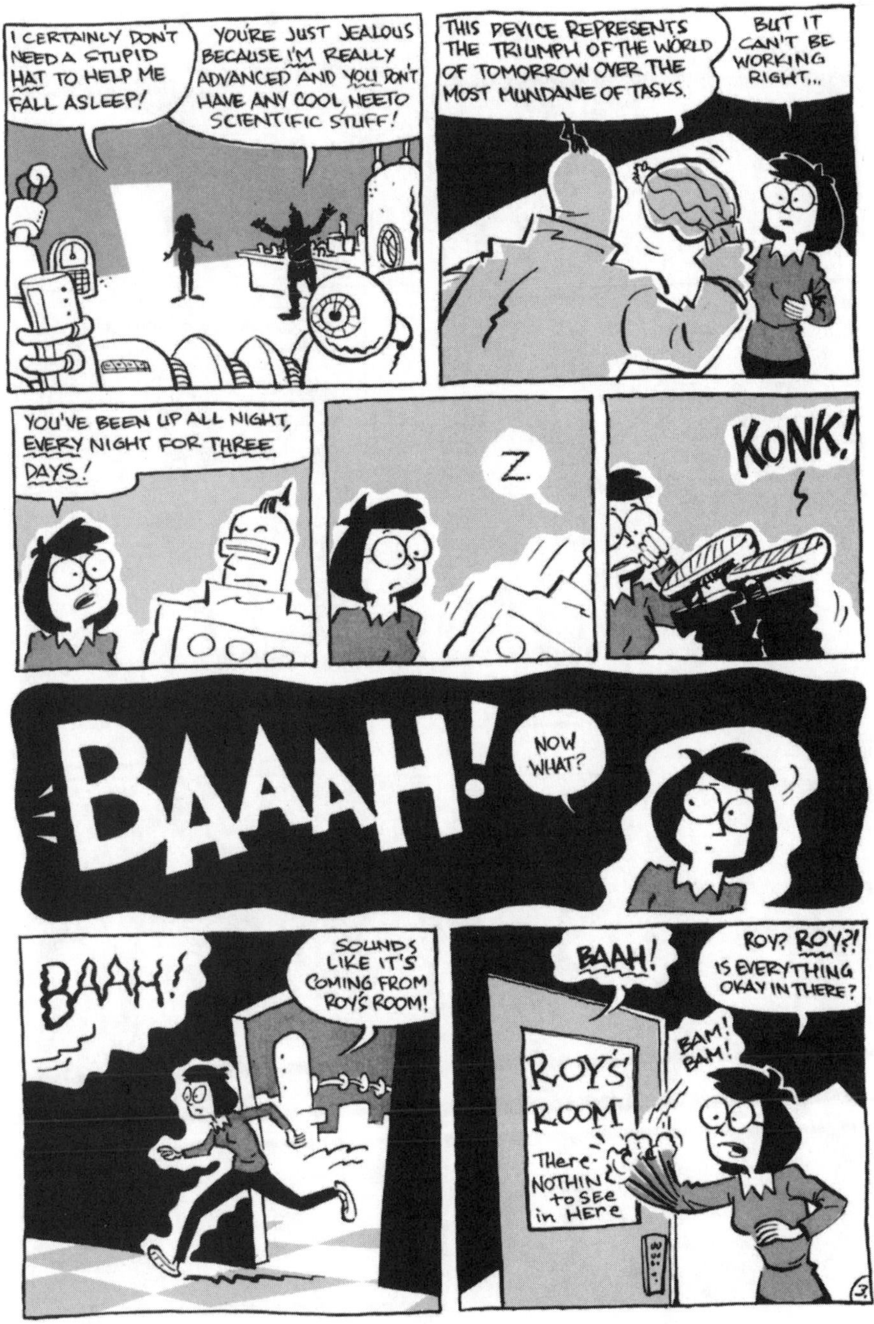
I CERTAINLY DON'T NEED A STUPID HAT TO HELP ME FALL ASLEEP!
YOU'RE JUST JEALOUS BECAUSE I'M REALLY ADVANCED AND YOU DON'T HAVE ANY COOL NEETO SCIENTIFIC STUFF!
THIS DEVICE REPRESENTS THE TRIUMPH OF THE WORLD OF TOMORROW OVER THE MOST MUNDANE OF TASKS.
BUT IT CAN'T BE WORKING RIGHT...
YOU'VE BEEN UP ALL NIGHT, EVERY NIGHT FOR THREE DAYS!
Z
KONK!
BAAAH!
NOW WHAT?
BAAH!
SOUNDS LIKE IT'S COMING FROM ROY'S ROOM!
BAAH!
ROY? ROY?!
IS EVERYTHING OKAY IN THERE?
BAM! BAM!
ROY'S ROOM
There NOTHIN to SEE in HEre
3.

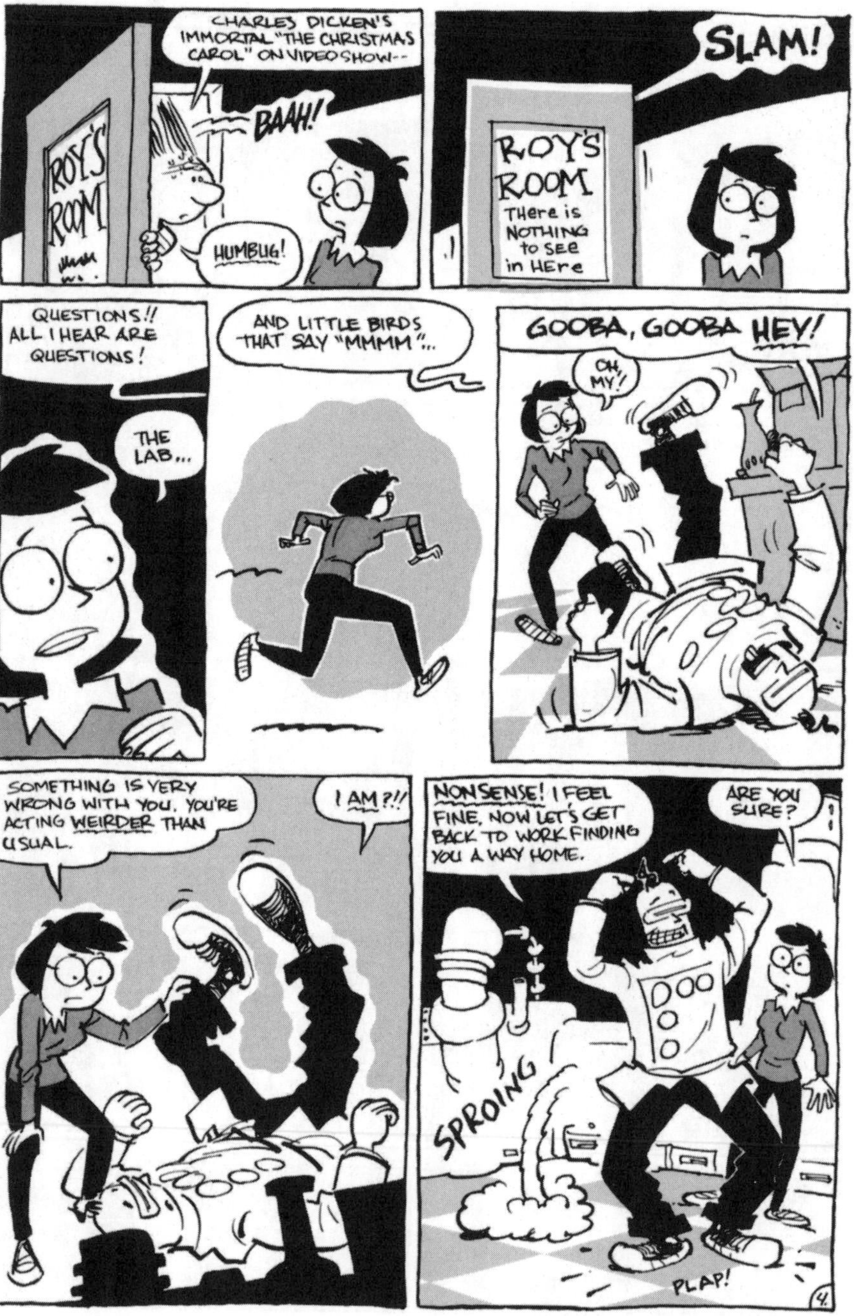

CHARLES DICKEN'S IMMORTAL "THE CHRISTMAS CAROL" ON VIDEO SHOW--
ROY'S ROOM
BAAH!
HUMBUG!
SLAM!
ROY'S ROOM
There is NOTHING to see in HEre
QUESTIONS!! ALL I HEAR ARE QUESTIONS!
THE LAB...
AND LITTLE BIRDS THAT SAY "MMMM"...
GOOBA, GOOBA HEY!
OH, MY!
SOMETHING IS VERY WRONG WITH YOU. YOU'RE ACTING WEIRDER THAN USUAL.
I AM?!!
NONSENSE! I FEEL FINE. NOW LET'S GET BACK TO WORK FINDING YOU A WAY HOME.
ARE YOU SURE?
SPROING
PLAP!
4.

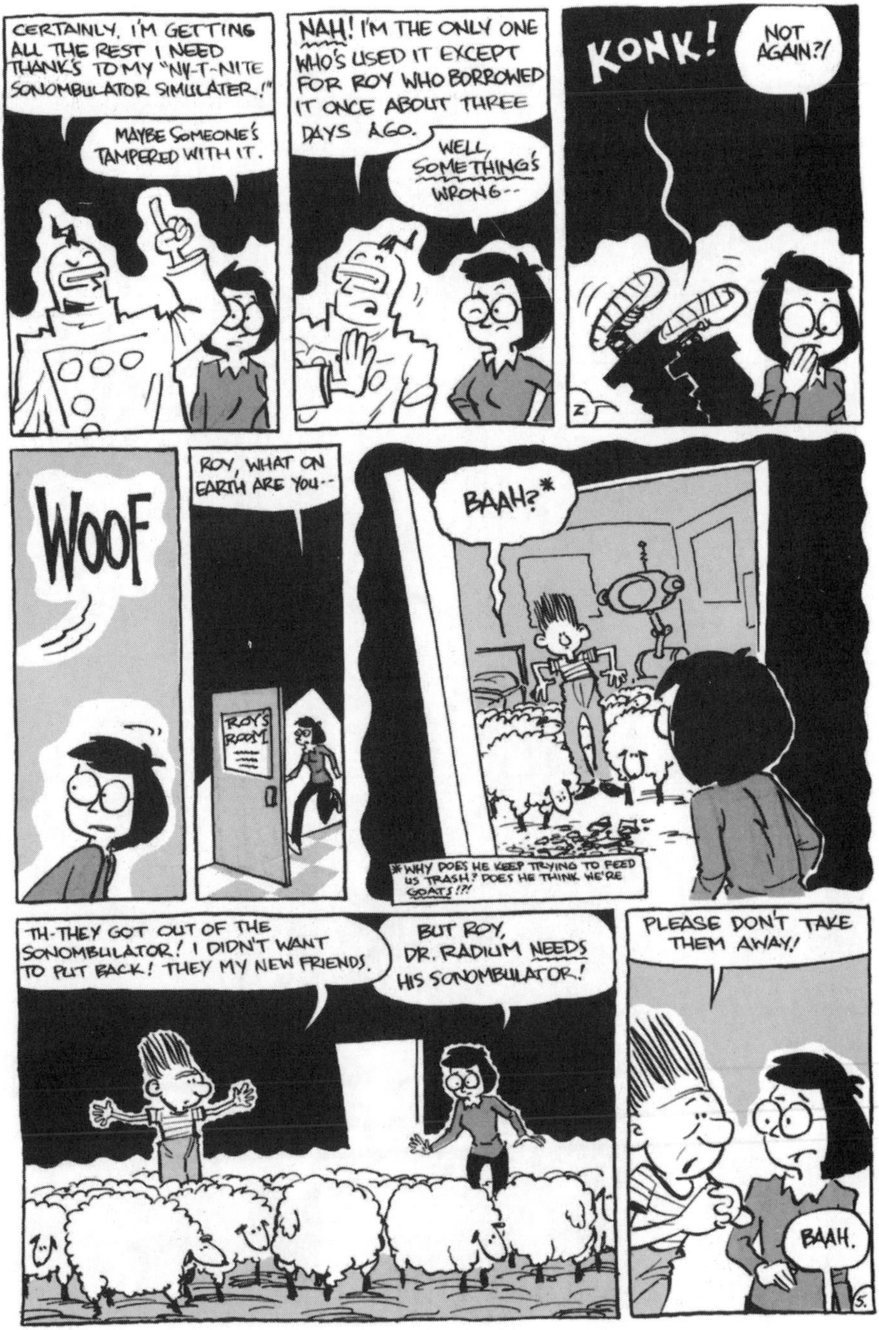
CERTAINLY, I'M GETTING ALL THE REST I NEED THANKS TO MY "NI-T-NITE SONOMBULATOR SIMULATER!"
MAYBE SOMEONE'S TAMPERED WITH IT.
NAH! I'M THE ONLY ONE WHO'S USED IT EXCEPT FOR ROY WHO BORROWED IT ONCE ABOUT THREE DAYS AGO.
WELL, SOMETHING'S WRONG--
KONK!
NOT AGAIN?!
Z
WOOF
ROY, WHAT ON EARTH ARE YOU--
ROY'S ROOM
BAAH?*
*WHY DOES HE KEEP TRYING TO FEED US TRASH? DOES HE THINK WE'RE GOATS!?!
TH-THEY GOT OUT OF THE SONOMBULATOR! I DIDN'T WANT TO PUT BACK! THEY MY NEW FRIENDS.
BUT ROY, DR. RADIUM NEEDS HIS SONOMBULATOR!
PLEASE DON'T TAKE THEM AWAY!
BAAH.
5.

IF THERE WERE SOME WAY TO--

PLEASE-O PLEASE-O PLEASE-O

REZ!

YOU'RE PRETTY SMART AREN'T YOU?

SURE, I'M A COMPUTER.

ROY'S ROOM

I NEED YOUR HELP WITH SOMETHING

LATER.

LAMBAHDAH!

KENNETH, WHAT IS THE--

BAAH

BAAH

WOOF!

ONE...

HE'S ASLEEP... BUT WEREN'T THE TWO OF YOU GOING TO BE WORKING ON SOMETHING TODAY?

OH, WELL...

LIGHT

...THERE'S ALWAYS TOMORROW.

CLICK!

Z!

52

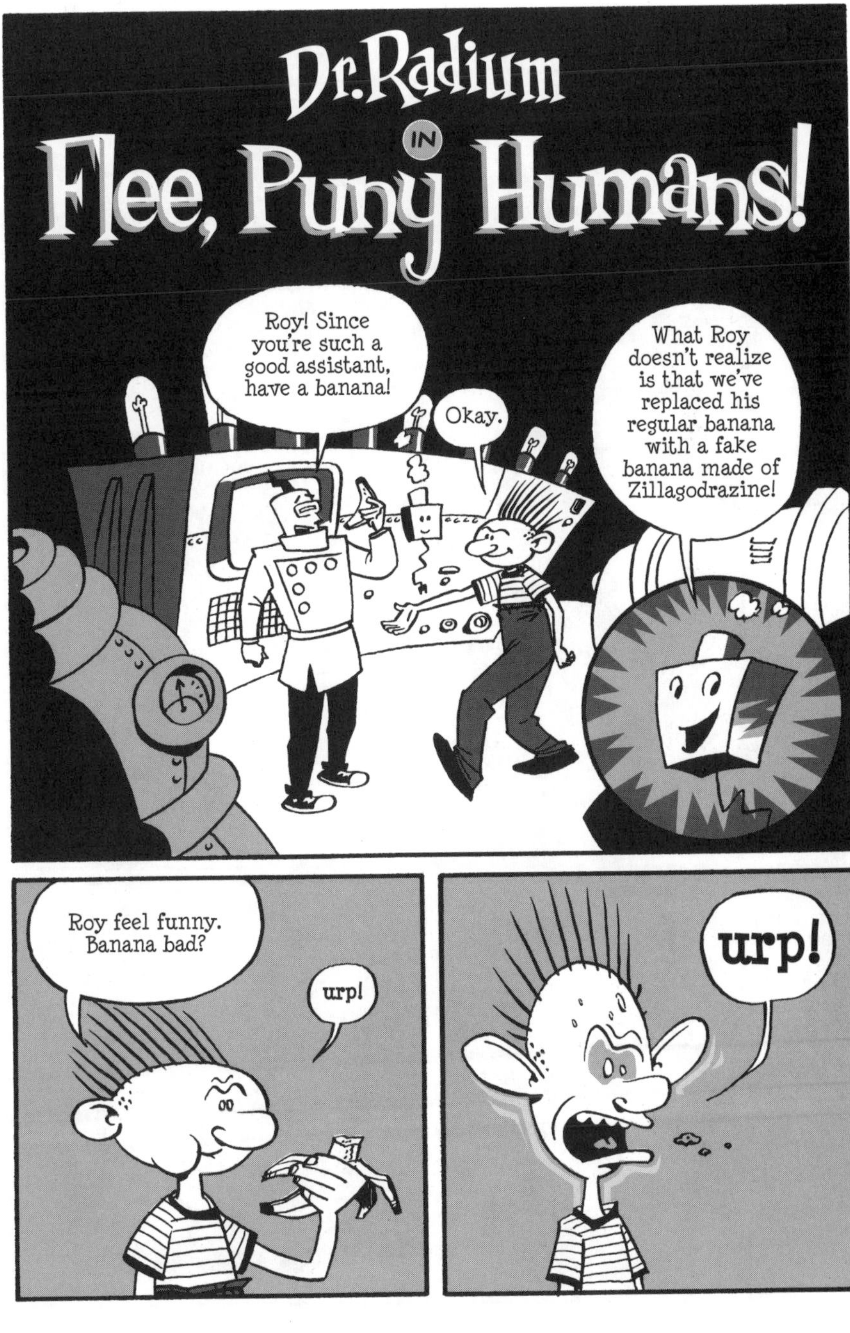
Dr. Radium
IN
Flee, Puny Humans!
Roy! Since you're such a good assistant, have a banana!
Okay.
What Roy doesn't realize is that we've replaced his regular banana with a fake banana made of Zillagodrazine!
Roy feel funny. Banana bad?
urp!
urp!

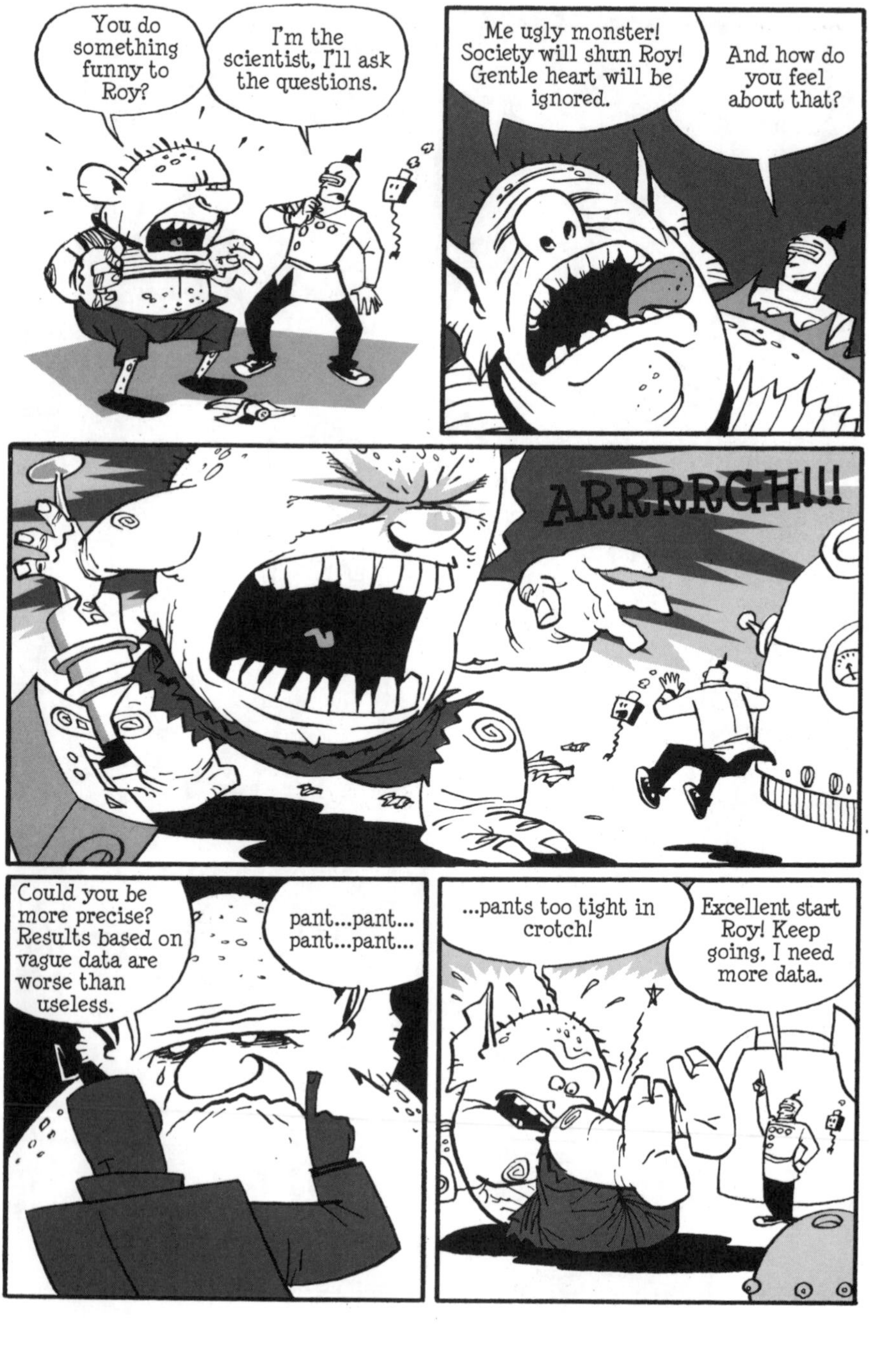
You do something funny to Roy?
I'm the scientist, I'll ask the questions.
Me ugly monster! Society will shun Roy! Gentle heart will be ignored.
And how do you feel about that?
ARRRRGH!!!
Could you be more precise? Results based on vague data are worse than useless.
pant...pant... pant...pant...
...pants too tight in crotch!
Excellent start Roy! Keep going, I need more data.

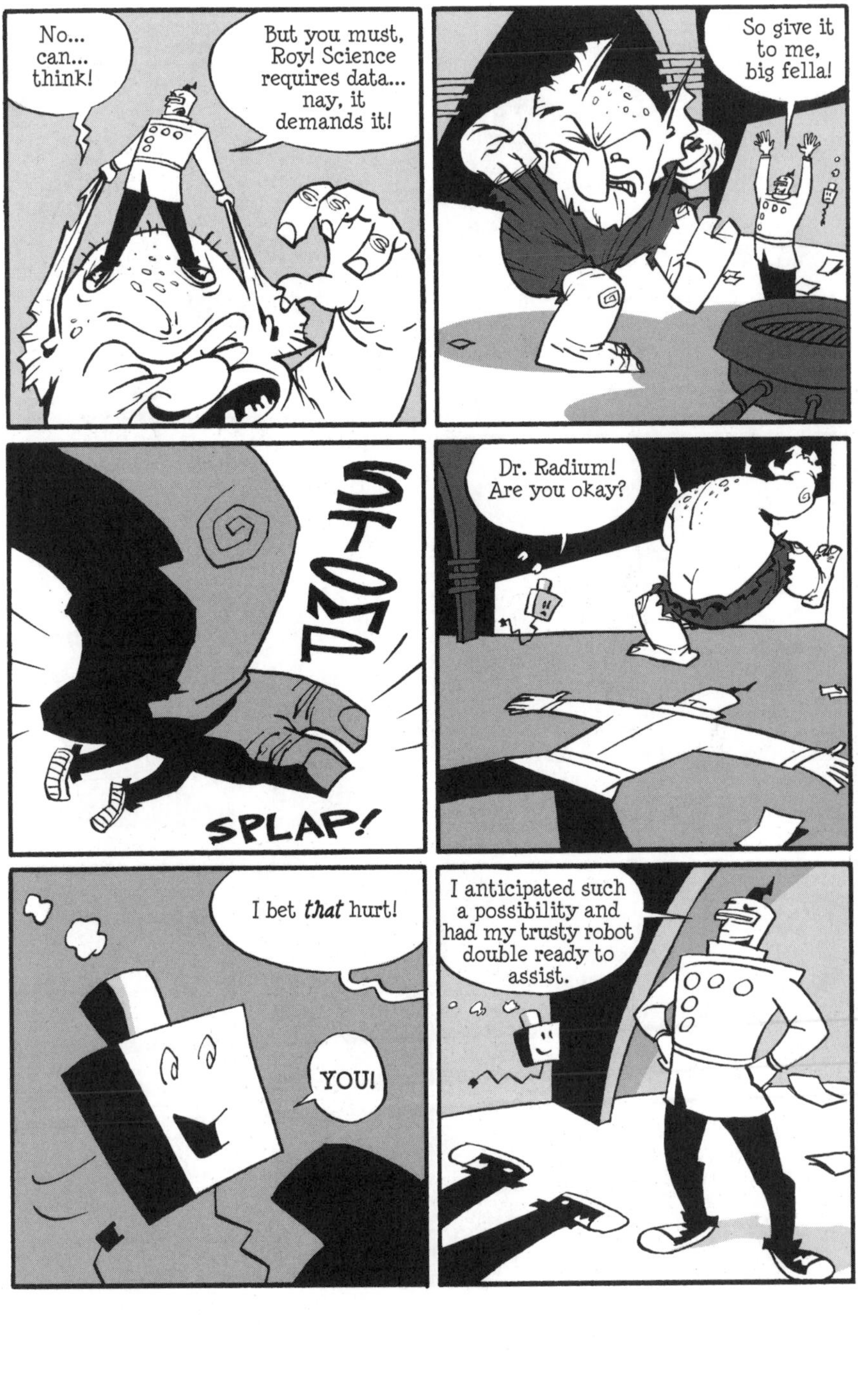

No... can... think!
But you must, Roy! Science requires data... nay, it demands it!
So give it to me, big fella!
STOMP
SPLAP!
Dr. Radium! Are you okay?
I bet *that* hurt!
YOU!
I anticipated such a possibility and had my trusty robot double ready to assist.

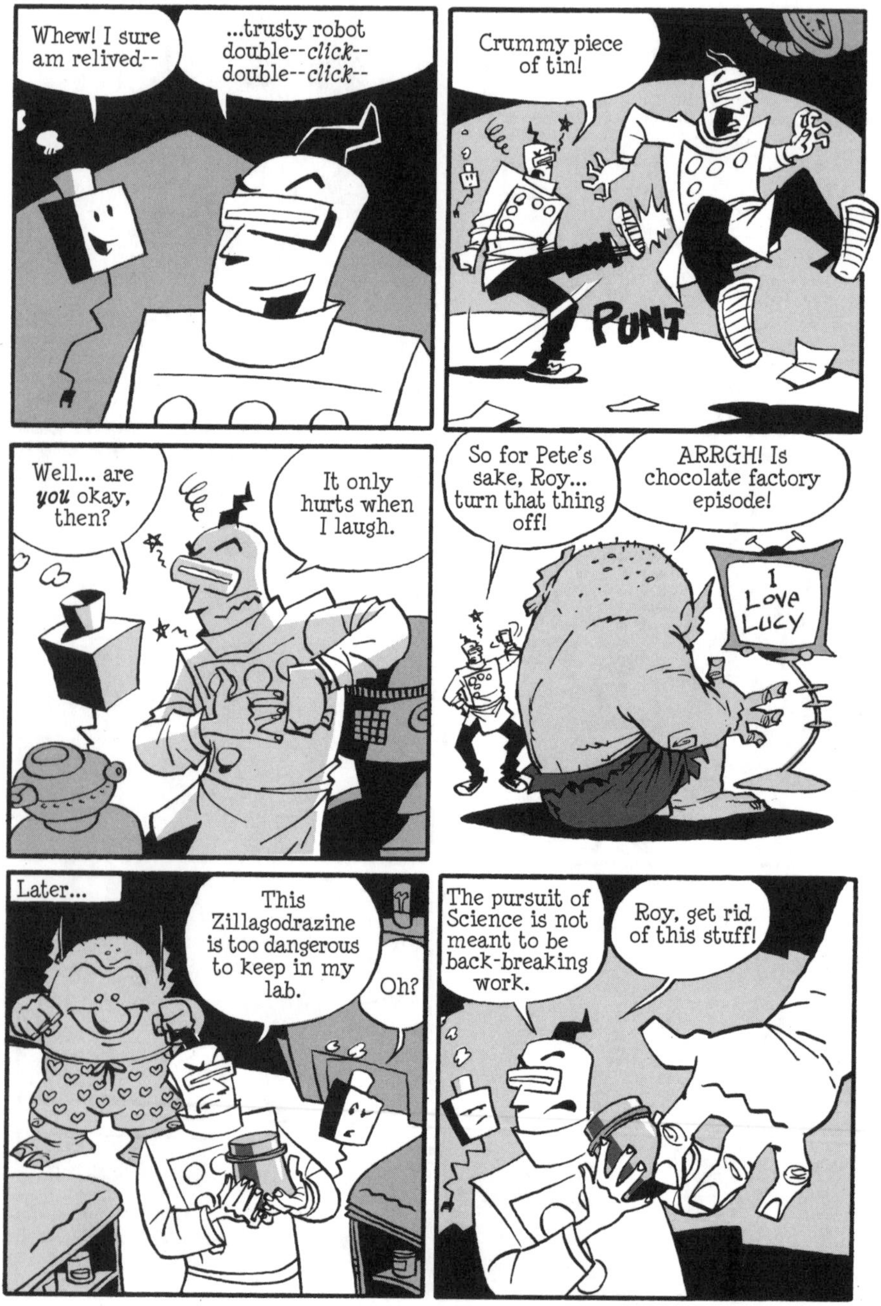
Whew! I sure am relived--
...trusty robot double--click-- double--click--
Crummy piece of tin!
PUNT
Well... are you okay, then?
It only hurts when I laugh.
So for Pete's sake, Roy... turn that thing off!
ARRGH! Is chocolate factory episode!
I Love Lucy
Later...
This Zillagodrazine is too dangerous to keep in my lab.
Oh?
The pursuit of Science is not meant to be back-breaking work.
Roy, get rid of this stuff!

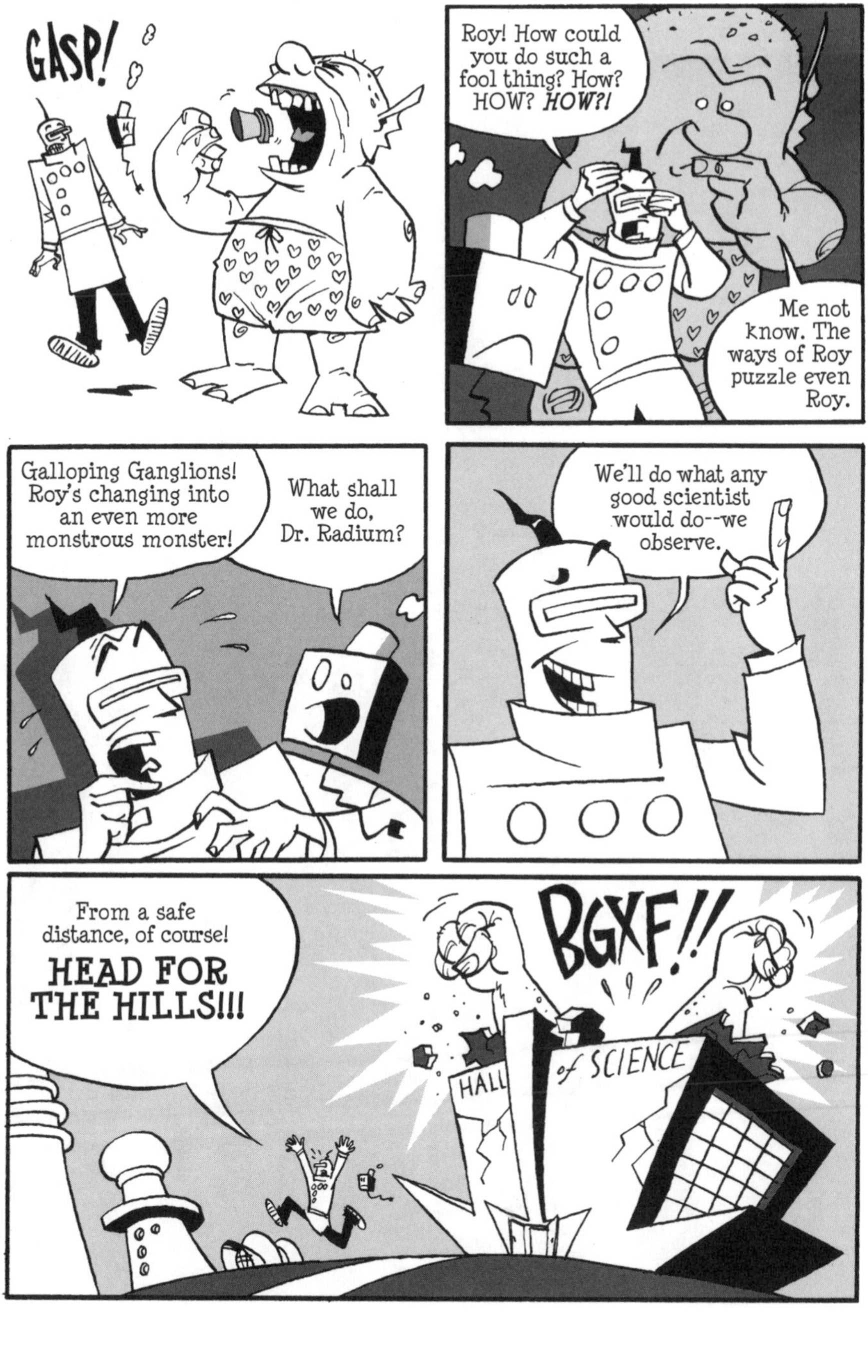
GASP!
Roy! How could you do such a fool thing? How? HOW? *HOW?!*
Me not know. The ways of Roy puzzle even Roy.
Galloping Ganglions! Roy's changing into an even more monstrous monster!
What shall we do, Dr. Radium?
We'll do what any good scientist would do--we observe.
From a safe distance, of course!
HEAD FOR THE HILLS!!!
BGXF!!
HALL of SCIENCE

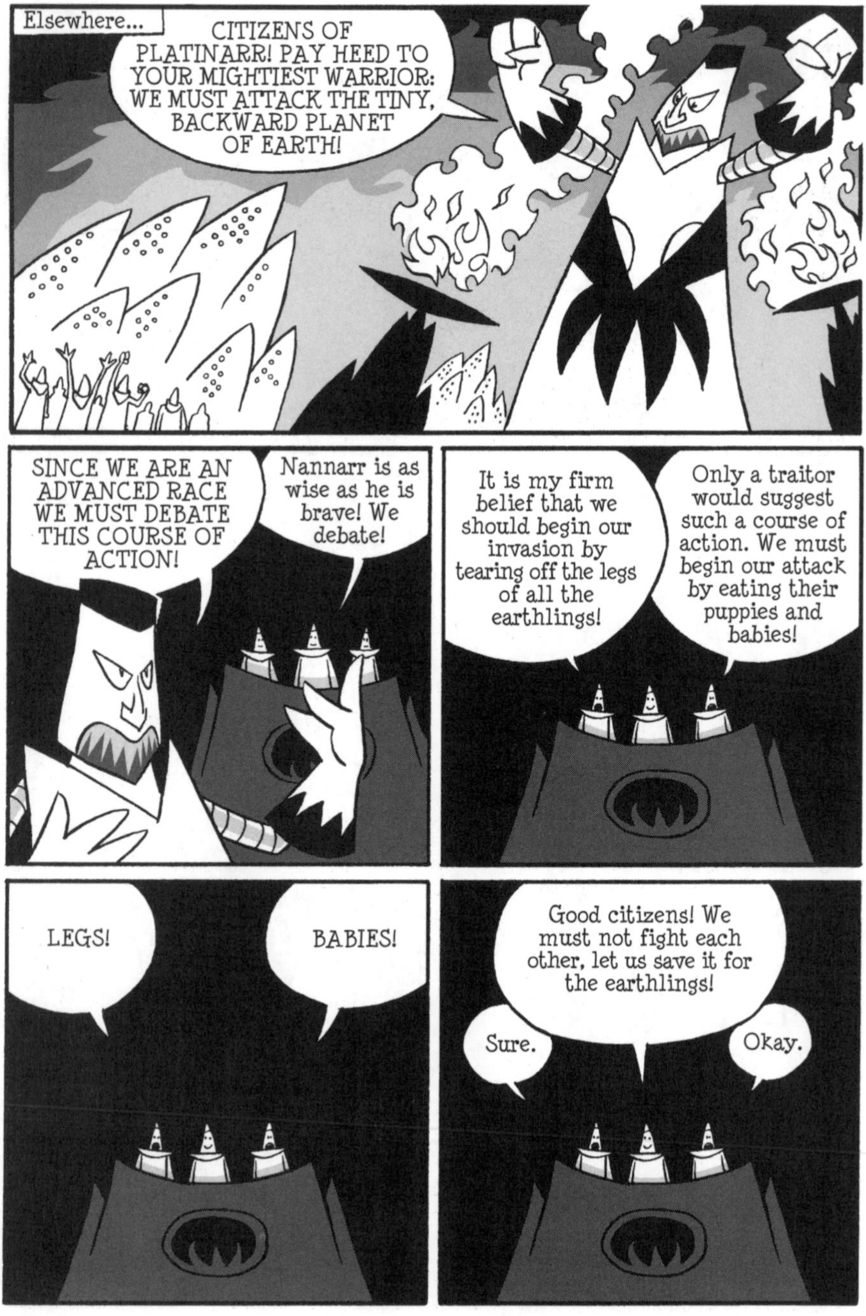

Elsewhere...
CITIZENS OF PLATINARR! PAY HEED TO YOUR MIGHTIEST WARRIOR: WE MUST ATTACK THE TINY, BACKWARD PLANET OF EARTH!
SINCE WE ARE AN ADVANCED RACE WE MUST DEBATE THIS COURSE OF ACTION!
Nannarr is as wise as he is brave! We debate!
It is my firm belief that we should begin our invasion by tearing off the legs of all the earthlings!
Only a traitor would suggest such a course of action. We must begin our attack by eating their puppies and babies!
LEGS!
BABIES!
Good citizens! We must not fight each other, let us save it for the earthlings!
Sure.
Okay.

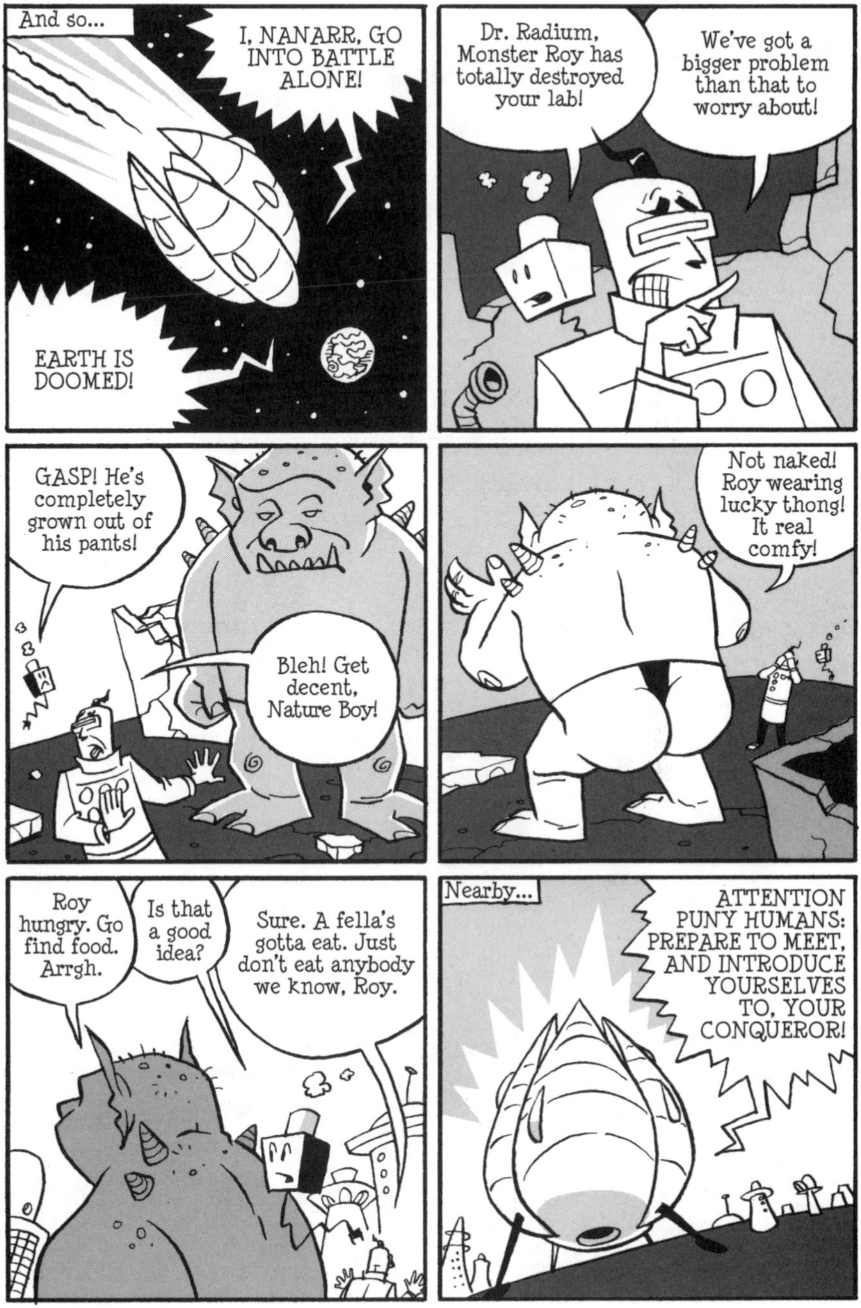
And so...
I, NANARR, GO INTO BATTLE ALONE!
EARTH IS DOOMED!
Dr. Radium, Monster Roy has totally destroyed your lab!
We've got a bigger problem than that to worry about!
GASP! He's completely grown out of his pants!
Bleh! Get decent, Nature Boy!
Not naked! Roy wearing lucky thong! It real comfy!
Roy hungry. Go find food. Arrgh.
Is that a good idea?
Sure. A fella's gotta eat. Just don't eat anybody we know, Roy.
Nearby...
ATTENTION PUNY HUMANS: PREPARE TO MEET, AND INTRODUCE YOURSELVES TO, YOUR CONQUEROR!

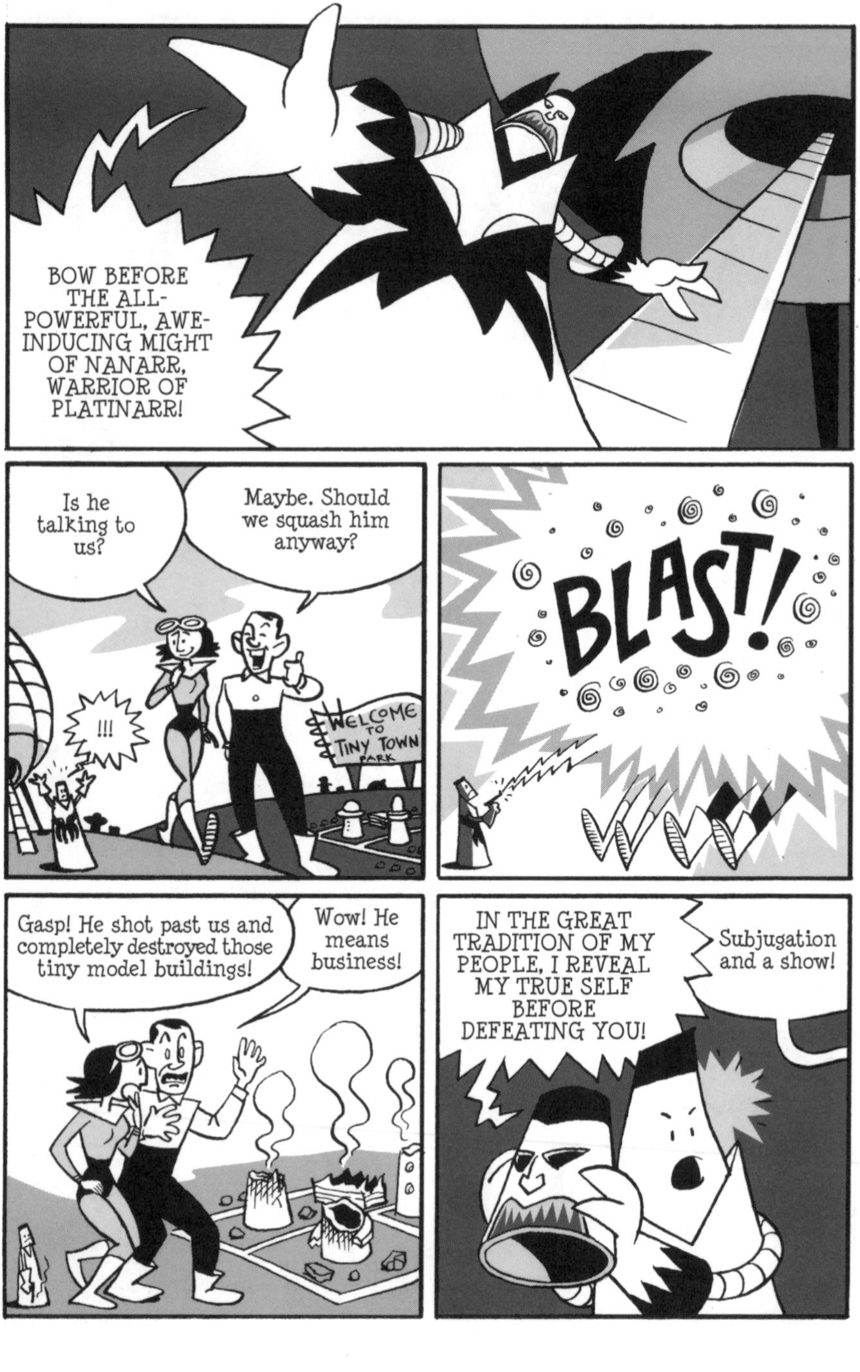
BOW BEFORE THE ALL-POWERFUL, AWE-INDUCING MIGHT OF NANARR, WARRIOR OF PLATINARR!
Is he talking to us?
Maybe. Should we squash him anyway?
!!!
WELCOME TO TINY TOWN PARK
BLAST!
Gasp! He shot past us and completely destroyed those tiny model buildings!
Wow! He means business!
IN THE GREAT TRADITION OF MY PEOPLE, I REVEAL MY TRUE SELF BEFORE DEFEATING YOU!
Subjugation and a show!

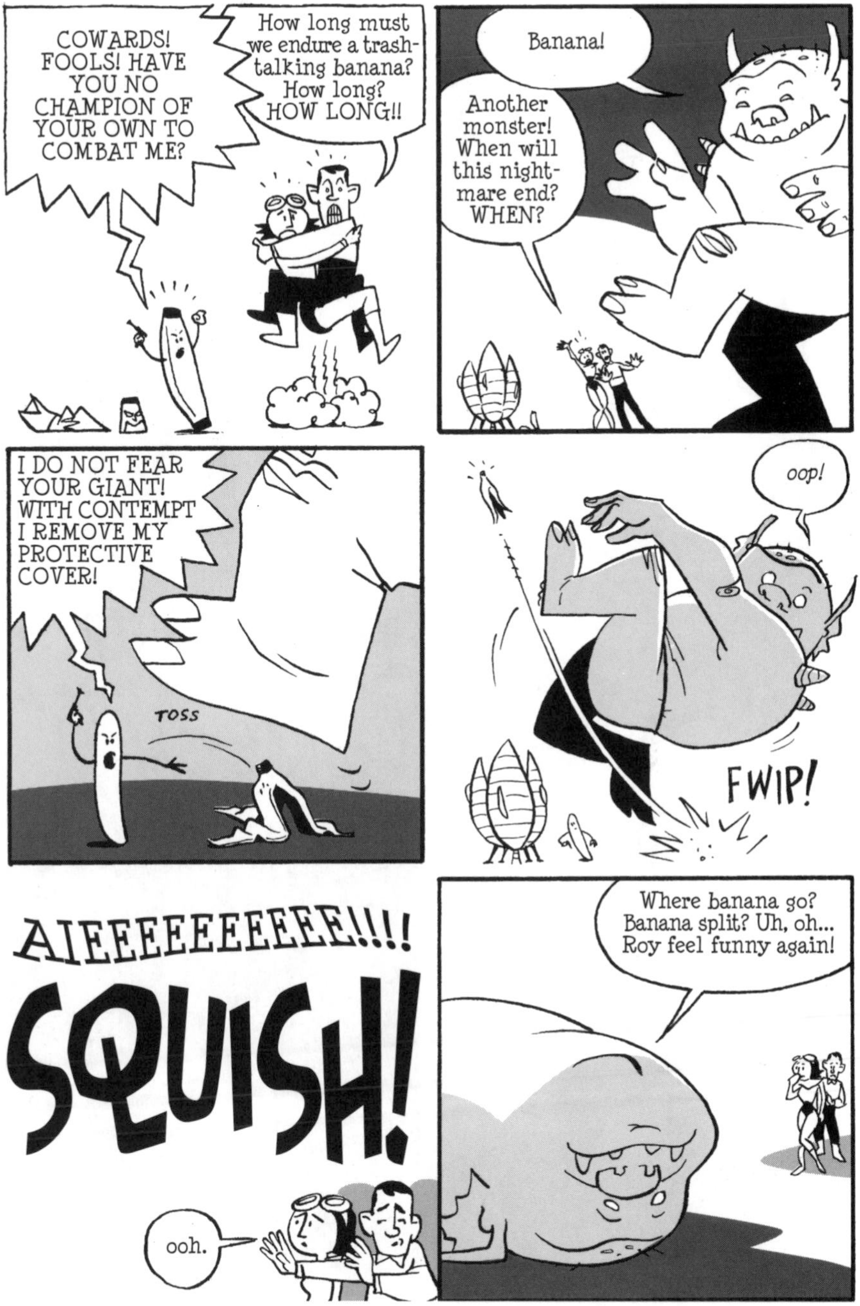
COWARDS! FOOLS! HAVE YOU NO CHAMPION OF YOUR OWN TO COMBAT ME?
How long must we endure a trash-talking banana? How long? HOW LONG!!
Banana!
Another monster! When will this night-mare end? WHEN?
I DO NOT FEAR YOUR GIANT! WITH CONTEMPT I REMOVE MY PROTECTIVE COVER!
TOSS
oop!
FWIP!
AIEEEEEEEEEEE!!!!
SQUISH!
ooh.
Where banana go? Banana split? Uh, oh... Roy feel funny again!

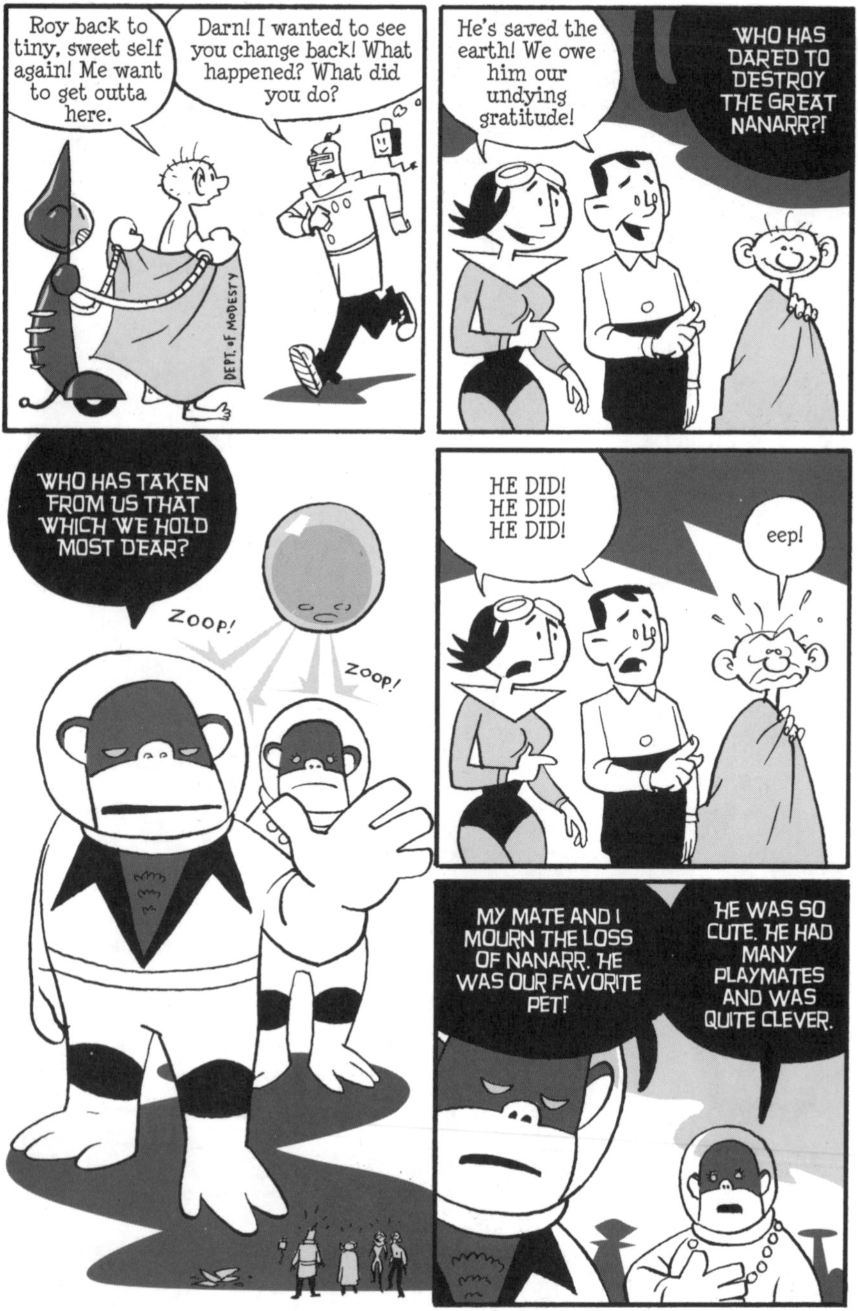
Roy back to tiny, sweet self again! Me want to get outta here.
Darn! I wanted to see you change back! What happened? What did you do?
DEPT. of MODESTY
He's saved the earth! We owe him our undying gratitude!
WHO HAS DARED TO DESTROY THE GREAT NANARR?!
WHO HAS TAKEN FROM US THAT WHICH WE HOLD MOST DEAR?
ZOOP!
ZOOP!
HE DID! HE DID! HE DID!
eep!
MY MATE AND I MOURN THE LOSS OF NANARR. HE WAS OUR FAVORITE PET!
HE WAS SO CUTE. HE HAD MANY PLAYMATES AND WAS QUITE CLEVER.

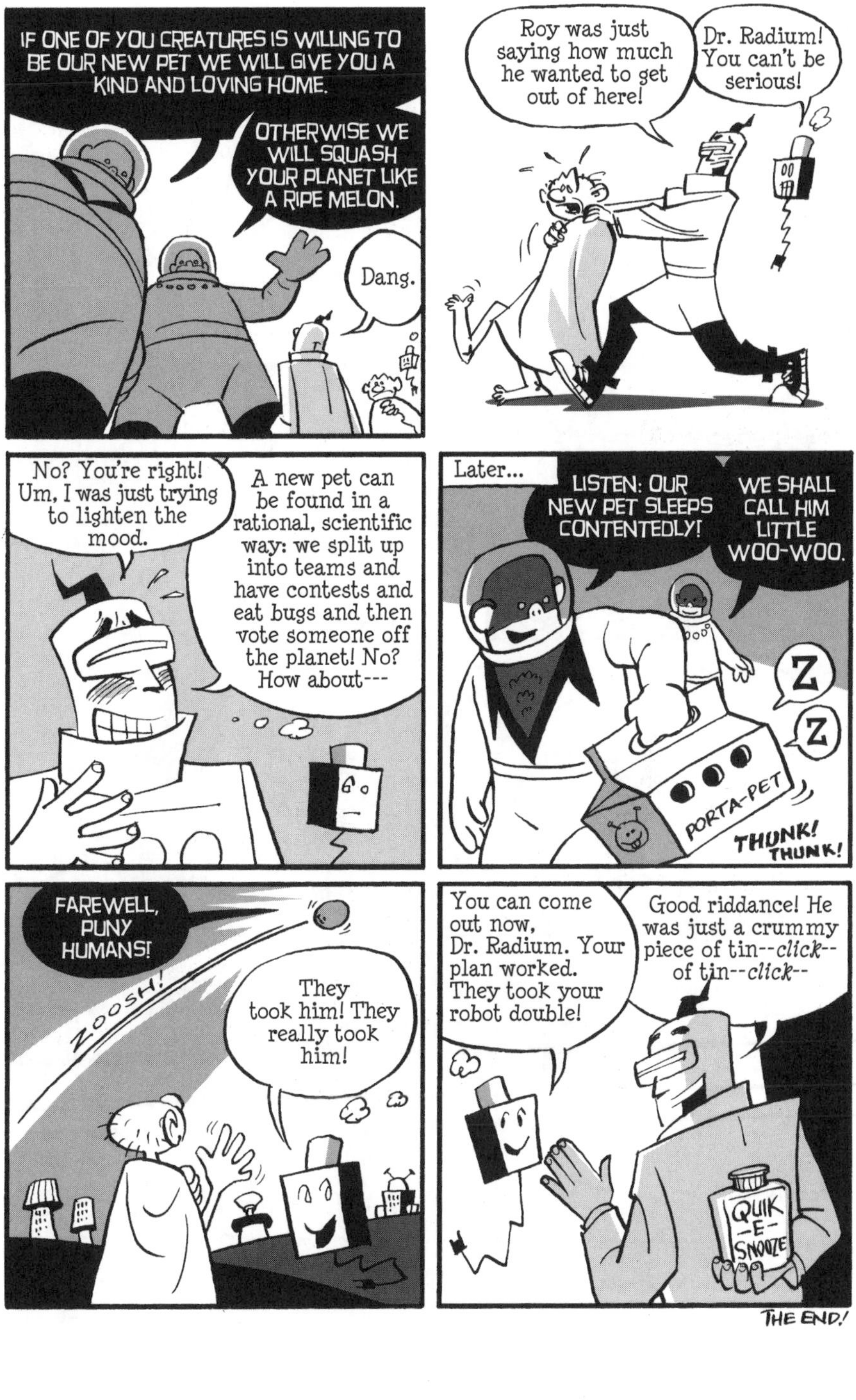
IF ONE OF YOU CREATURES IS WILLING TO BE OUR NEW PET WE WILL GIVE YOU A KIND AND LOVING HOME.
OTHERWISE WE WILL SQUASH YOUR PLANET LIKE A RIPE MELON.
Dang.
Roy was just saying how much he wanted to get out of here!
Dr. Radium! You can't be serious!
No? You're right! Um, I was just trying to lighten the mood.
A new pet can be found in a rational, scientific way: we split up into teams and have contests and eat bugs and then vote someone off the planet! No? How about---
Later...
LISTEN: OUR NEW PET SLEEPS CONTENTEDLY!
WE SHALL CALL HIM LITTLE WOO-WOO.
Z
Z
PORTA-PET
THUNK! THUNK!
FAREWELL, PUNY HUMANS!
ZOOSH!
They took him! They really took him!
You can come out now, Dr. Radium. Your plan worked. They took your robot double!
Good riddance! He was just a crummy piece of tin--*click*--of tin--*click*--
QUIK -E- SNOOZE
THE END!

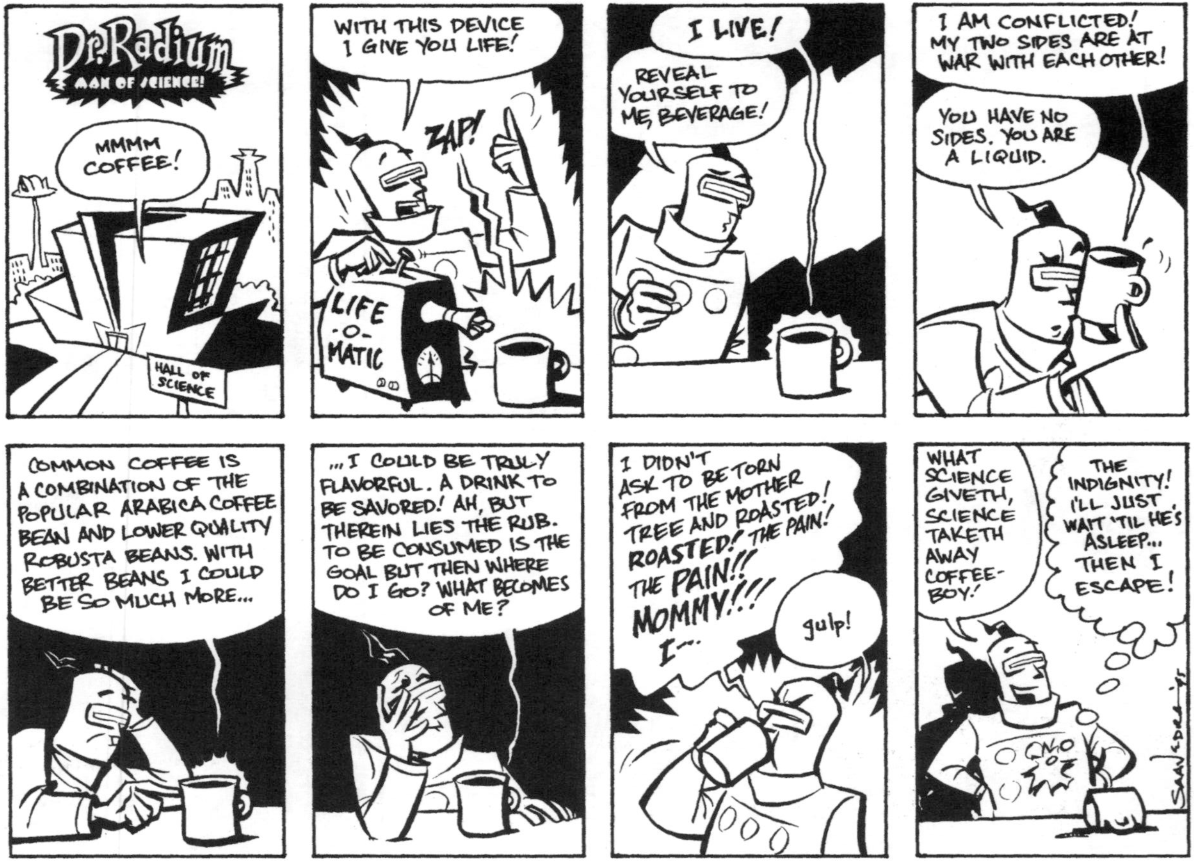
Dr. Radium
MAN OF SCIENCE!
MMMM COFFEE!
HALL OF SCIENCE
WITH THIS DEVICE I GIVE YOU LIFE!
ZAP!
LIFE -O- MATIC
I LIVE!
REVEAL YOURSELF TO ME, BEVERAGE!
I AM CONFLICTED! MY TWO SIDES ARE AT WAR WITH EACH OTHER!
YOU HAVE NO SIDES. YOU ARE A LIQUID.
COMMON COFFEE IS A COMBINATION OF THE POPULAR ARABICA COFFEE BEAN AND LOWER QUALITY ROBUSTA BEANS. WITH BETTER BEANS I COULD BE SO MUCH MORE...
...I COULD BE TRULY FLAVORFUL. A DRINK TO BE SAVORED! AH, BUT THEREIN LIES THE RUB. TO BE CONSUMED IS THE GOAL BUT THEN WHERE DO I GO? WHAT BECOMES OF ME?
I DIDN'T ASK TO BE TORN FROM THE MOTHER TREE AND ROASTED! ROASTED! THE PAIN! THE PAIN!!! MOMMY!!! I—
gulp!
WHAT SCIENCE GIVETH, SCIENCE TAKETH AWAY COFFEE-BOY!
THE INDIGNITY! I'LL JUST WAIT 'TIL HE'S ASLEEP... THEN I ESCAPE!

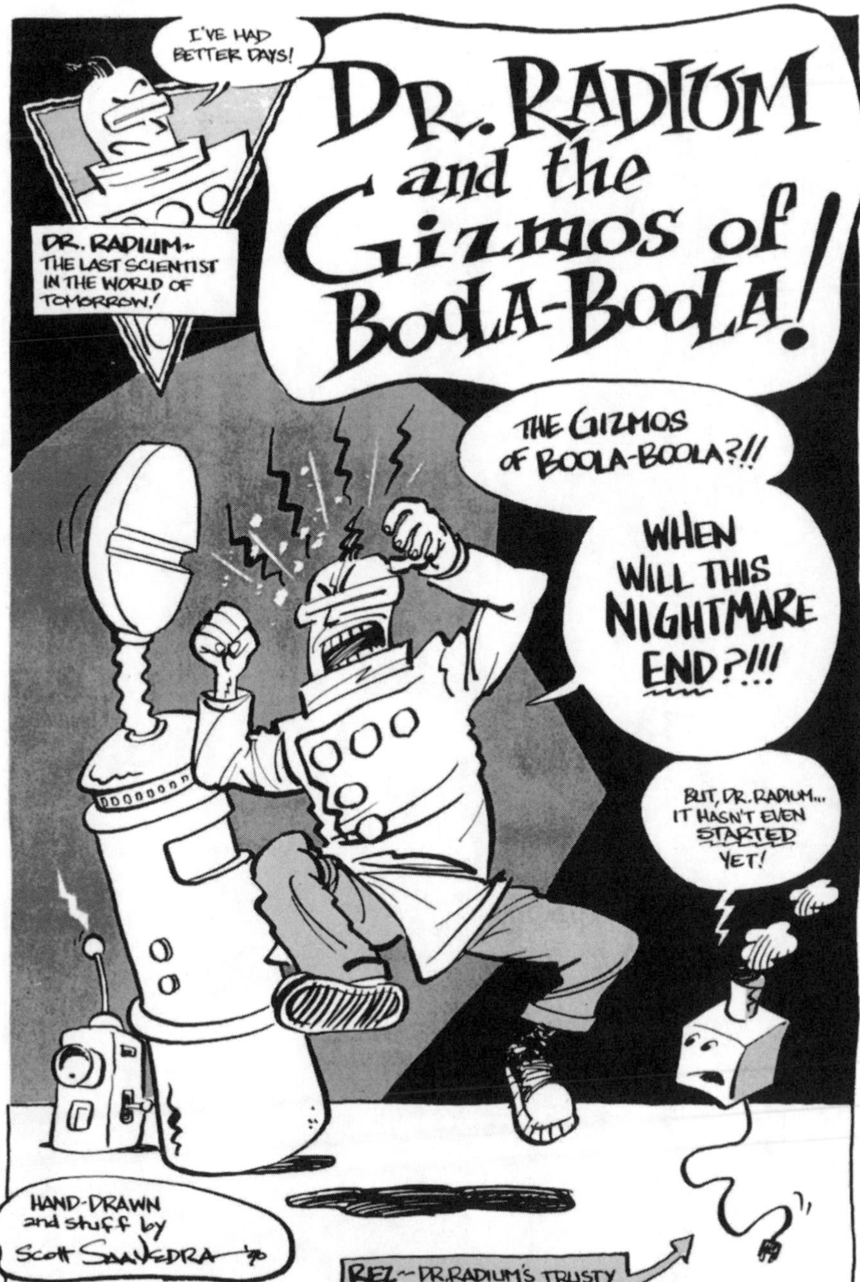
I'VE HAD BETTER DAYS!
DR. RADIUM and the GIZMOS of BOOLA-BOOLA!
DR. RADIUM - THE LAST SCIENTIST IN THE WORLD OF TOMORROW!
THE GIZMOS OF BOOLA-BOOLA?!!
WHEN WILL THIS NIGHTMARE END?!!!...
BUT, DR. RADIUM... IT HASN'T EVEN STARTED YET!
HAND-DRAWN and stuff by Scott Saavedra '90
REZ -- DR. RADIUM'S TRUSTY COMPUTER PAL!

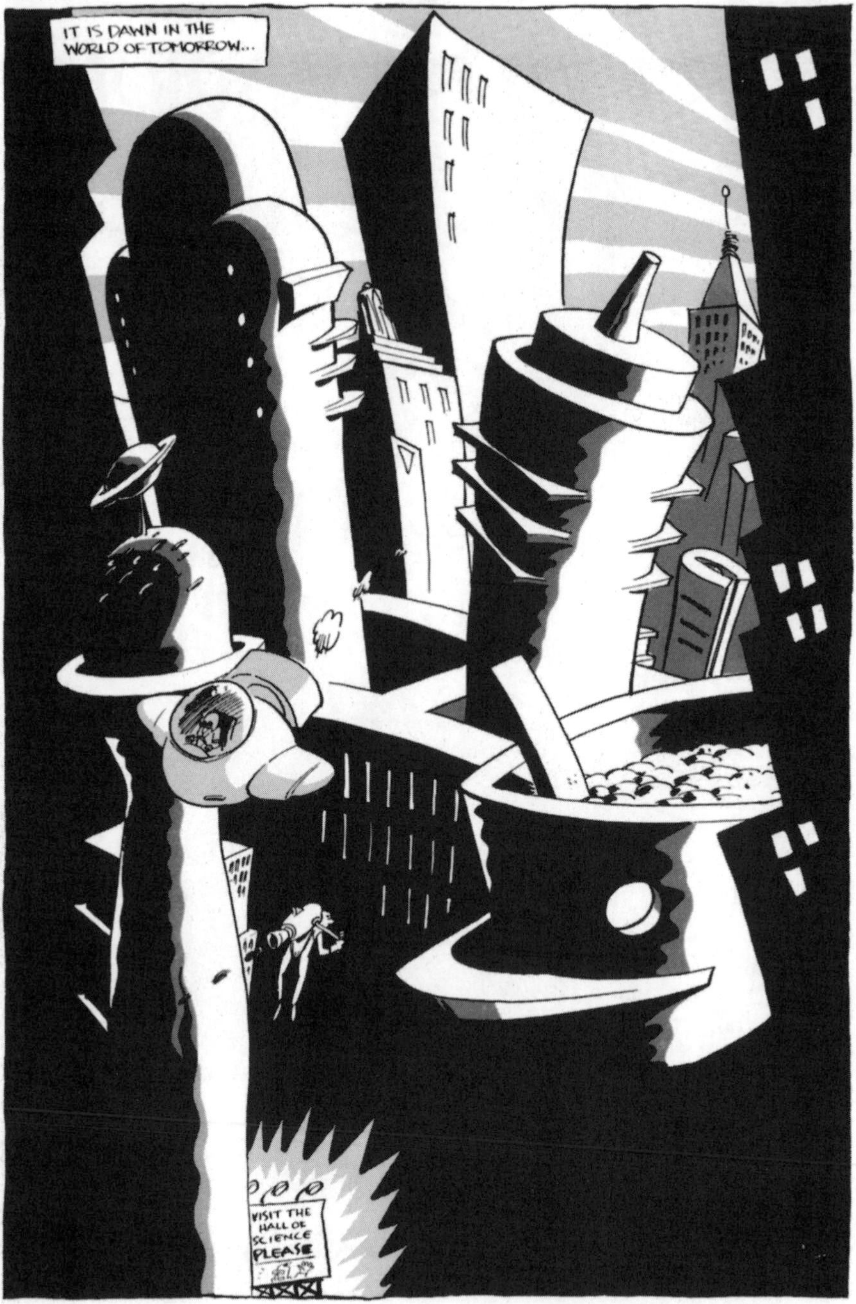
IT IS DAWN IN THE WORLD OF TOMORROW...
VISIT THE HALL OF SCIENCE PLEASE

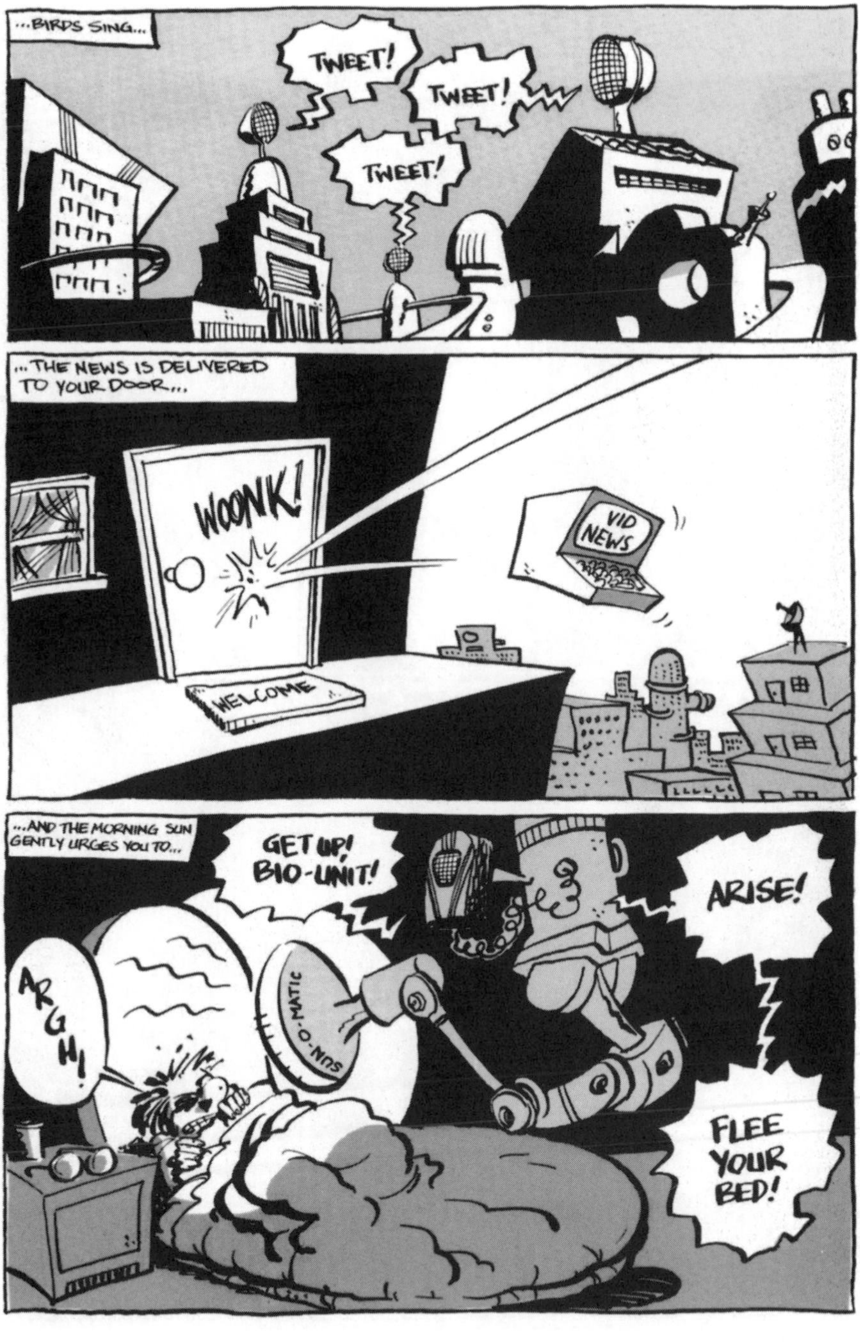
...BIRDS SING...
TWEET!
TWEET!
TWEET!
...THE NEWS IS DELIVERED TO YOUR DOOR...
WOONK!
VID NEWS
WELCOME
...AND THE MORNING SUN GENTLY URGES YOU TO...
GET UP! BIO-UNIT!
ARISE!
ARGH!
SUN-O-MATIC
FLEE YOUR BED!

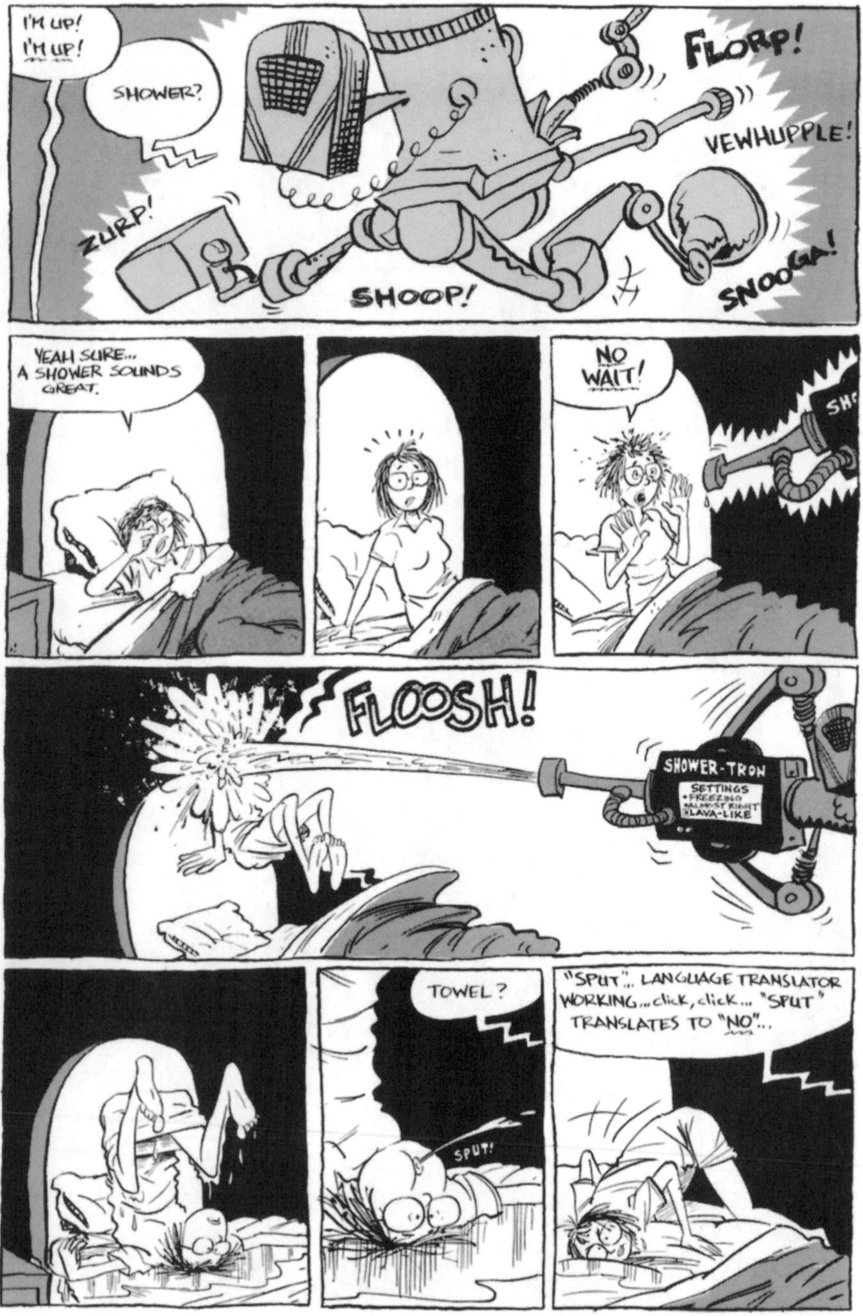
I'M UP! I'M UP!
SHOWER?
FLORP!
VEWHUPPLE!
ZURP!
SHOOP!
SNOOGA!
YEAH SURE... A SHOWER SOUNDS GREAT.
NO WAIT!
FLOOSH!
SHOWER-TRON
SETTINGS
• FREEZING
• ALMOST RIGHT
• LAVA-LIKE
TOWEL?
SPUT!
"SPUT".. LANGUAGE TRANSLATOR WORKING... click, click... "SPUT" TRANSLATES TO "NO"..

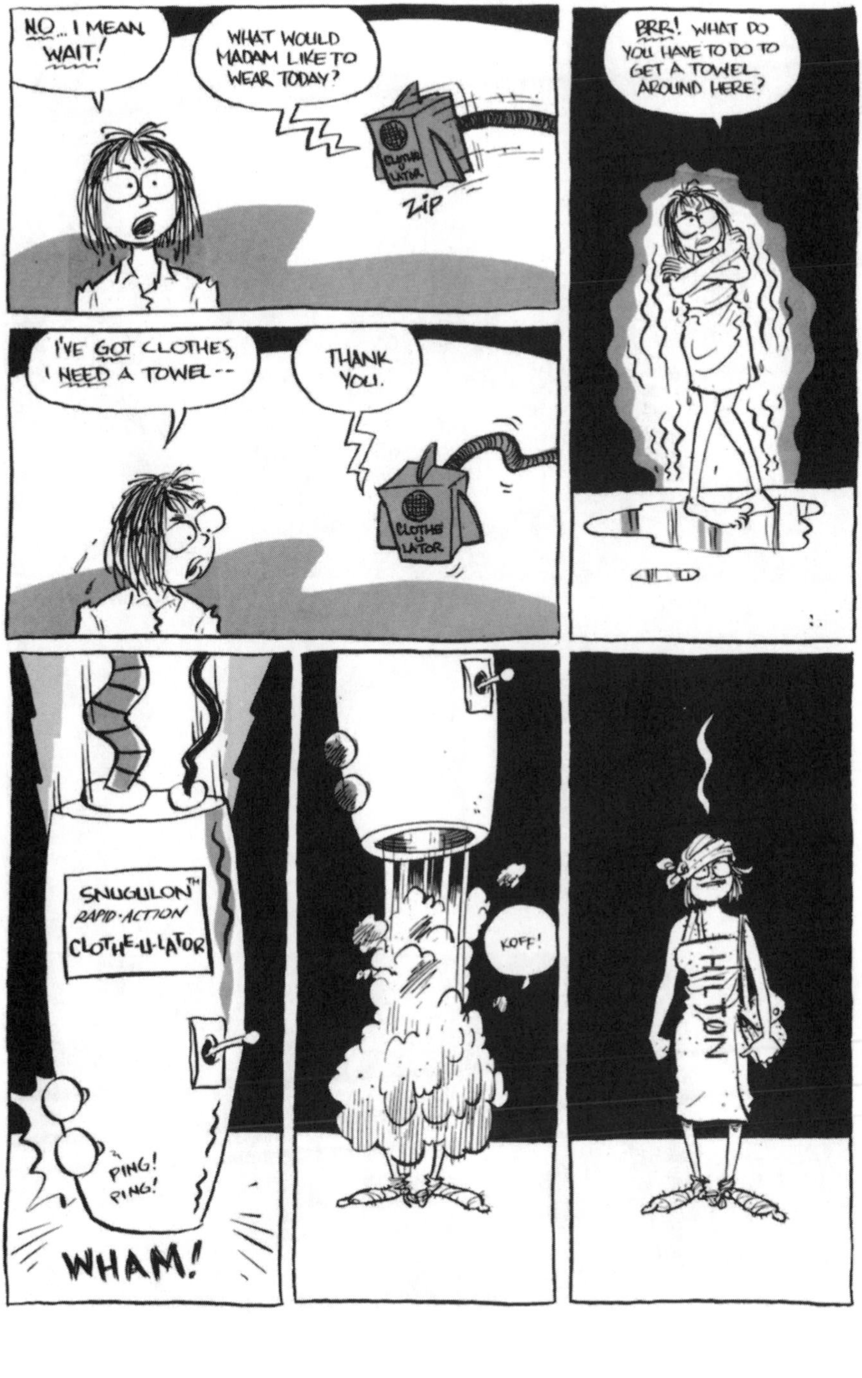
NO... I MEAN WAIT!
WHAT WOULD MADAM LIKE TO WEAR TODAY?
CLOTHE-U-LATOR
ZIP
I'VE GOT CLOTHES, I NEED A TOWEL--
THANK YOU.
CLOTHE-U-LATOR
BRR! WHAT DO YOU HAVE TO DO TO GET A TOWEL AROUND HERE?
SNUGULON™ RAPID-ACTION CLOTHE-U-LATOR
PING! PING!
WHAM!
KOFF!
HILTON

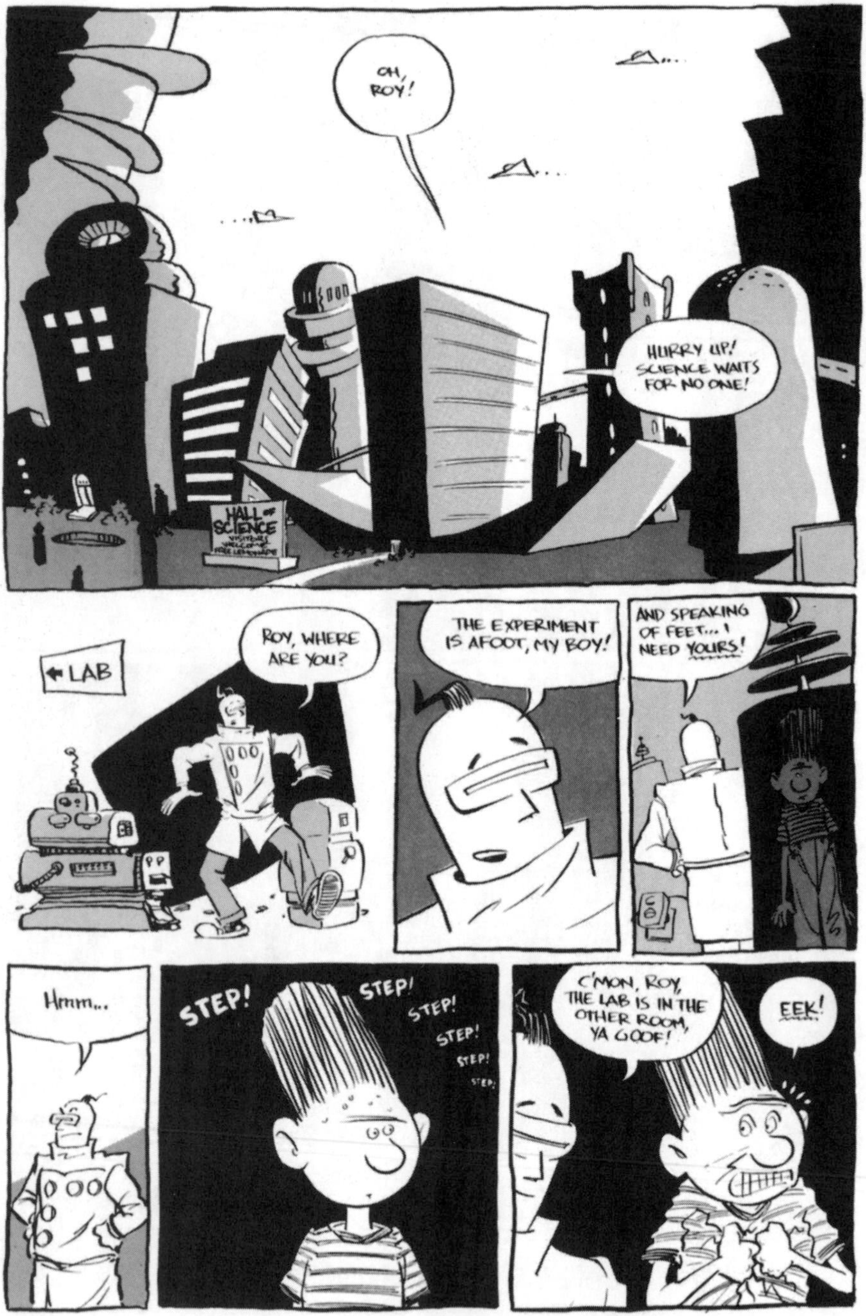
OH, ROY!
HURRY UP! SCIENCE WAITS FOR NO ONE!
HALL of SCIENCE
LAB
ROY, WHERE ARE YOU?
THE EXPERIMENT IS AFOOT, MY BOY!
AND SPEAKING OF FEET... I NEED YOURS!
Hmm...
STEP! STEP! STEP! STEP! STEP! STEP!
C'MON, ROY, THE LAB IS IN THE OTHER ROOM, YA GOOF!
EEK!

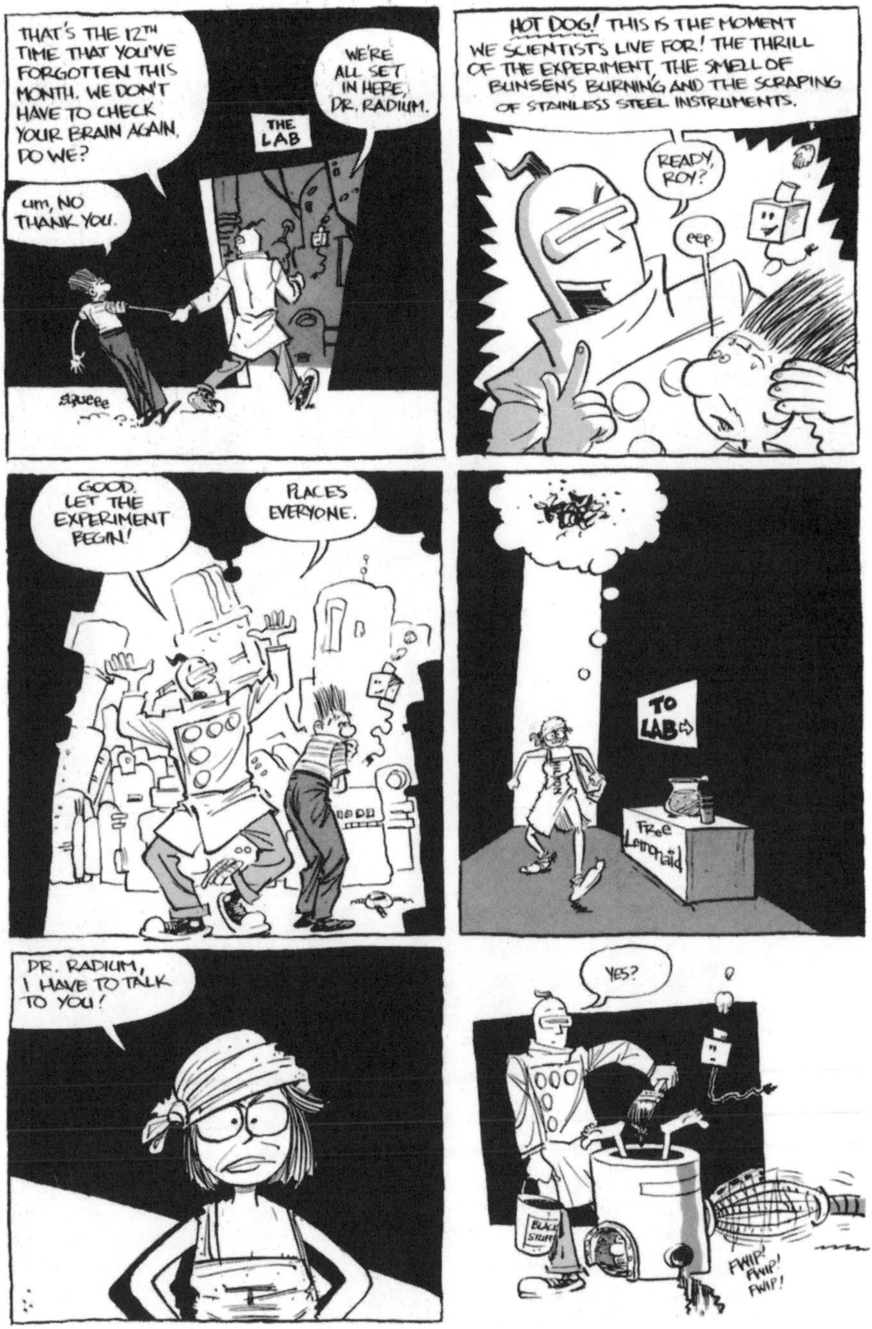
THAT'S THE 12TH TIME THAT YOU'VE FORGOTTEN THIS MONTH. WE DON'T HAVE TO CHECK YOUR BRAIN AGAIN, DO WE?
WE'RE ALL SET IN HERE, DR. RADIUM.
THE LAB
um, NO THANK YOU.
squeee
HOT DOG! THIS IS THE MOMENT WE SCIENTISTS LIVE FOR! THE THRILL OF THE EXPERIMENT, THE SMELL OF BUNSENS BURNING AND THE SCRAPING OF STAINLESS STEEL INSTRUMENTS.
READY, ROY?
eep.
GOOD. LET THE EXPERIMENT BEGIN!
PLACES EVERYONE.
TO LAB
Free Lemonaid
DR. RADIUM, I HAVE TO TALK TO YOU!
YES?
BLACK STUFF
FWIP! FWIP! FWIP!

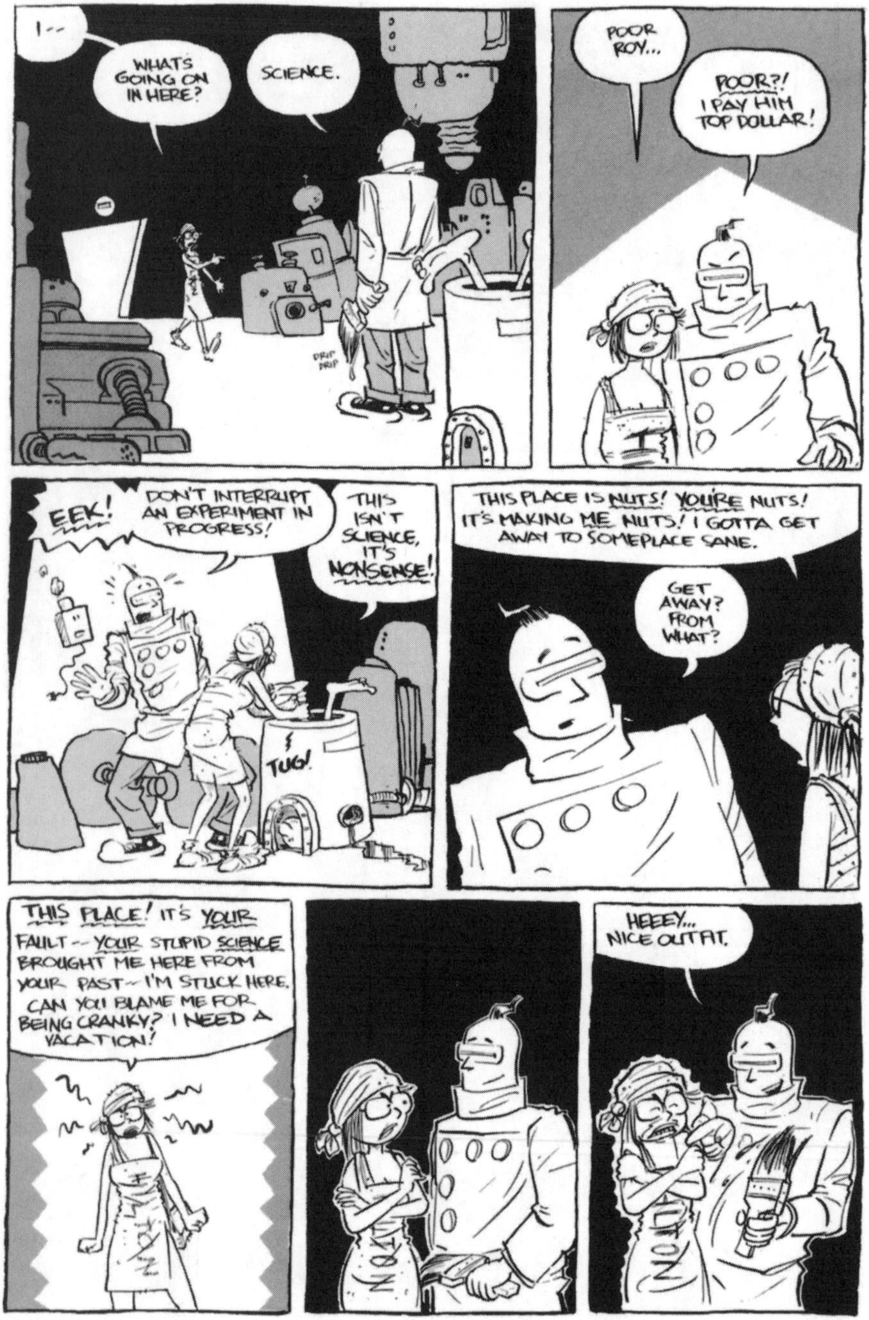
I--
WHATS GOING ON IN HERE?
SCIENCE.
DRIP DRIP
POOR ROY...
POOR?! I PAY HIM TOP DOLLAR!
EEK!
DON'T INTERRUPT AN EXPERIMENT IN PROGRESS!
THIS ISN'T SCIENCE, IT'S NONSENSE!
TUG!
THIS PLACE IS NUTS! YOU'RE NUTS! IT'S MAKING ME NUTS! I GOTTA GET AWAY TO SOMEPLACE SANE.
GET AWAY? FROM WHAT?
THIS PLACE! IT'S YOUR FAULT -- YOUR STUPID SCIENCE BROUGHT ME HERE FROM YOUR PAST -- I'M STUCK HERE. CAN YOU BLAME ME FOR BEING CRANKY? I NEED A VACATION!
HEEEY... NICE OUTFIT.

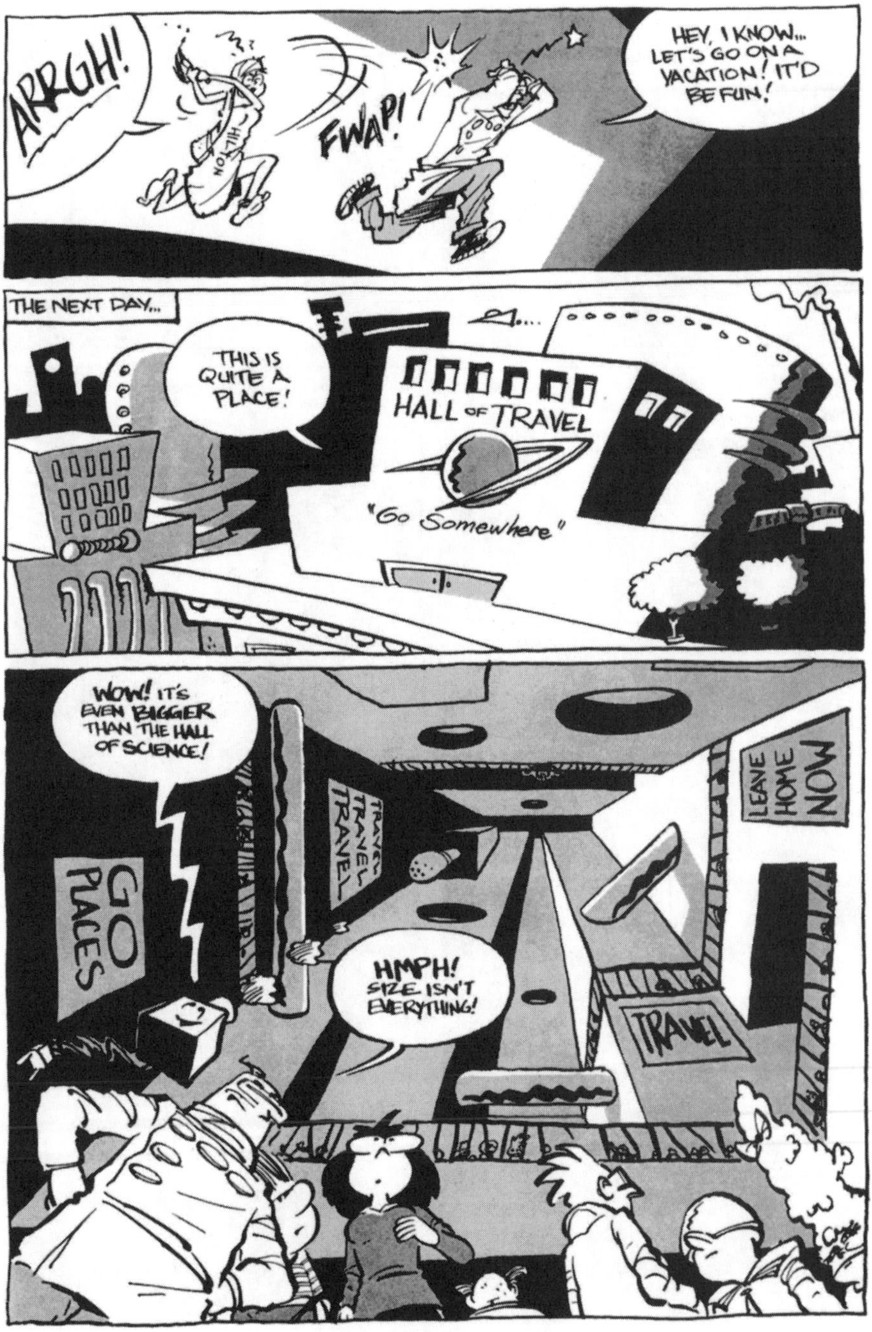
ARRGH!
HILTON
FWAP!
HEY, I KNOW... LET'S GO ON A VACATION! IT'D BE FUN!
THE NEXT DAY...
THIS IS QUITE A PLACE!
HALL OF TRAVEL
"Go Somewhere"
WOW! IT'S EVEN BIGGER THAN THE HALL OF SCIENCE!
LEAVE HOME NOW
TRAVEL TRAVEL TRAVEL
GO PLACES
HMPH! SIZE ISN'T EVERYTHING!
TRAVEL

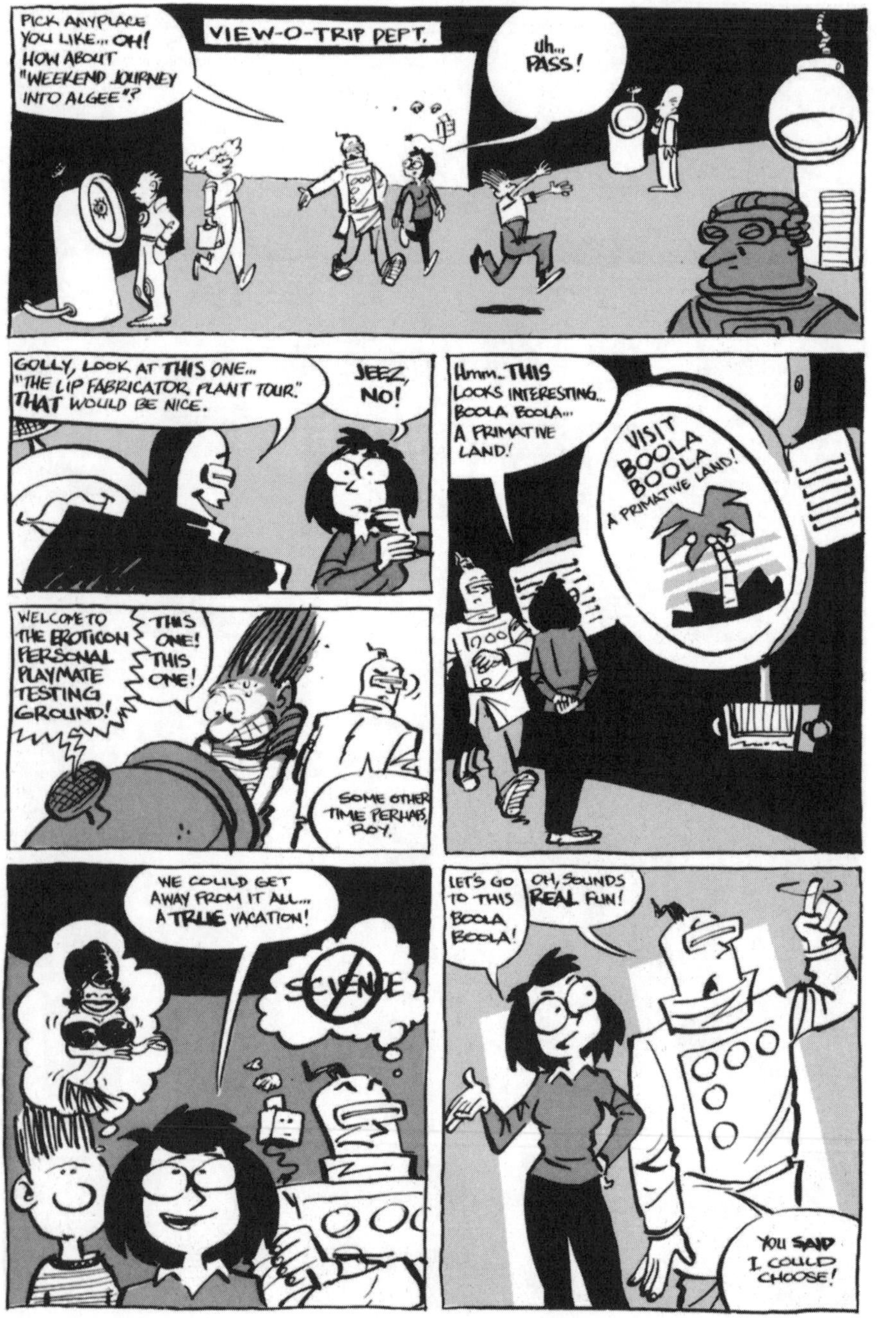
PICK ANYPLACE YOU LIKE... OH! HOW ABOUT "WEEKEND JOURNEY INTO ALGEE"?
VIEW-O-TRIP DEPT.
uh... PASS!
GOLLY, LOOK AT THIS ONE... "THE LIP FABRICATOR PLANT TOUR." THAT WOULD BE NICE.
JEEZ, NO!
Hmm.. THIS LOOKS INTERESTING... BOOLA BOOLA... A PRIMATIVE LAND!
VISIT BOOLA BOOLA A PRIMATIVE LAND!
WELCOME TO THE EROTICON PERSONAL PLAYMATE TESTING GROUND!
THIS ONE! THIS ONE!
SOME OTHER TIME PERHAPS, ROY.
WE COULD GET AWAY FROM IT ALL... A TRUE VACATION!
SCIENCE
LET'S GO TO THIS BOOLA BOOLA!
OH, SOUNDS REAL FUN!
YOU SAID I COULD CHOOSE!

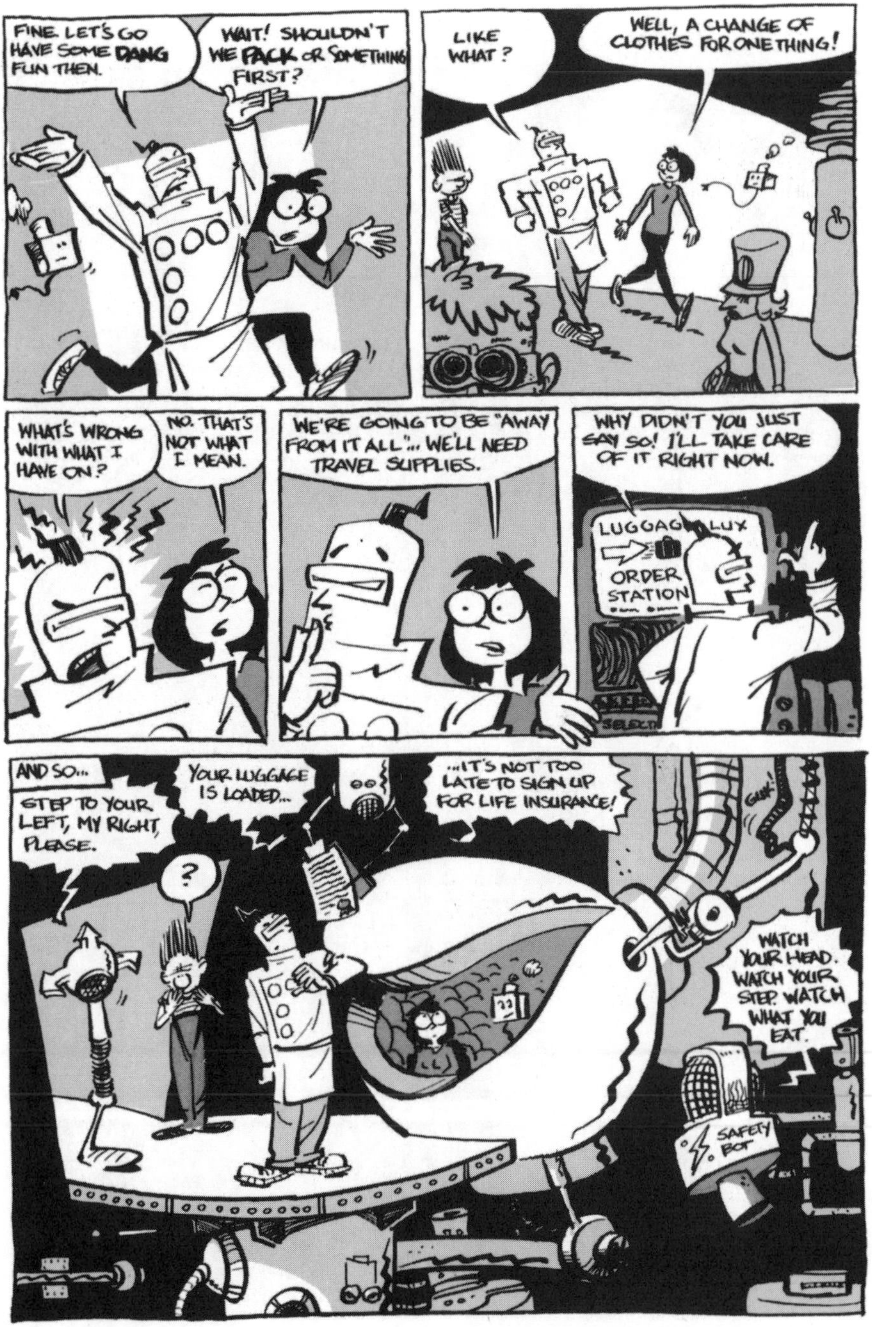
FINE. LET'S GO HAVE SOME DANG FUN THEN.
WAIT! SHOULDN'T WE PACK OR SOMETHING FIRST?
LIKE WHAT?
WELL, A CHANGE OF CLOTHES FOR ONE THING!
WHAT'S WRONG WITH WHAT I HAVE ON?
NO. THAT'S NOT WHAT I MEAN.
WE'RE GOING TO BE "AWAY FROM IT ALL"... WE'LL NEED TRAVEL SUPPLIES.
WHY DIDN'T YOU JUST SAY SO! I'LL TAKE CARE OF IT RIGHT NOW.
LUGGAG LUX
ORDER STATION
AND SO...
STEP TO YOUR LEFT, MY RIGHT, PLEASE.
?
YOUR LUGGAGE IS LOADED...
...IT'S NOT TOO LATE TO SIGN UP FOR LIFE INSURANCE!
WATCH YOUR HEAD. WATCH YOUR STEP. WATCH WHAT YOU EAT.
SAFETY BOT

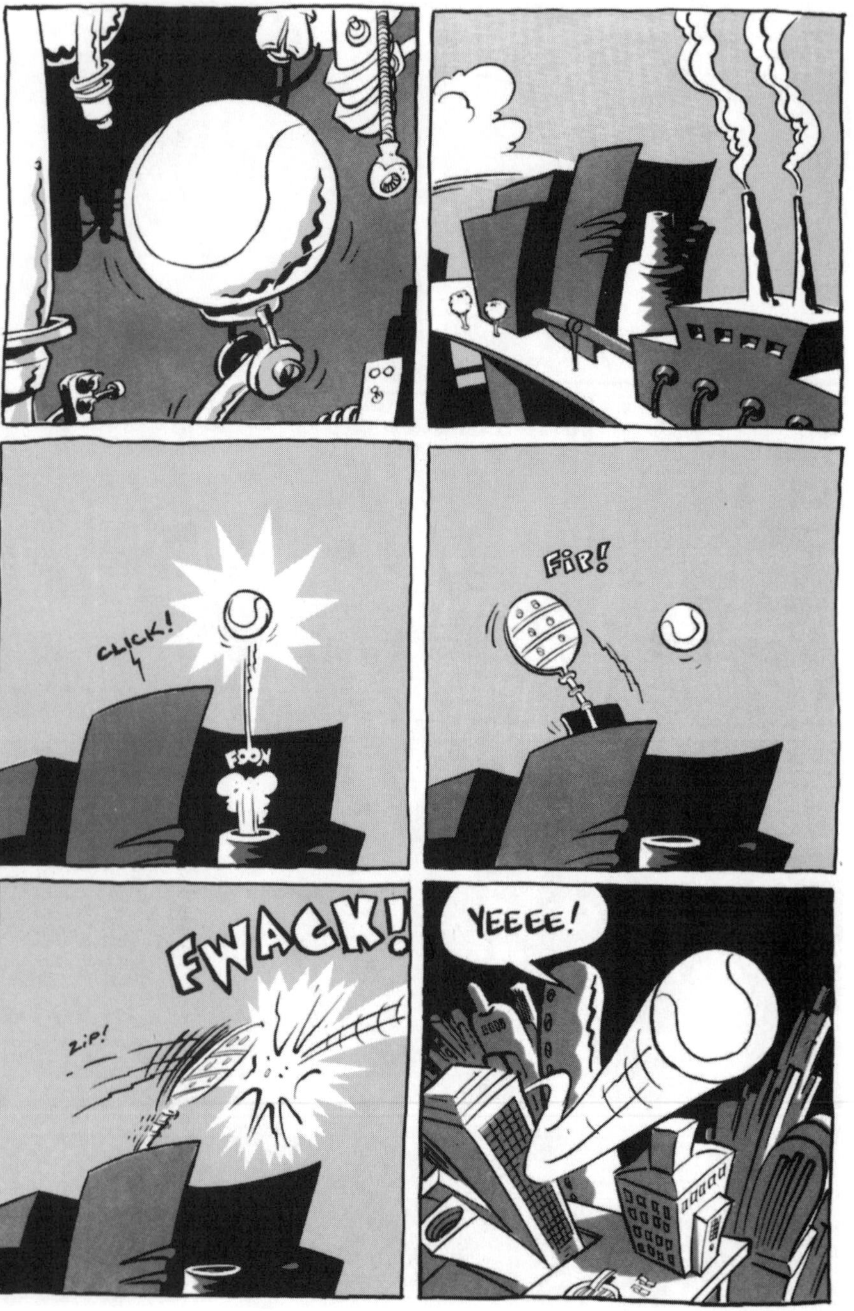
CLICK!
FOON
FIP!
FWACK!
ZIP!
YEEEE!

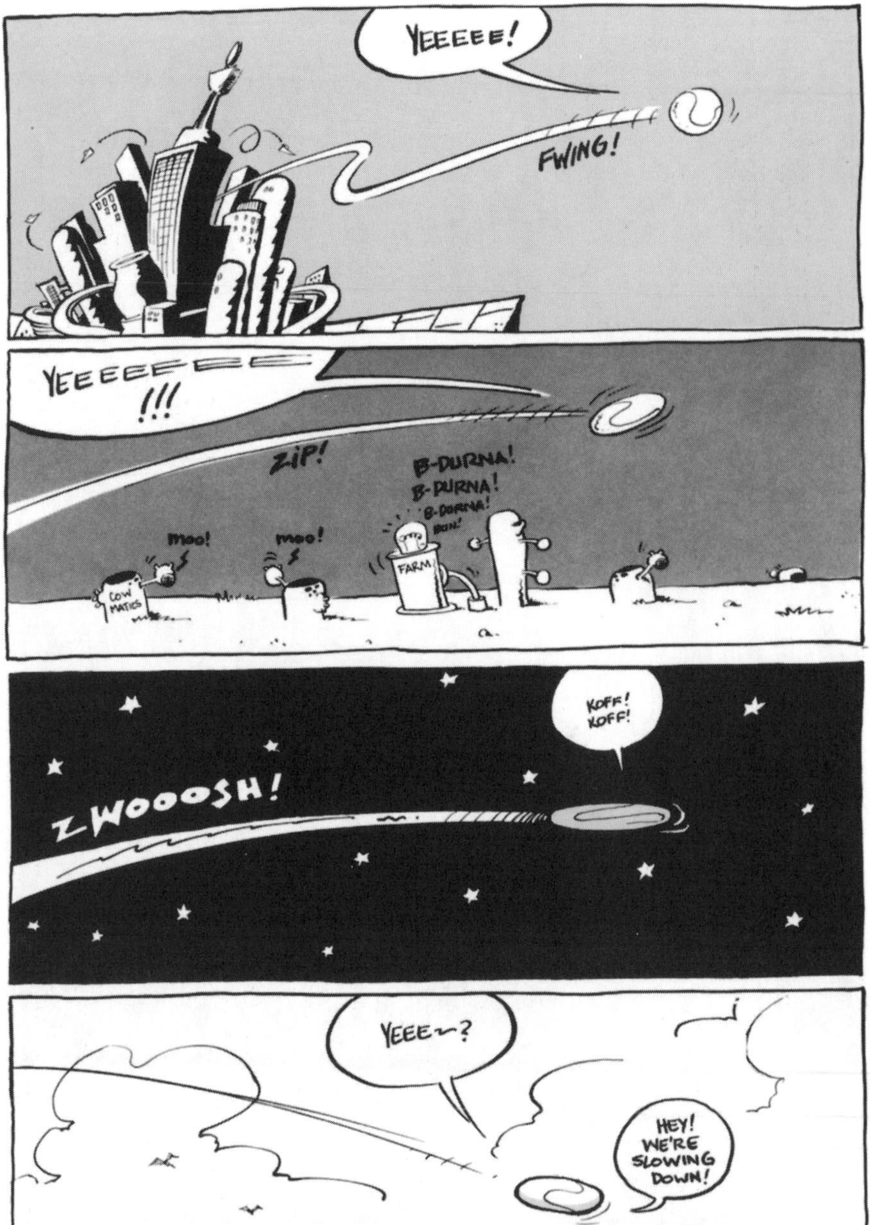
YEEEEE!
FWING!
YEEEEEEEEE !!!
ZIP!
moo!
moo!
COW MATICS
B-DURNA!
B-DURNA!
B-DURNA!
FARM
KOFF! KOFF!
ZWOOOSH!
YEEE~?
HEY! WE'RE SLOWING DOWN!

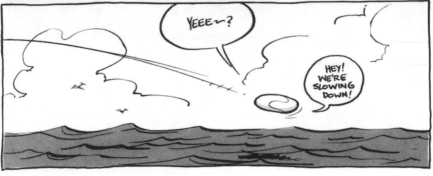

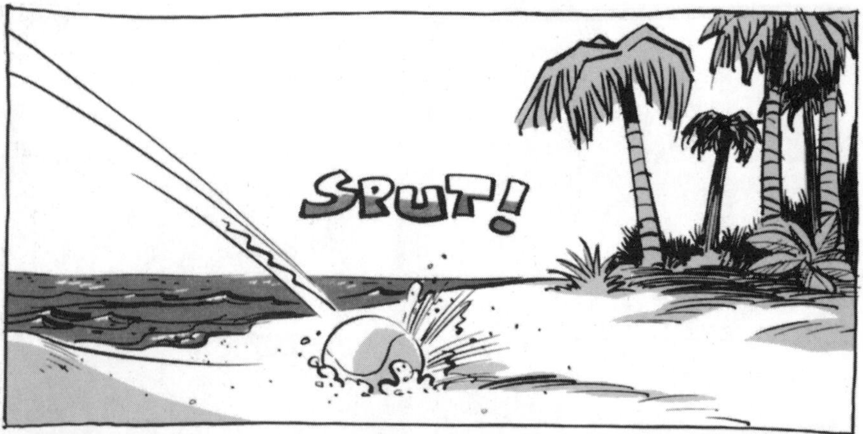
SPUT!

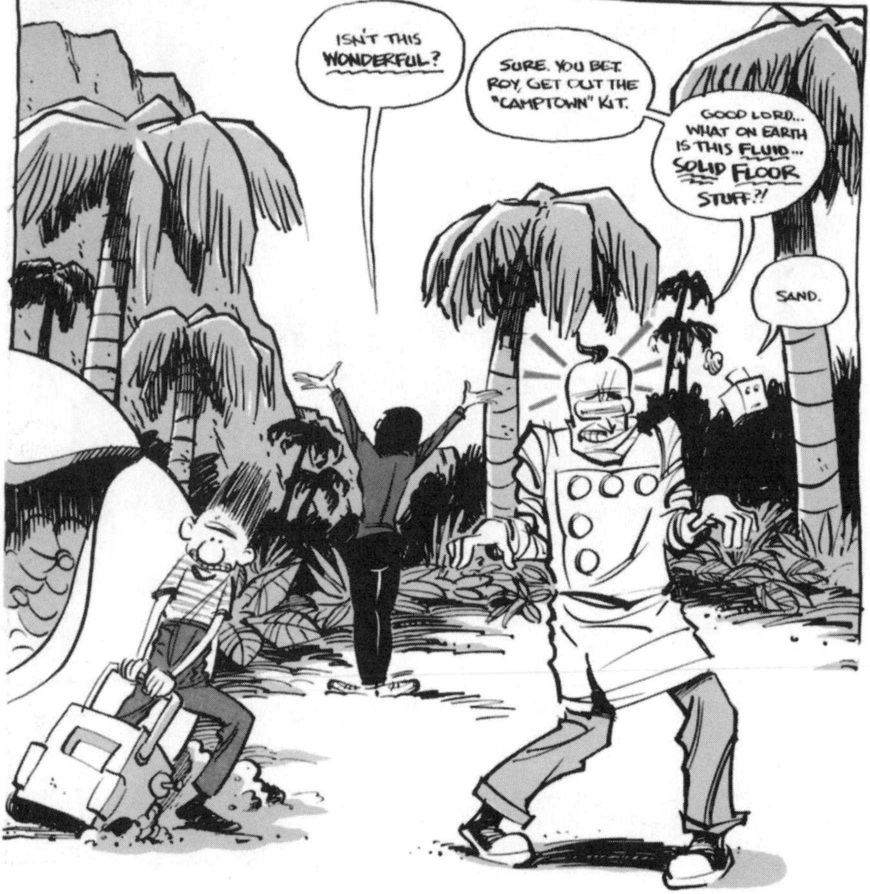
ISN'T THIS WONDERFUL?
SURE. YOU BET. ROY, GET OUT THE "CAMPTOWN" KIT.
GOOD LORD... WHAT ON EARTH IS THIS FLUID... SOLID FLOOR STUFF?!
SAND.

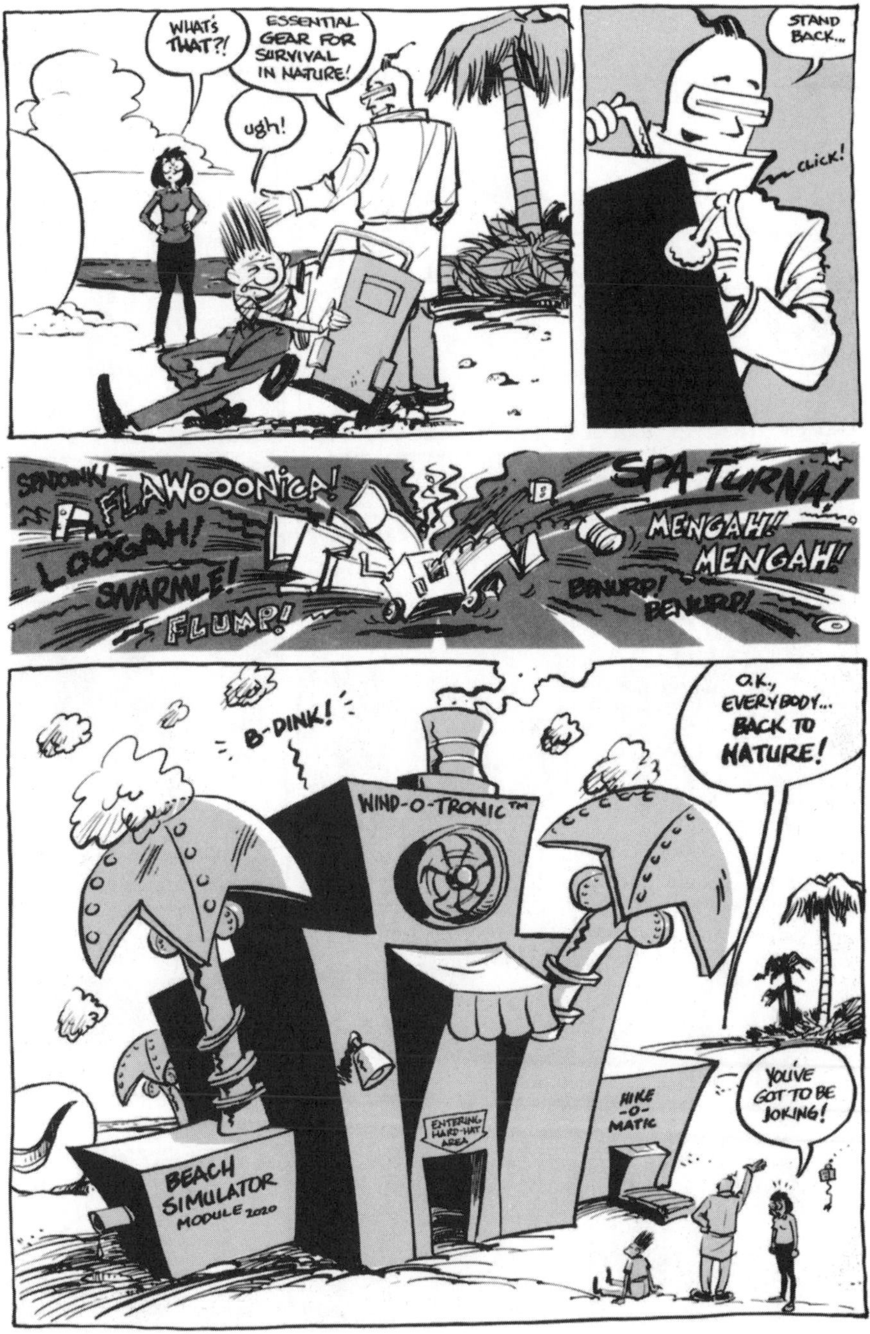
WHAT'S THAT?!
ESSENTIAL GEAR FOR SURVIVAL IN NATURE!
ugh!
STAND BACK...
CLICK!
FLAWOOONICA!
LOOGAH!
SWARMLE!
FLUMP!
SPA-TURNA!
MENGAH!
MENGAH!
BENURP!
BENURP!
B-DINK!
O.K., EVERYBODY... BACK TO NATURE!
WIND-O-TRONIC™
ENTERING HARD-HAT AREA
HIKE -O- MATIC
BEACH SIMULATOR MODULE 2020
YOU'VE GOT TO BE JOKING!

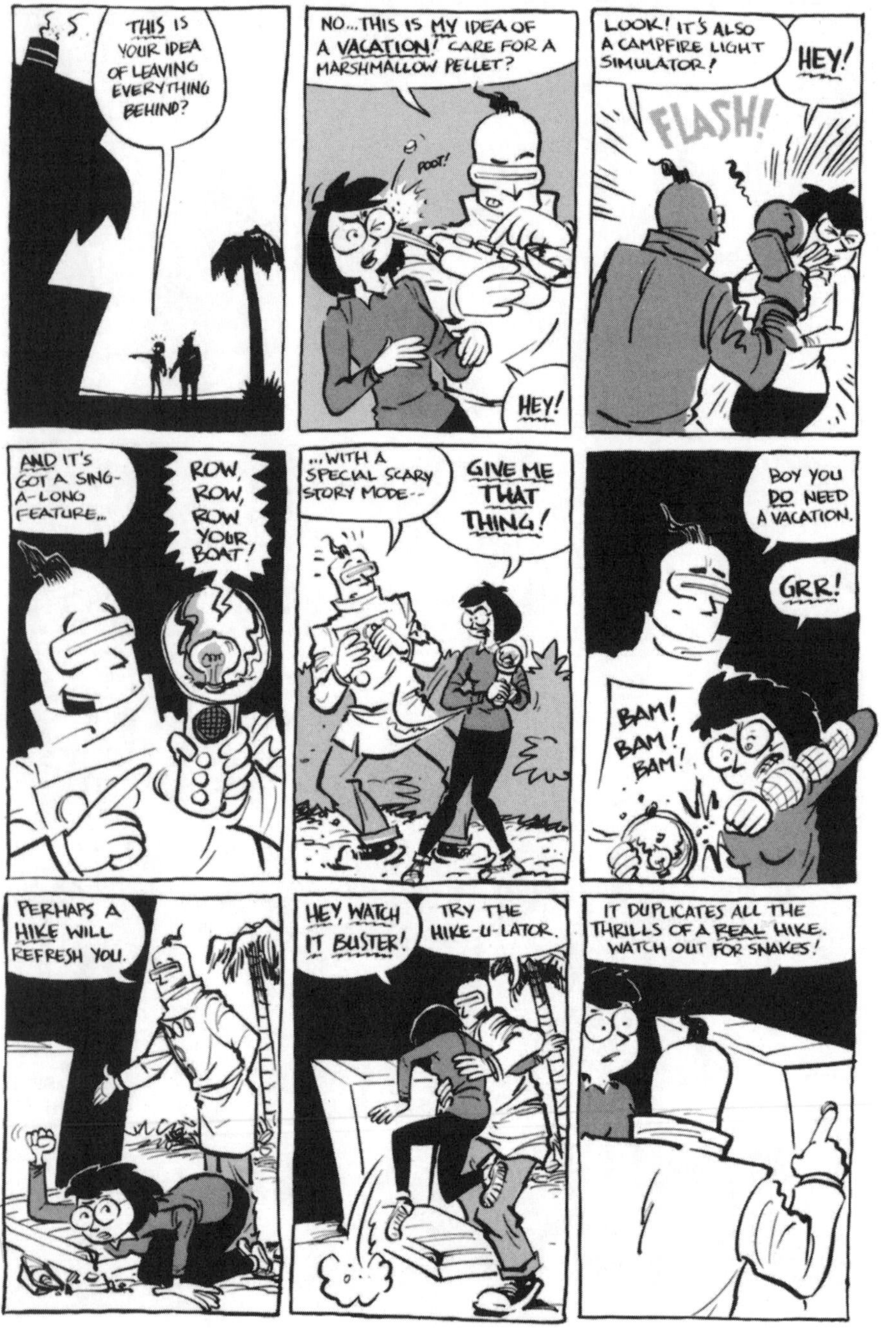
THIS IS YOUR IDEA OF LEAVING EVERYTHING BEHIND?
NO... THIS IS MY IDEA OF A VACATION! CARE FOR A MARSHMALLOW PELLET?
POOT!
HEY!
LOOK! IT'S ALSO A CAMPFIRE LIGHT SIMULATOR!
HEY!
FLASH!
AND IT'S GOT A SING-A-LONG FEATURE...
ROW, ROW, ROW YOUR BOAT!
...WITH A SPECIAL SCARY STORY MODE--
GIVE ME THAT THING!
BOY YOU DO NEED A VACATION.
GRR!
BAM! BAM! BAM!
PERHAPS A HIKE WILL REFRESH YOU.
HEY, WATCH IT BUSTER!
TRY THE HIKE-U-LATOR.
IT DUPLICATES ALL THE THRILLS OF A REAL HIKE. WATCH OUT FOR SNAKES!

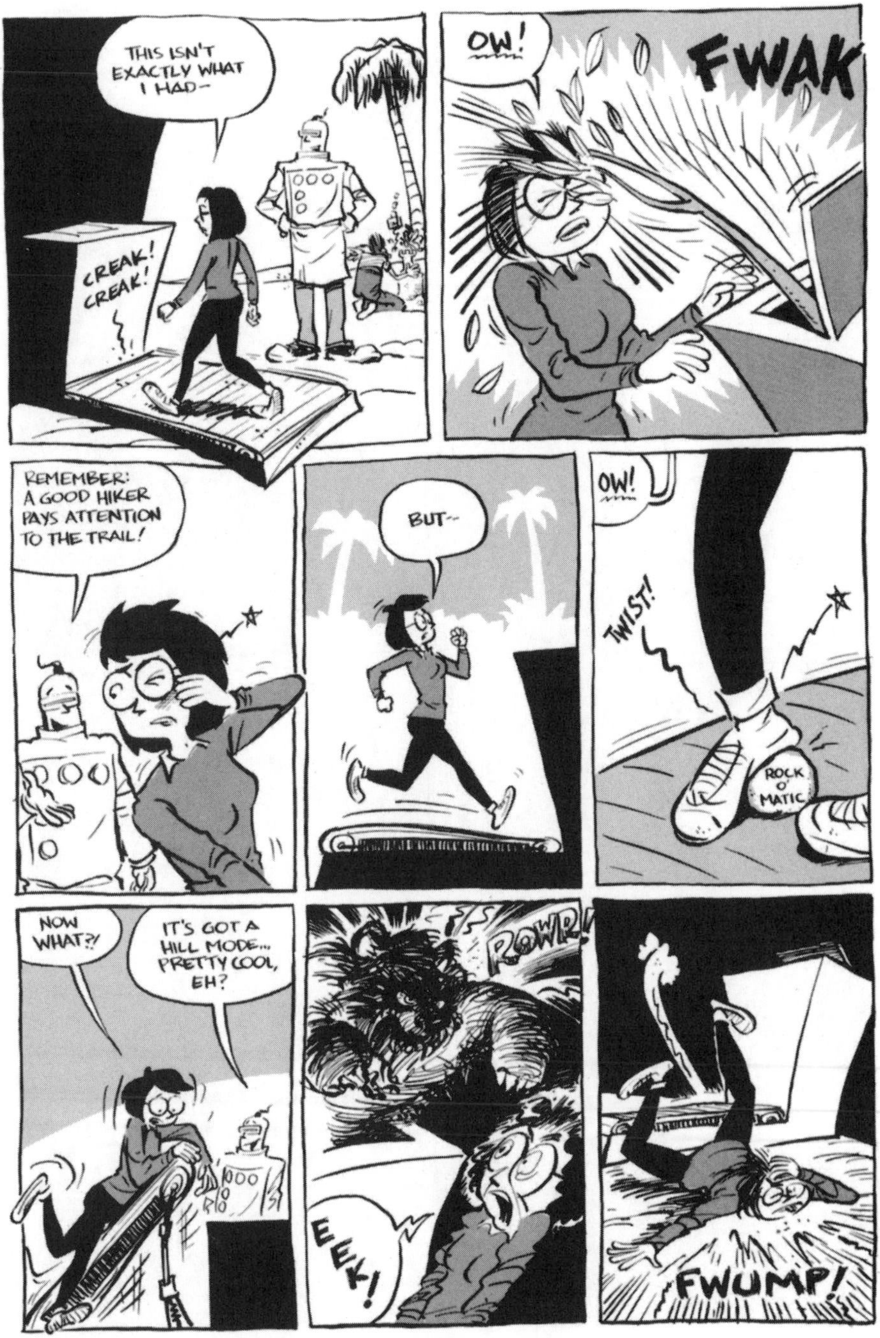
THIS ISN'T EXACTLY WHAT I HAD--
CREAK! CREAK!
OW!
FWAK
REMEMBER: A GOOD HIKER PAYS ATTENTION TO THE TRAIL!
BUT--
OW!
TWIST!
ROCK O' MATIC
NOW WHAT?!
IT'S GOT A HILL MODE... PRETTY COOL, EH?
ROWR!
EEK!
FWUMP!

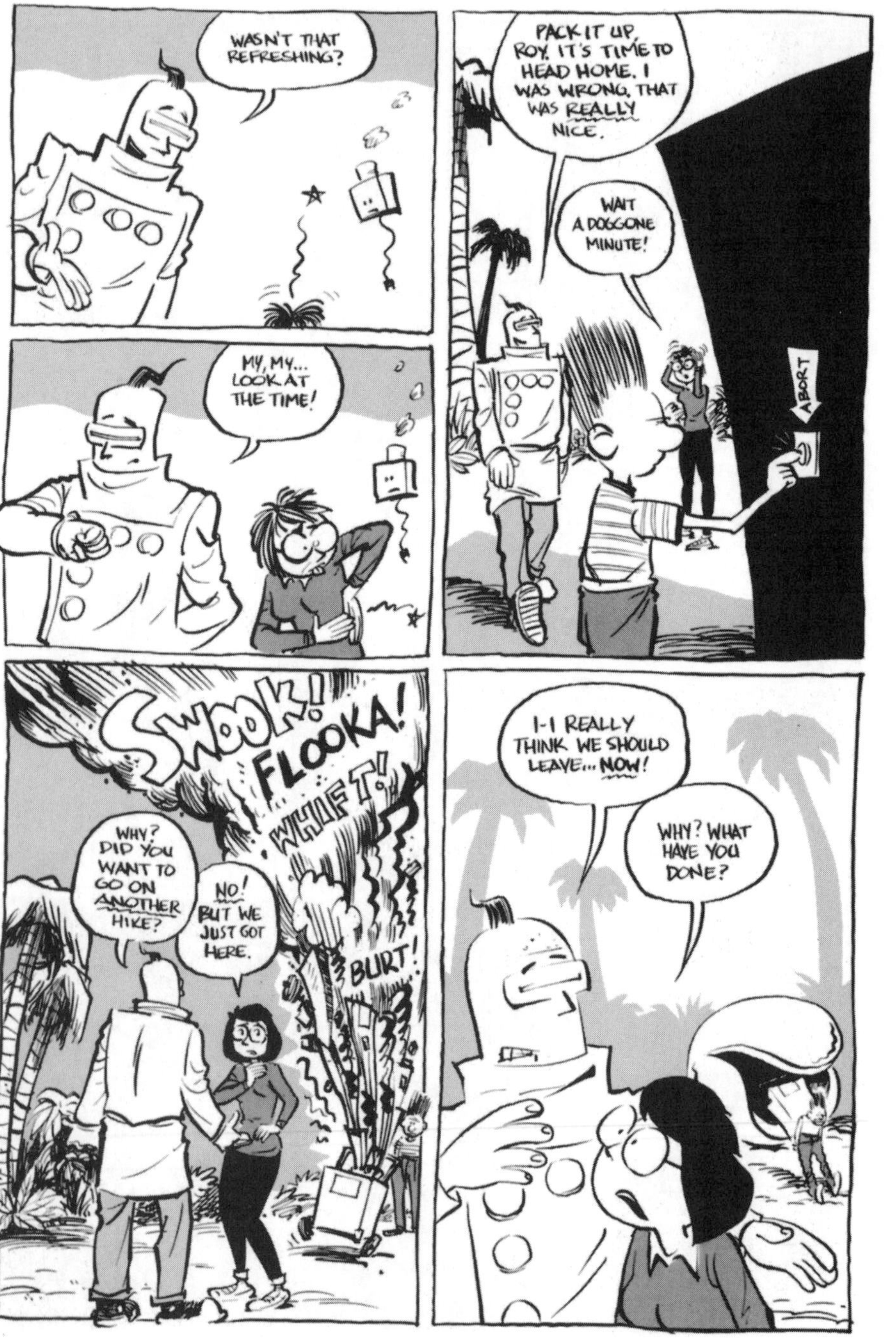
WASN'T THAT REFRESHING?
MY, MY... LOOK AT THE TIME!
PACK IT UP, ROY. IT'S TIME TO HEAD HOME. I WAS WRONG. THAT WAS REALLY NICE.
WAIT A DOGGONE MINUTE!
ABORT
SWOOK!
FLOOKA!
WHUFT!
BURT!
WHY? DID YOU WANT TO GO ON ANOTHER HIKE?
NO! BUT WE JUST GOT HERE.
I-I REALLY THINK WE SHOULD LEAVE... NOW!
WHY? WHAT HAVE YOU DONE?

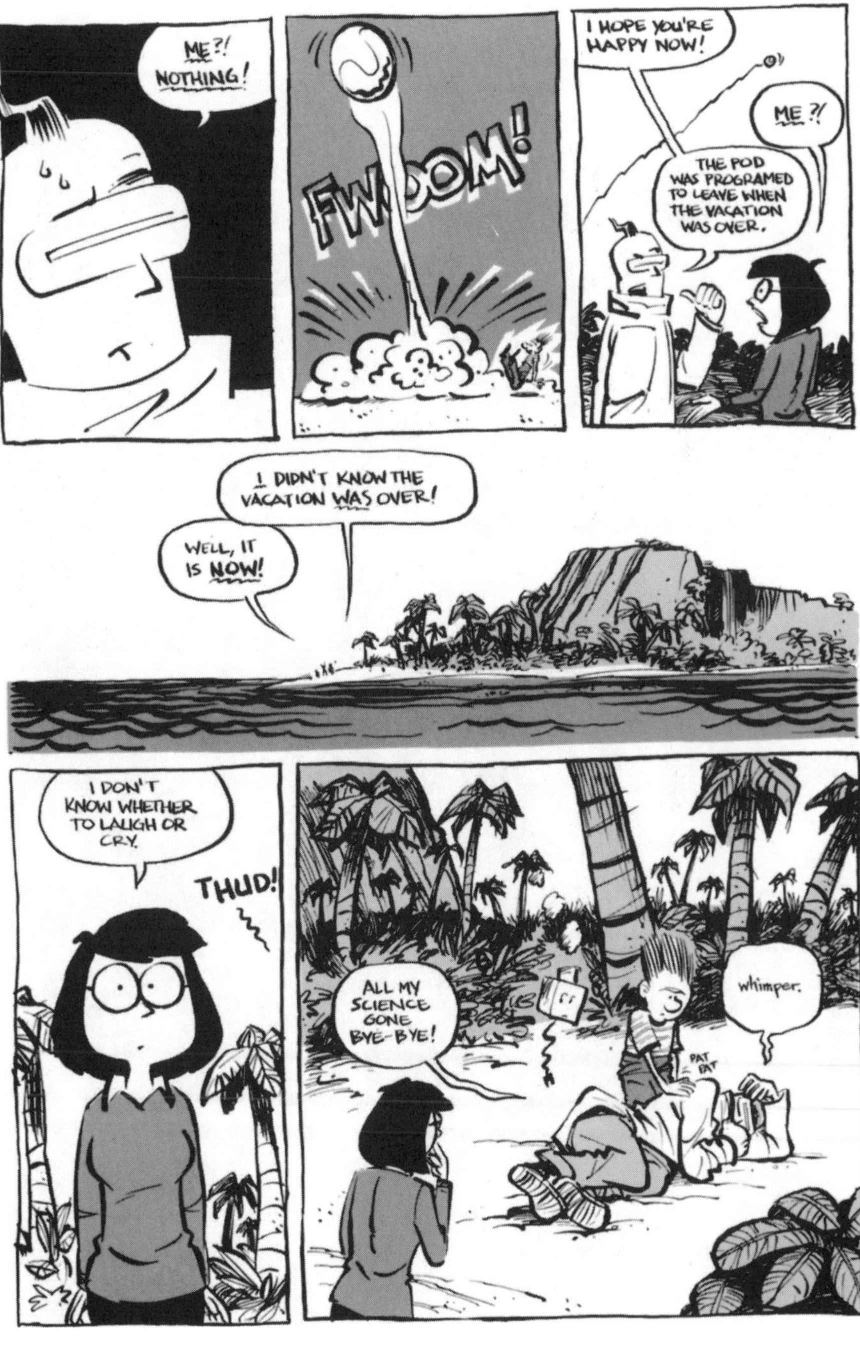
ME?! NOTHING!
FWOOM!
I HOPE YOU'RE HAPPY NOW!
THE POD WAS PROGRAMED TO LEAVE WHEN THE VACATION WAS OVER.
ME ?!
I DIDN'T KNOW THE VACATION WAS OVER!
WELL, IT IS NOW!
I DON'T KNOW WHETHER TO LAUGH OR CRY.
THUD!
ALL MY SCIENCE GONE BYE-BYE!
whimper.
PAT PAT

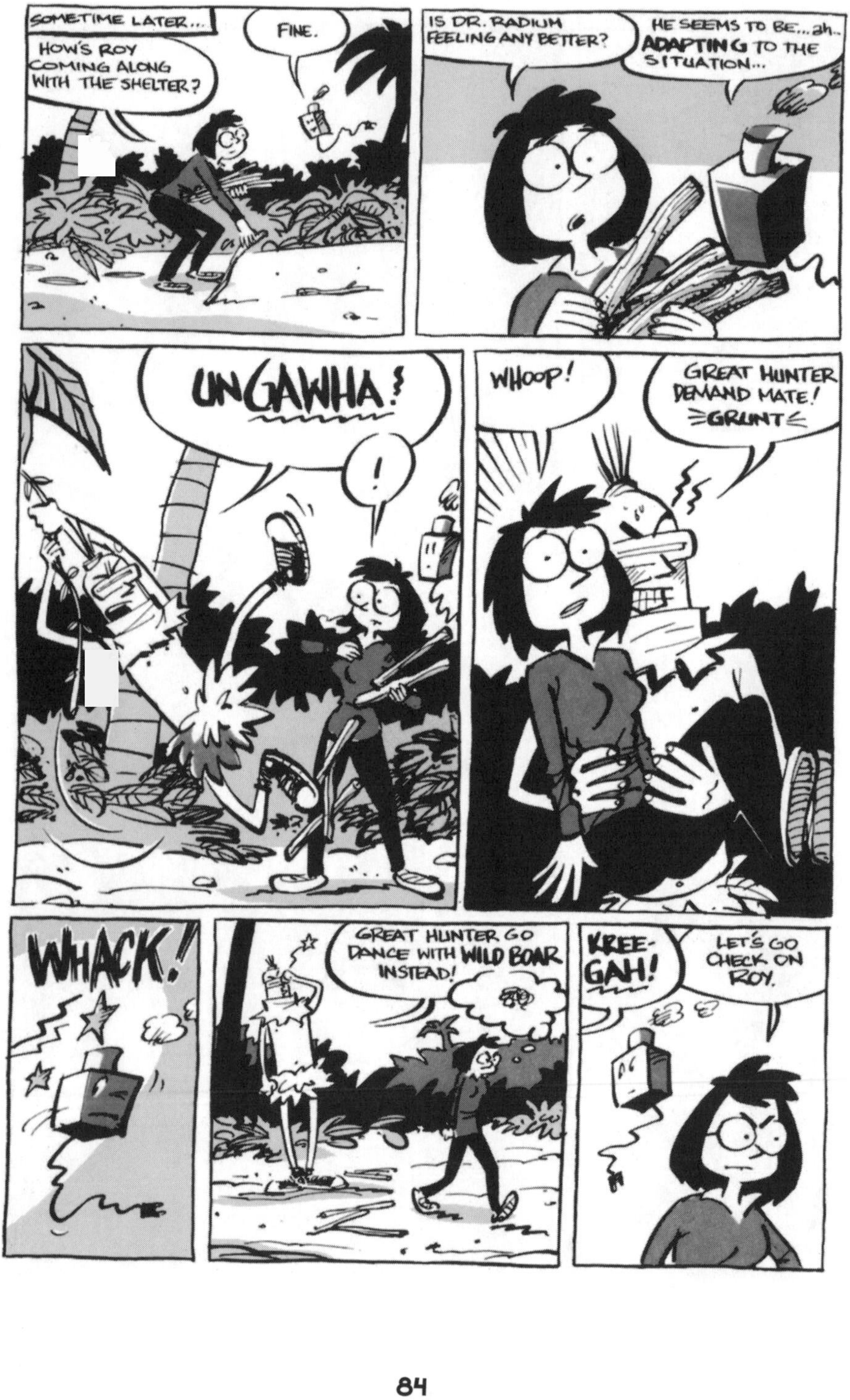
SOMETIME LATER...
HOW'S ROY COMING ALONG WITH THE SHELTER?
FINE.
IS DR. RADIUM FEELING ANY BETTER?
HE SEEMS TO BE... ah.. ADAPTING TO THE SITUATION...
UNGAWHA!
!
WHOOP!
GREAT HUNTER DEMAND MATE! GRUNT
WHACK!
GREAT HUNTER GO DANCE WITH WILD BOAR INSTEAD!
KREE-GAH!
LET'S GO CHECK ON ROY.

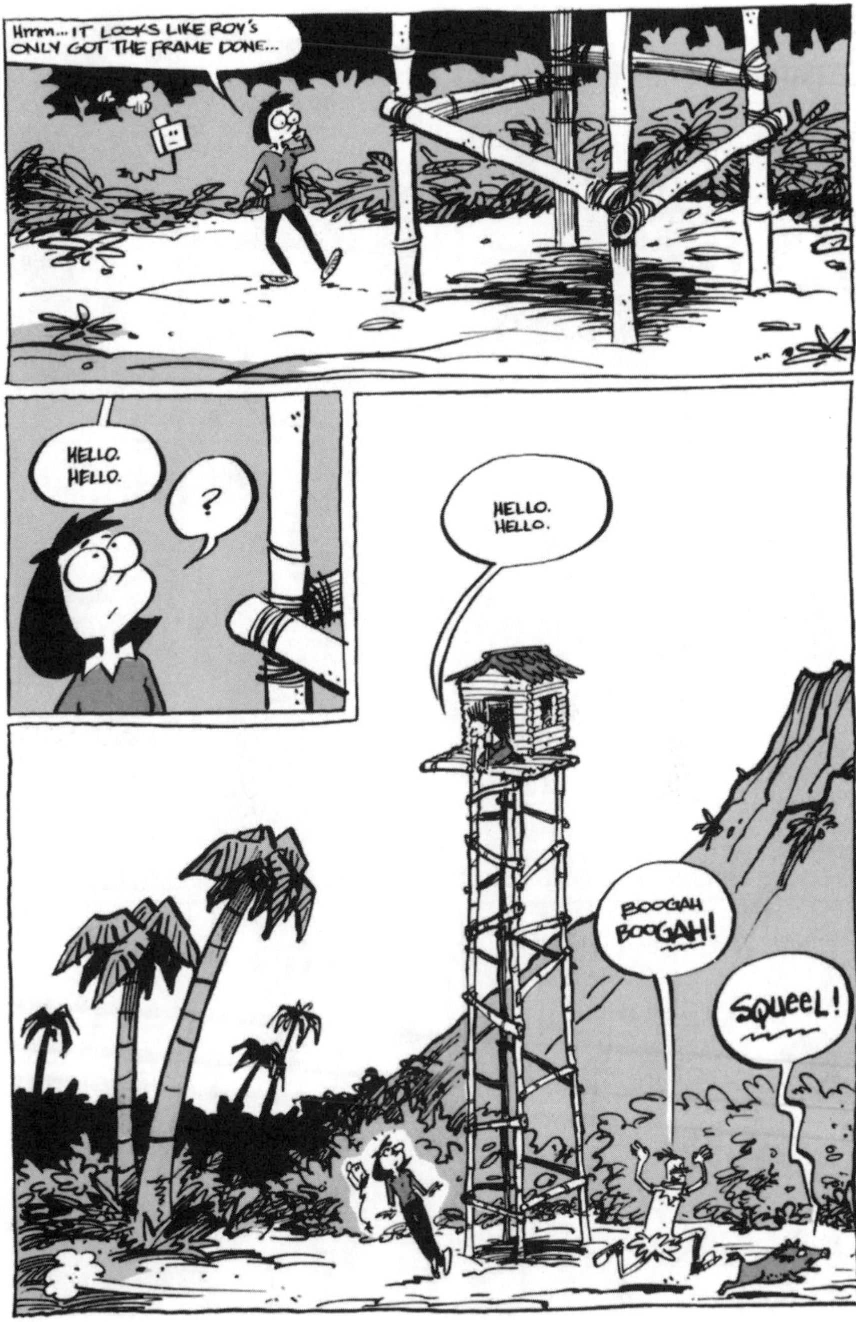
Hmm... IT LOOKS LIKE ROY'S ONLY GOT THE FRAME DONE...
HELLO. HELLO.
?
HELLO. HELLO.
BOOGAH BOOGAH!
SQUEEL!

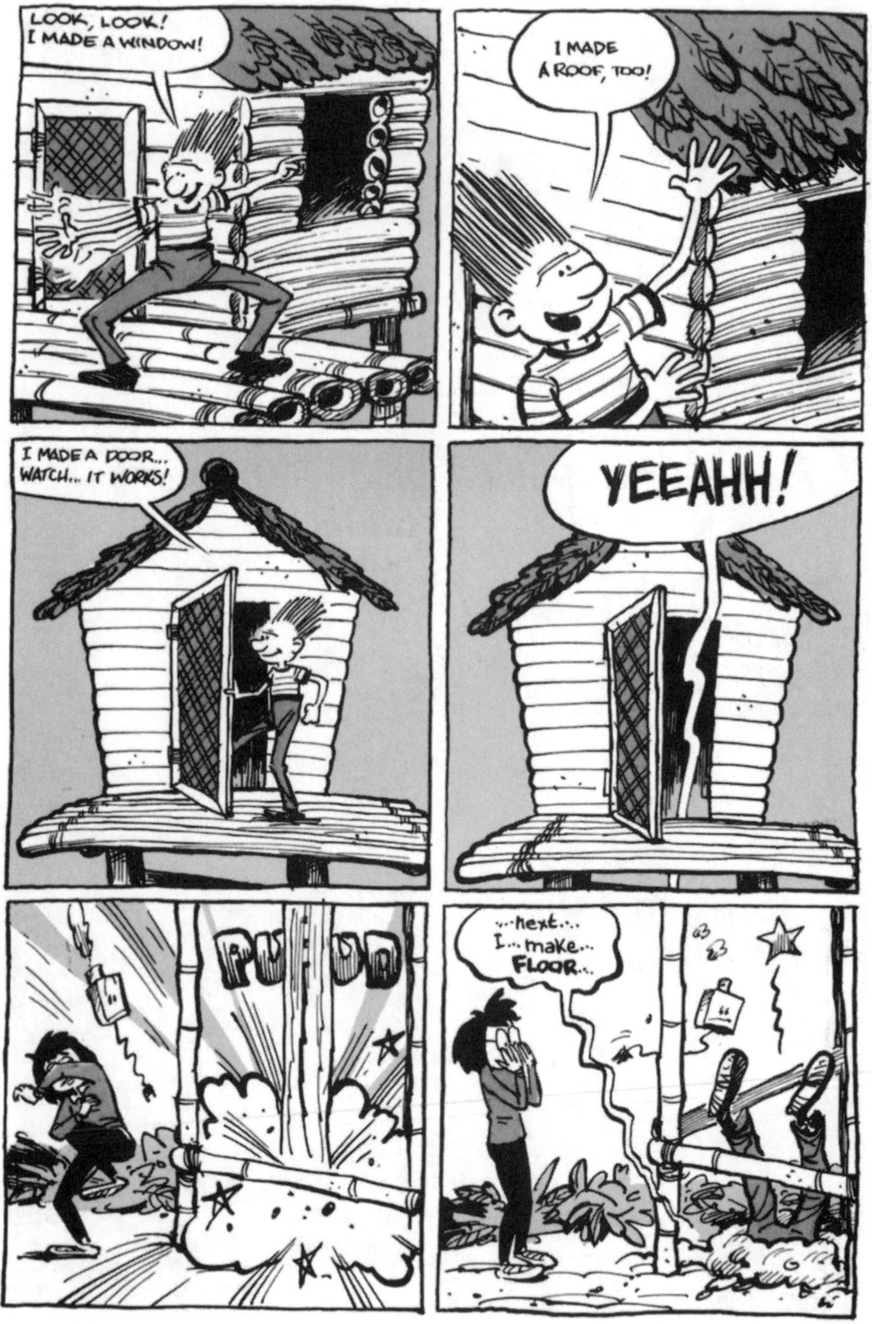
LOOK, LOOK! I MADE A WINDOW!
I MADE A ROOF, TOO!
I MADE A DOOR... WATCH... IT WORKS!
YEEAHH!
...next... I... make... FLOOR...

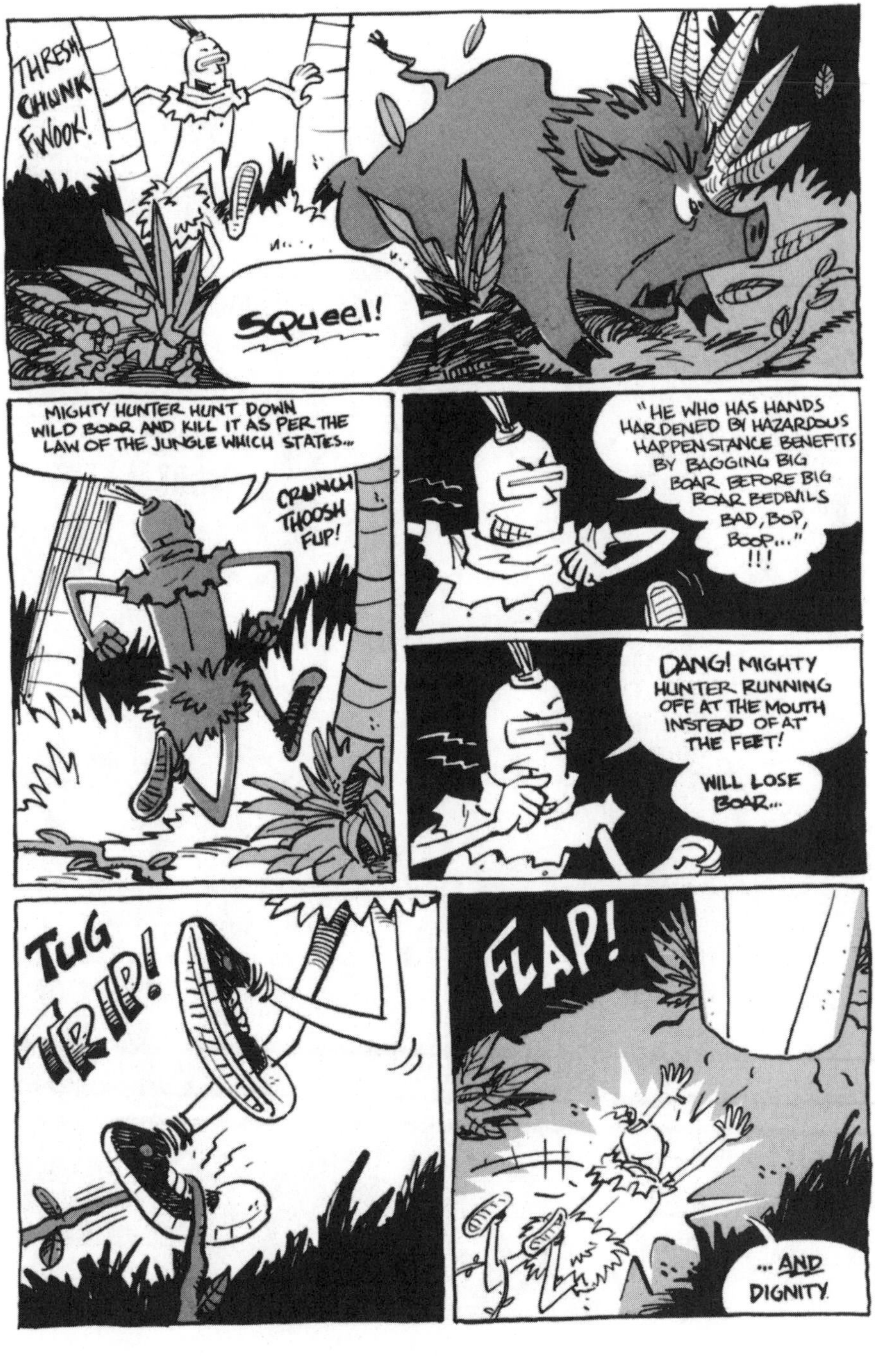

THRESH
CHUNK
FWOOK!
SQUEEL!
MIGHTY HUNTER HUNT DOWN WILD BOAR AND KILL IT AS PER THE LAW OF THE JUNGLE WHICH STATES...
CRUNCH
THOOSH
FLIP!
"HE WHO HAS HANDS HARDENED BY HAZARDOUS HAPPENSTANCE BENEFITS BY BAGGING BIG BOAR BEFORE BIG BOAR BEDEVILS BAD, BOP, BOOP..." !!!
DANG! MIGHTY HUNTER RUNNING OFF AT THE MOUTH INSTEAD OF AT THE FEET!
WILL LOSE BOAR...
TUG
TRIP!
FLAP!
...AND DIGNITY.

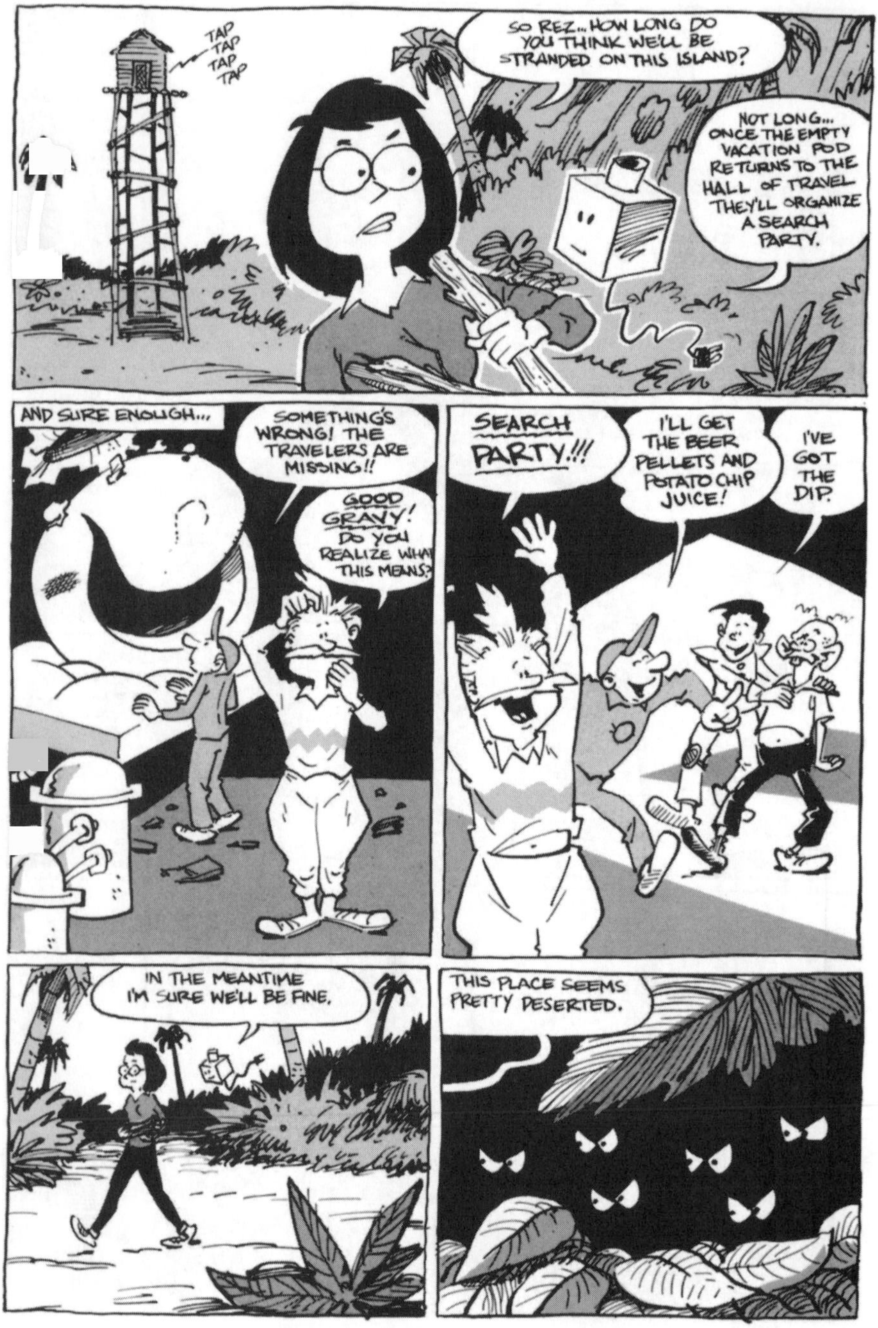
TAP TAP TAP TAP
SO REZ... HOW LONG DO YOU THINK WE'LL BE STRANDED ON THIS ISLAND?
NOT LONG... ONCE THE EMPTY VACATION POD RETURNS TO THE HALL OF TRAVEL THEY'LL ORGANIZE A SEARCH PARTY.
AND SURE ENOUGH...
SOMETHING'S WRONG! THE TRAVELERS ARE MISSING!!
GOOD GRAVY! DO YOU REALIZE WHAT THIS MEANS?
SEARCH PARTY!!!
I'LL GET THE BEER PELLETS AND POTATO CHIP JUICE!
I'VE GOT THE DIP.
IN THE MEANTIME I'M SURE WE'LL BE FINE.
THIS PLACE SEEMS PRETTY DESERTED.

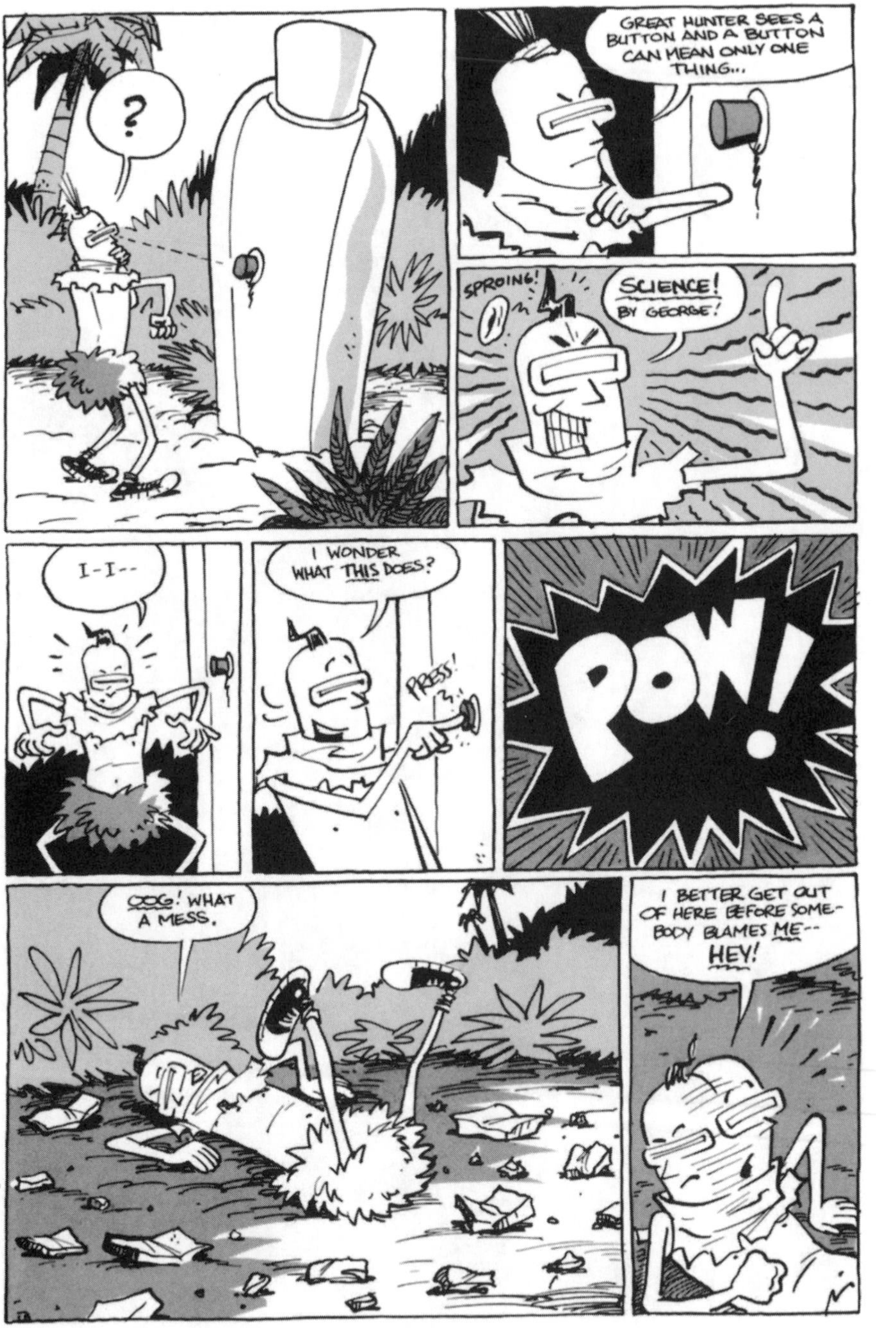
?
GREAT HUNTER SEES A BUTTON AND A BUTTON CAN MEAN ONLY ONE THING...
SPROING!
SCIENCE! BY GEORGE!
I-I--
I WONDER WHAT THIS DOES?
PRESS!
POW!
OOG! WHAT A MESS.
I BETTER GET OUT OF HERE BEFORE SOME-BODY BLAMES ME-- HEY!

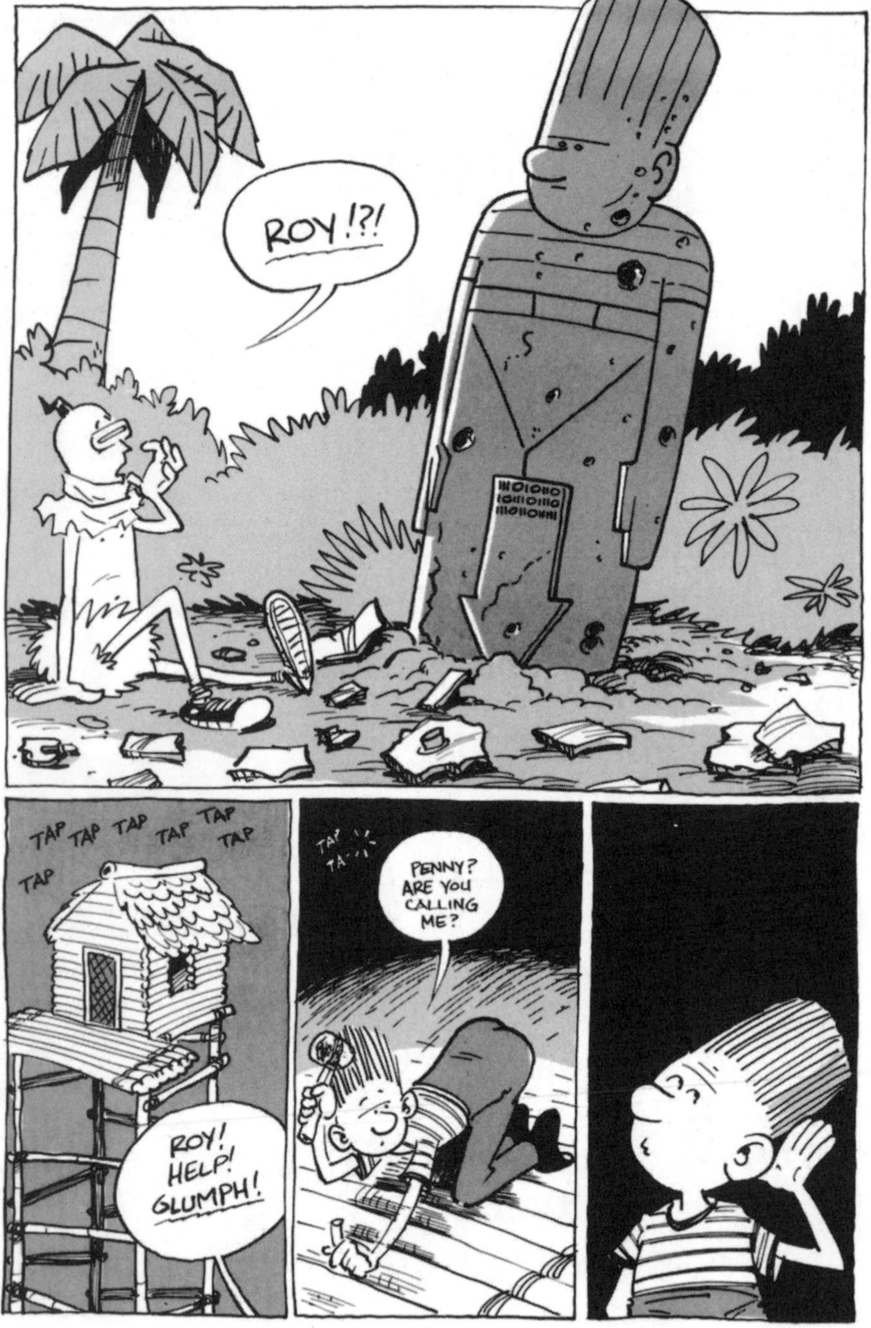
ROY!?!
TAP TAP TAP TAP TAP TAP TAP
ROY! HELP! GLUMPH!
TAP TA-
PENNY? ARE YOU CALLING ME?

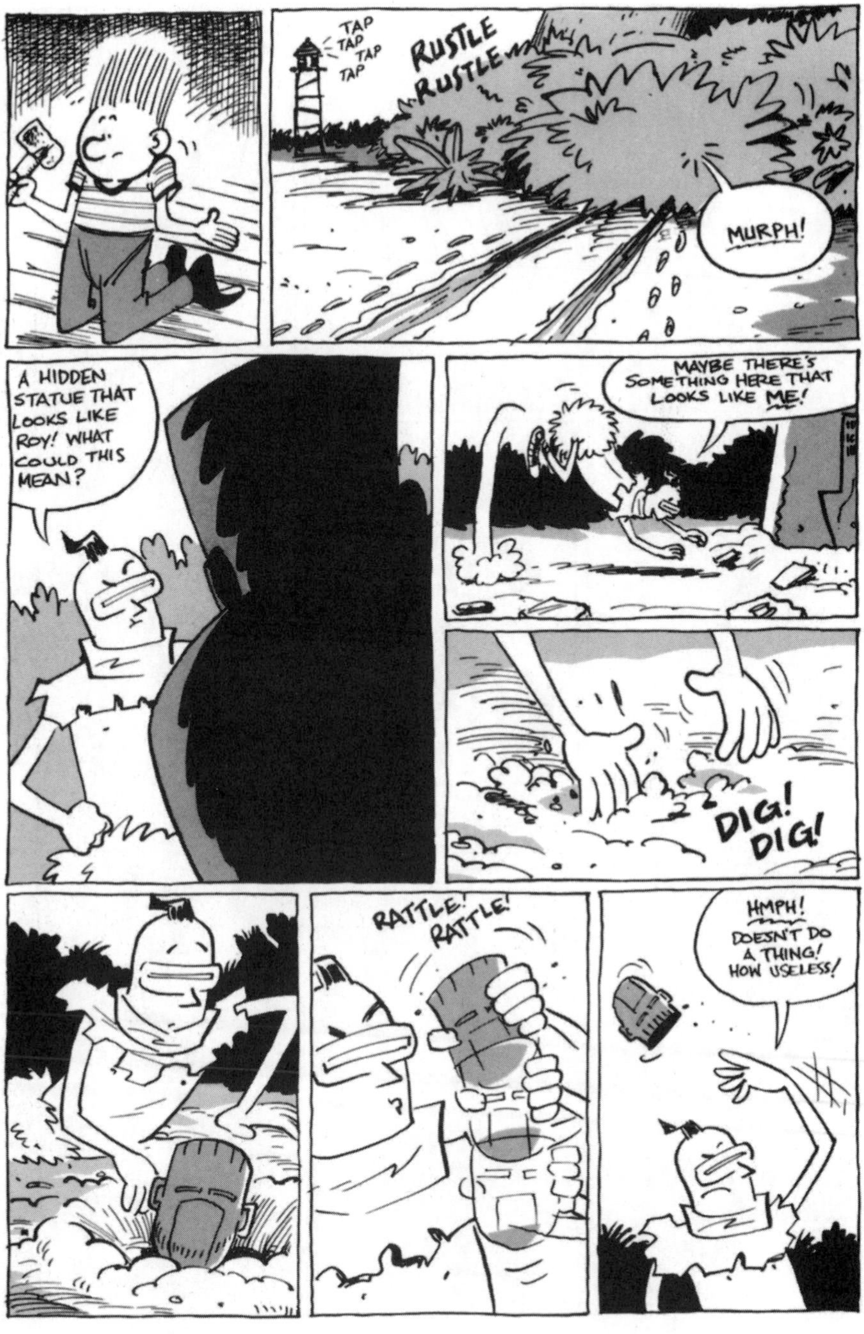
TAP
TAP
TAP
TAP
RUSTLE
RUSTLE
MURPH!
A HIDDEN STATUE THAT LOOKS LIKE ROY! WHAT COULD THIS MEAN?
MAYBE THERE'S SOMETHING HERE THAT LOOKS LIKE ME!
DIG! DIG!
RATTLE! RATTLE!
HMPH! DOESN'T DO A THING! HOW USELESS!

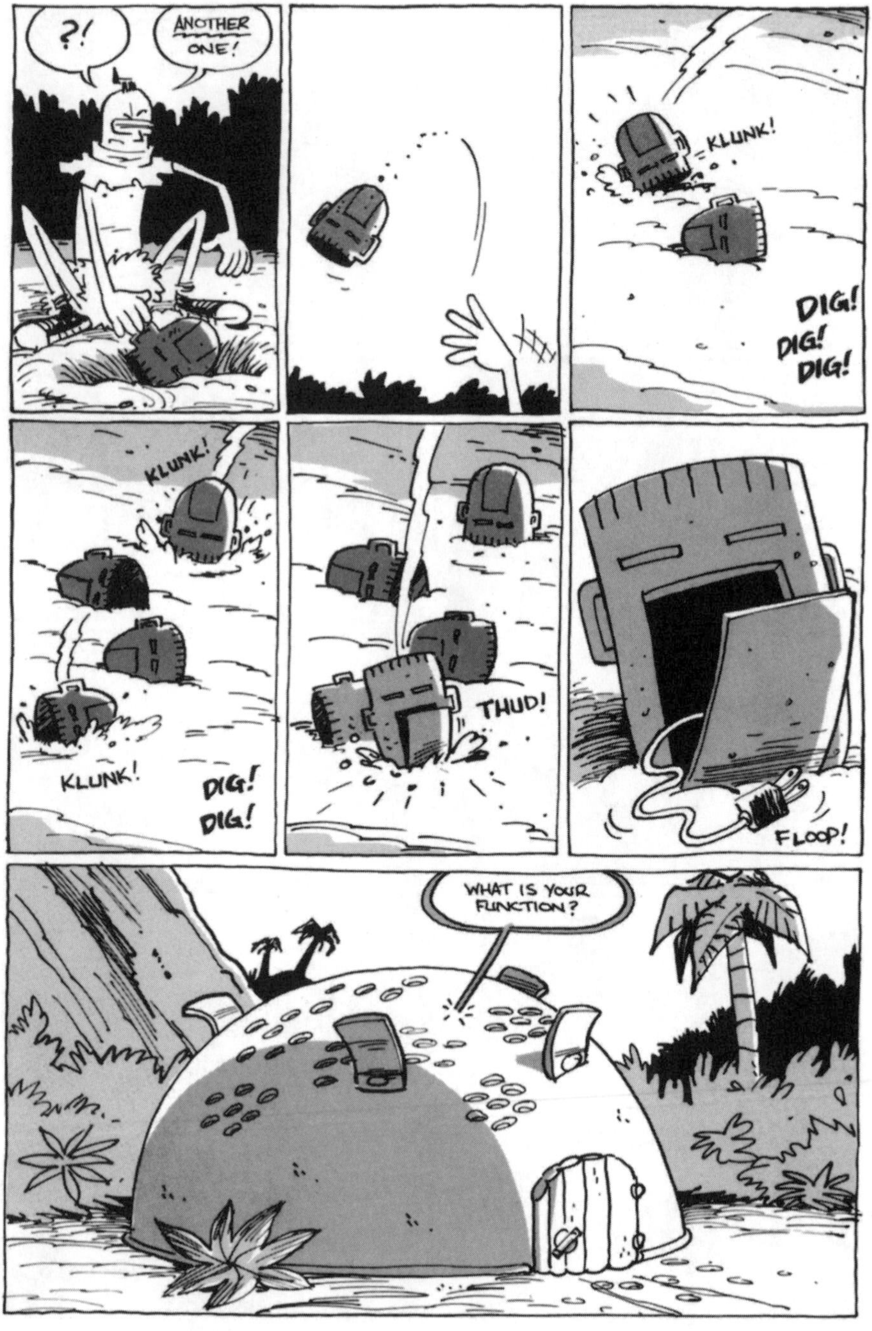
?!
ANOTHER ONE!
KLUNK!
DIG! DIG! DIG!
KLUNK!
KLUNK!
DIG! DIG!
THUD!
FLOOP!
WHAT IS YOUR FUNCTION?

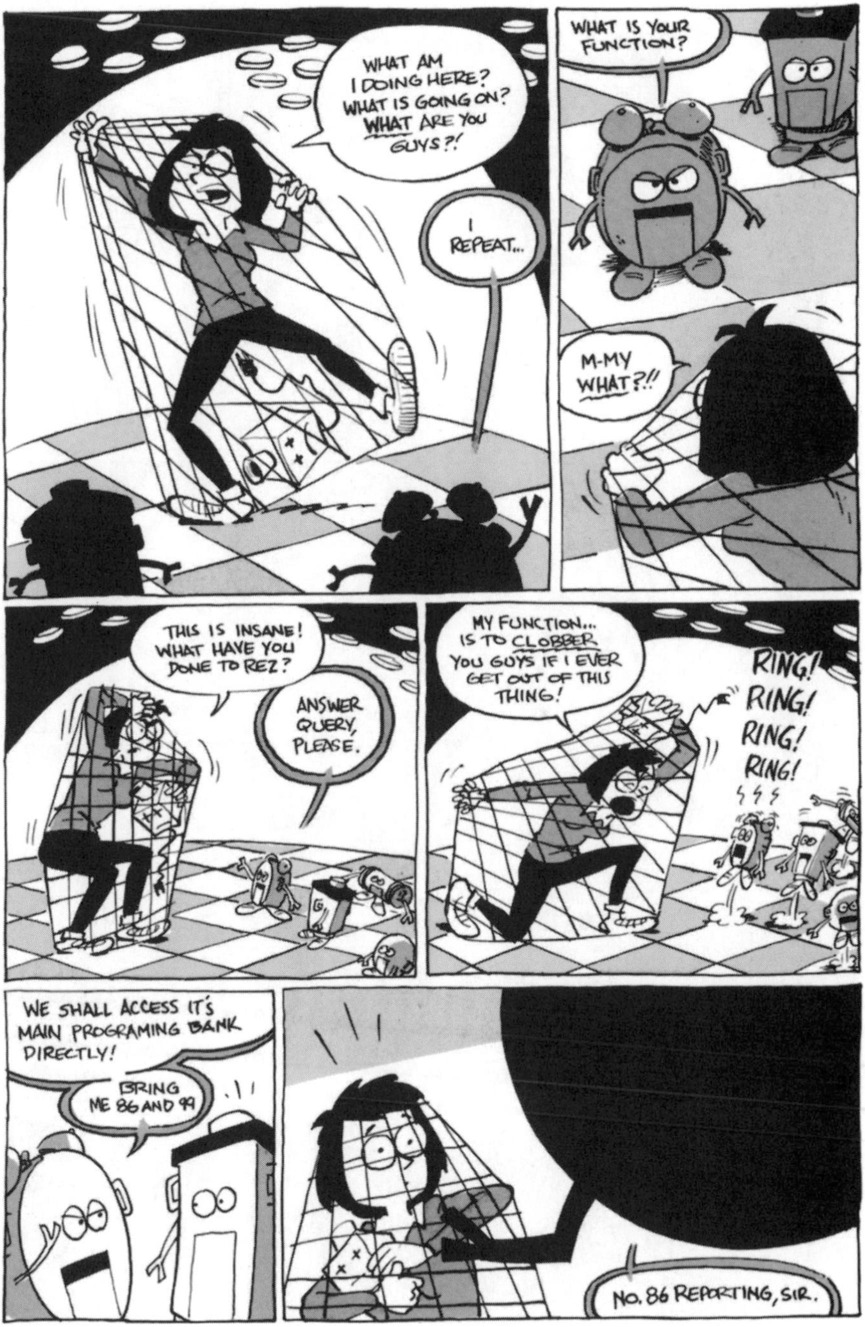
WHAT AM I DOING HERE? WHAT IS GOING ON? WHAT ARE YOU GUYS?!
I REPEAT...
WHAT IS YOUR FUNCTION?
M-MY WHAT?!!
THIS IS INSANE! WHAT HAVE YOU DONE TO REZ?
ANSWER QUERY, PLEASE.
MY FUNCTION... IS TO CLOBBER YOU GUYS IF I EVER GET OUT OF THIS THING!
RING! RING! RING! RING!
WE SHALL ACCESS IT'S MAIN PROGRAMING BANK DIRECTLY!
BRING ME 86 AND 99
NO. 86 REPORTING, SIR.

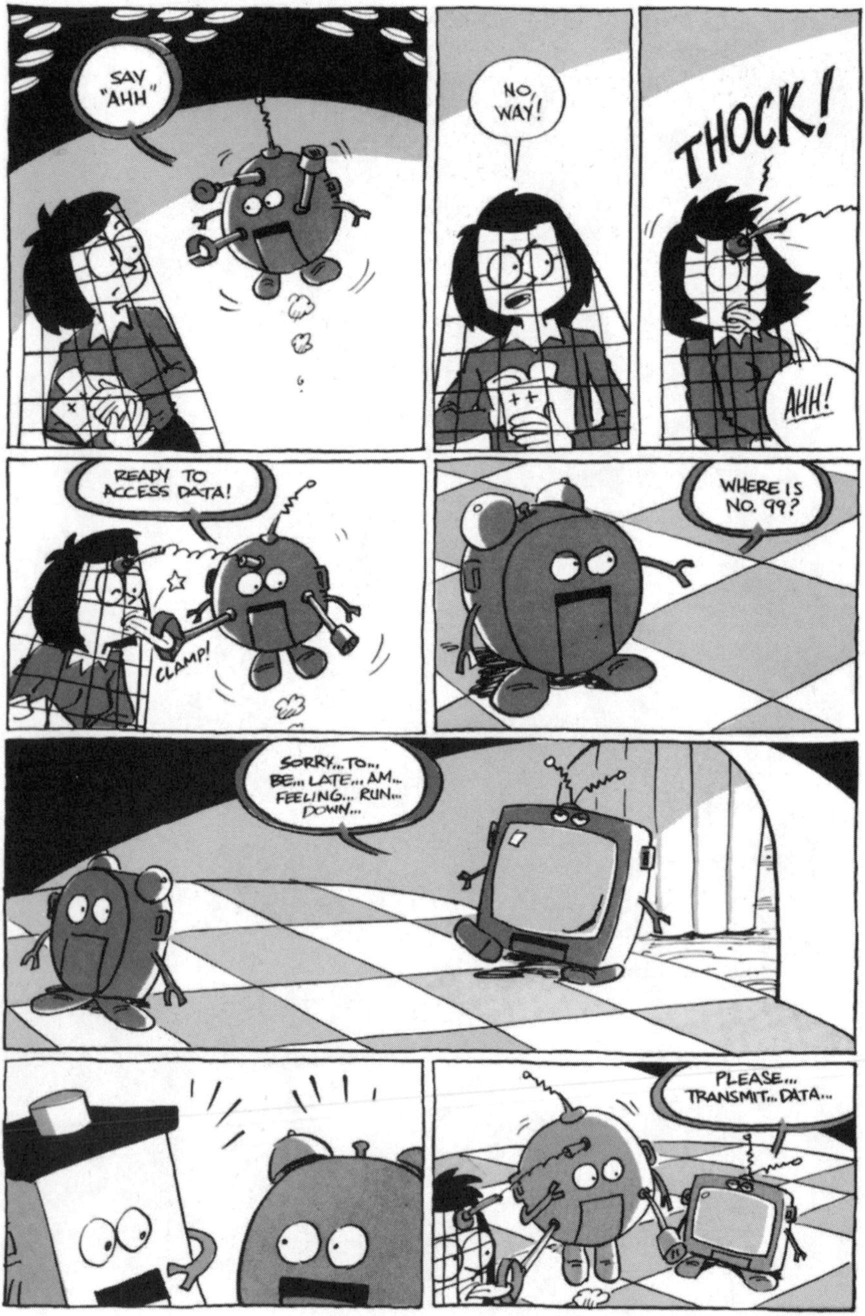
SAY "AHH"
NO, WAY!
THOCK!
AHH!
READY TO ACCESS DATA!
CLAMP!
WHERE IS NO. 99?
SORRY... TO... BE... LATE... AM... FEELING... RUN... DOWN...
PLEASE... TRANSMIT... DATA...

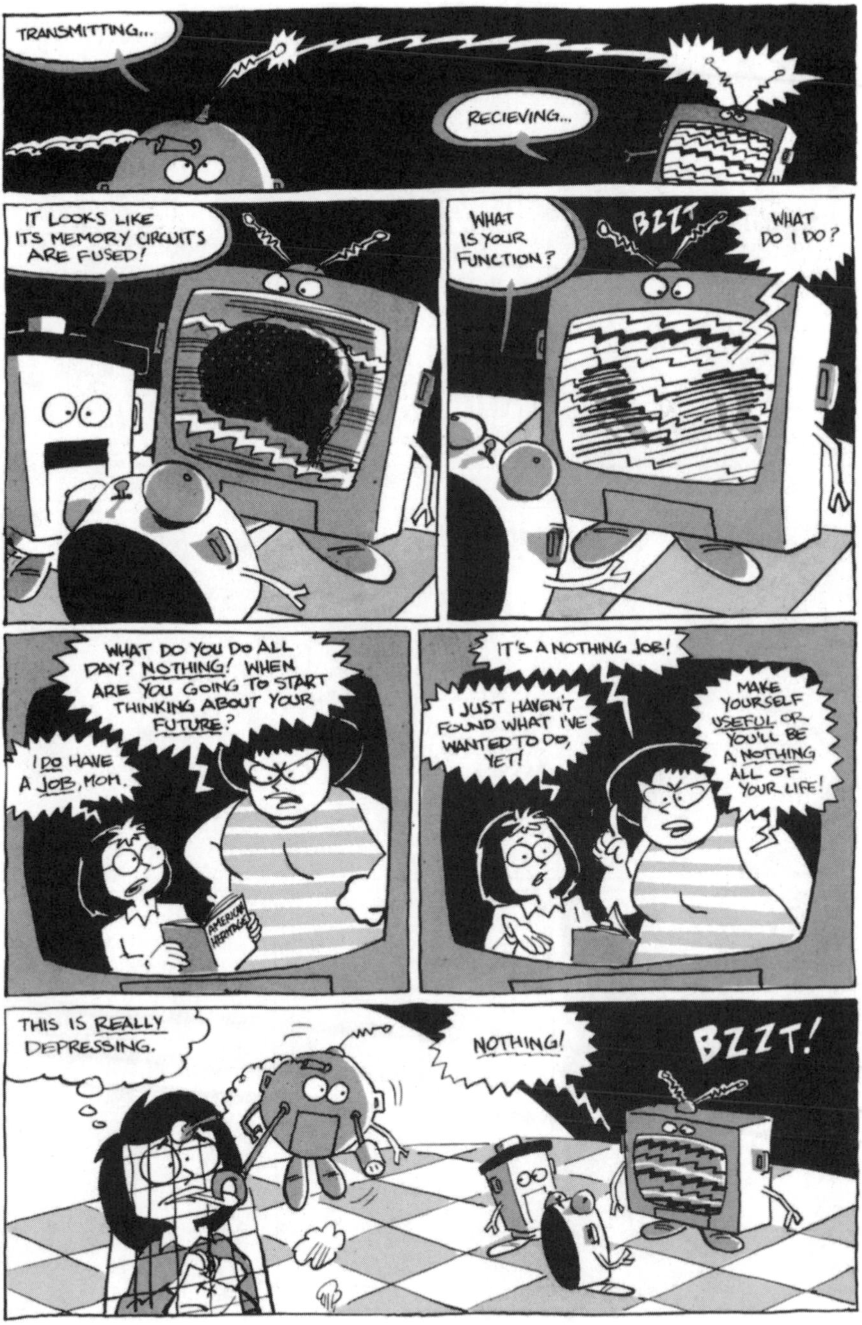
TRANSMITTING...
RECIEVING...
IT LOOKS LIKE ITS MEMORY CIRCUITS ARE FUSED!
WHAT IS YOUR FUNCTION?
BZZT
WHAT DO I DO?
WHAT DO YOU DO ALL DAY? NOTHING! WHEN ARE YOU GOING TO START THINKING ABOUT YOUR FUTURE?
I DO HAVE A JOB, MOM.
AMERICAN HERITAGE
IT'S A NOTHING JOB!
I JUST HAVEN'T FOUND WHAT I'VE WANTED TO DO, YET!
MAKE YOURSELF USEFUL OR YOU'LL BE A NOTHING ALL OF YOUR LIFE!
THIS IS REALLY DEPRESSING.
NOTHING!
BZZT!

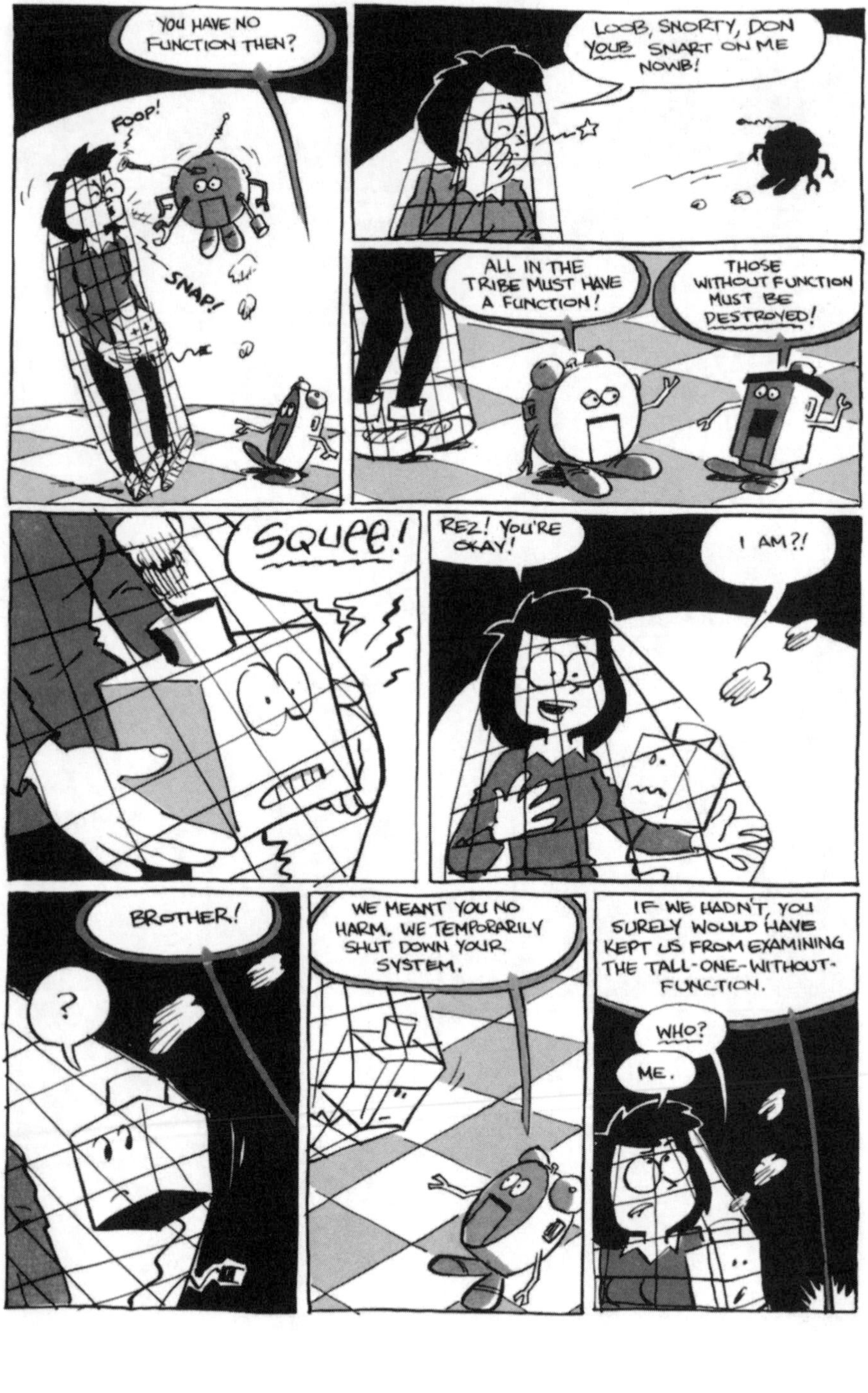

YOU HAVE NO FUNCTION THEN?
FOOP!
SNAP!
LOOB, SNORTY, DON YOUB SNART ON ME NOWB!
ALL IN THE TRIBE MUST HAVE A FUNCTION!
THOSE WITHOUT FUNCTION MUST BE DESTROYED!
SQUEE!
REZ! YOU'RE OKAY!
I AM?!
BROTHER!
?
WE MEANT YOU NO HARM. WE TEMPORARILY SHUT DOWN YOUR SYSTEM.
IF WE HADN'T, YOU SURELY WOULD HAVE KEPT US FROM EXAMINING THE TALL-ONE-WITHOUT-FUNCTION.
WHO?
ME.

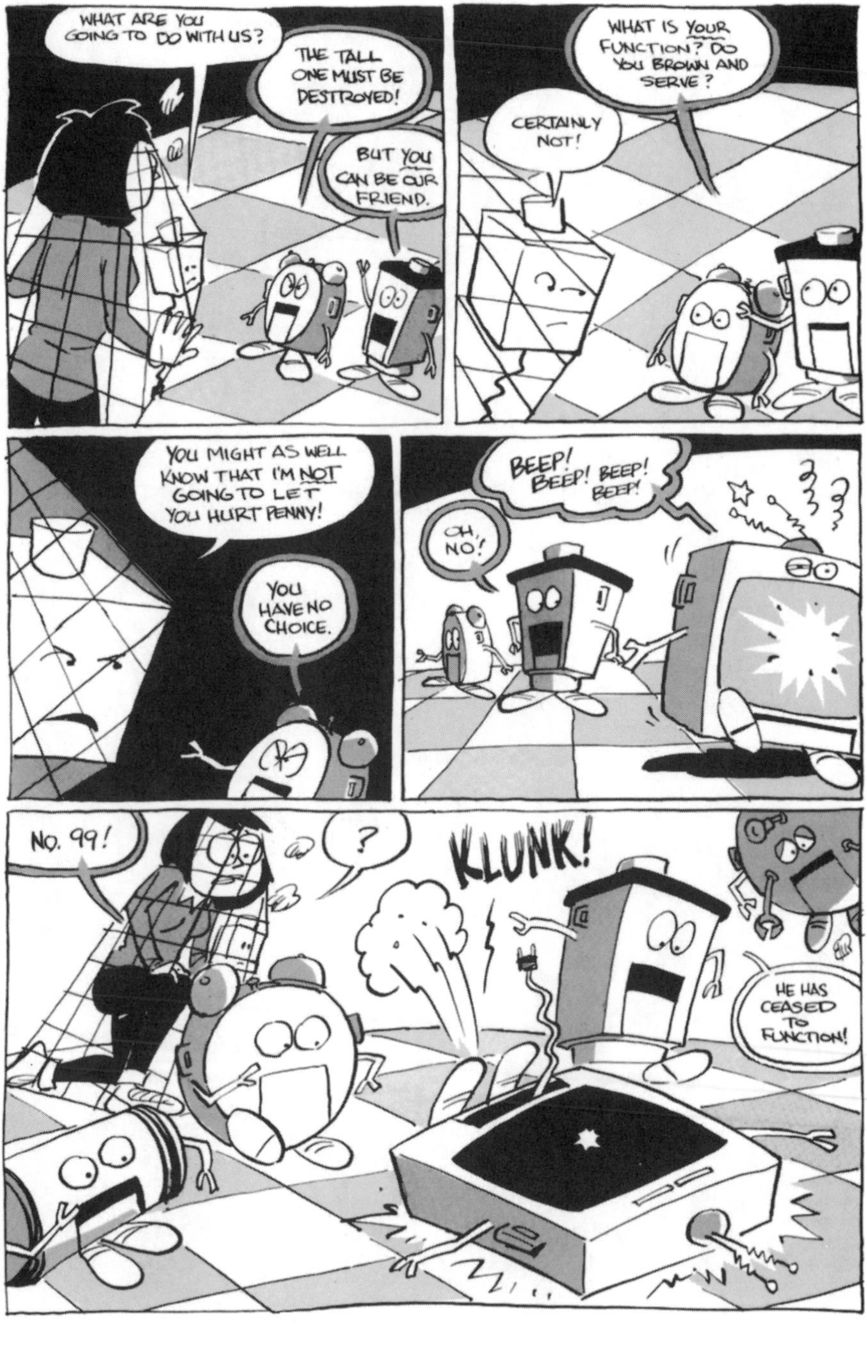
WHAT ARE YOU GOING TO DO WITH US?
THE TALL ONE MUST BE DESTROYED!
BUT YOU CAN BE OUR FRIEND.
WHAT IS YOUR FUNCTION? DO YOU BROWN AND SERVE?
CERTAINLY NOT!
YOU MIGHT AS WELL KNOW THAT I'M NOT GOING TO LET YOU HURT PENNY!
YOU HAVE NO CHOICE.
BEEP! BEEP! BEEP! BEEP!
OH, NO!
NO. 99!
?
KLUNK!
HE HAS CEASED TO FUNCTION!

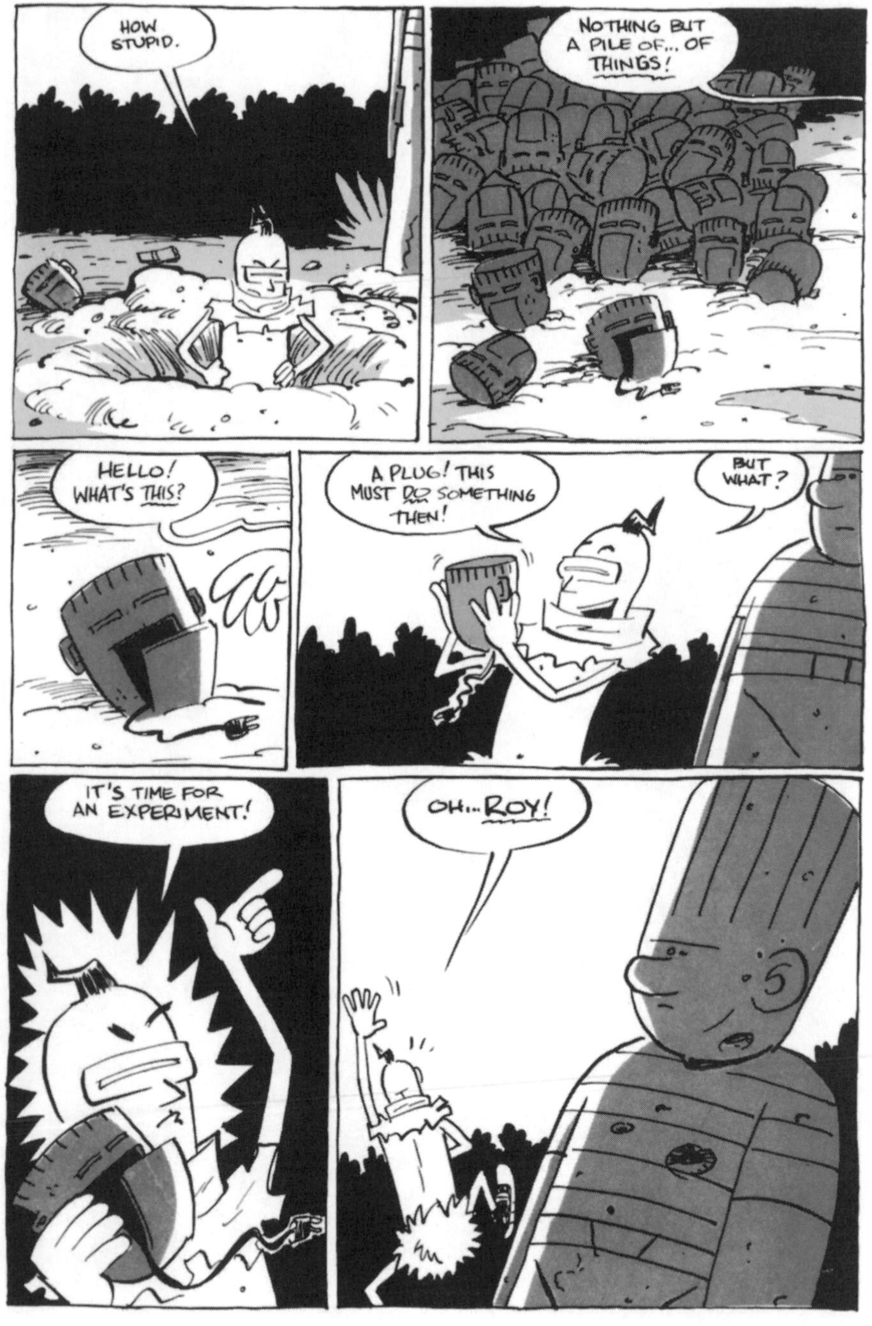
HOW STUPID.
NOTHING BUT A PILE OF... OF THINGS!
HELLO! WHAT'S THIS?
A PLUG! THIS MUST DO SOMETHING THEN!
BUT WHAT?
IT'S TIME FOR AN EXPERIMENT!
OH... ROY!

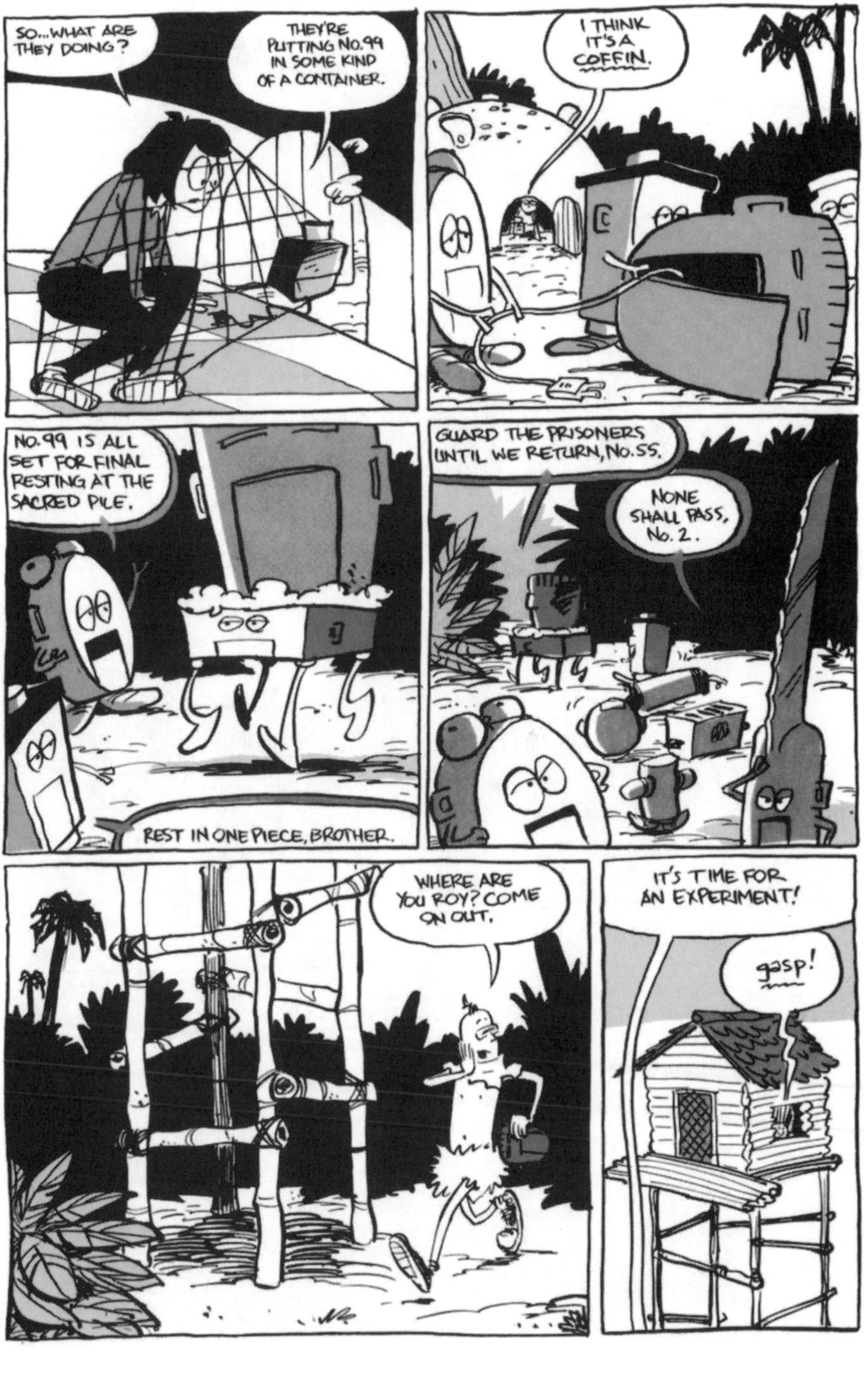
SO...WHAT ARE THEY DOING?
THEY'RE PUTTING No.99 IN SOME KIND OF A CONTAINER.
I THINK IT'S A COFFIN.
No.99 IS ALL SET FOR FINAL RESTING AT THE SACRED PILE.
REST IN ONE PIECE, BROTHER.
GUARD THE PRISONERS UNTIL WE RETURN, No.55.
NONE SHALL PASS, No. 2.
WHERE ARE YOU ROY? COME ON OUT.
IT'S TIME FOR AN EXPERIMENT!
gasp!

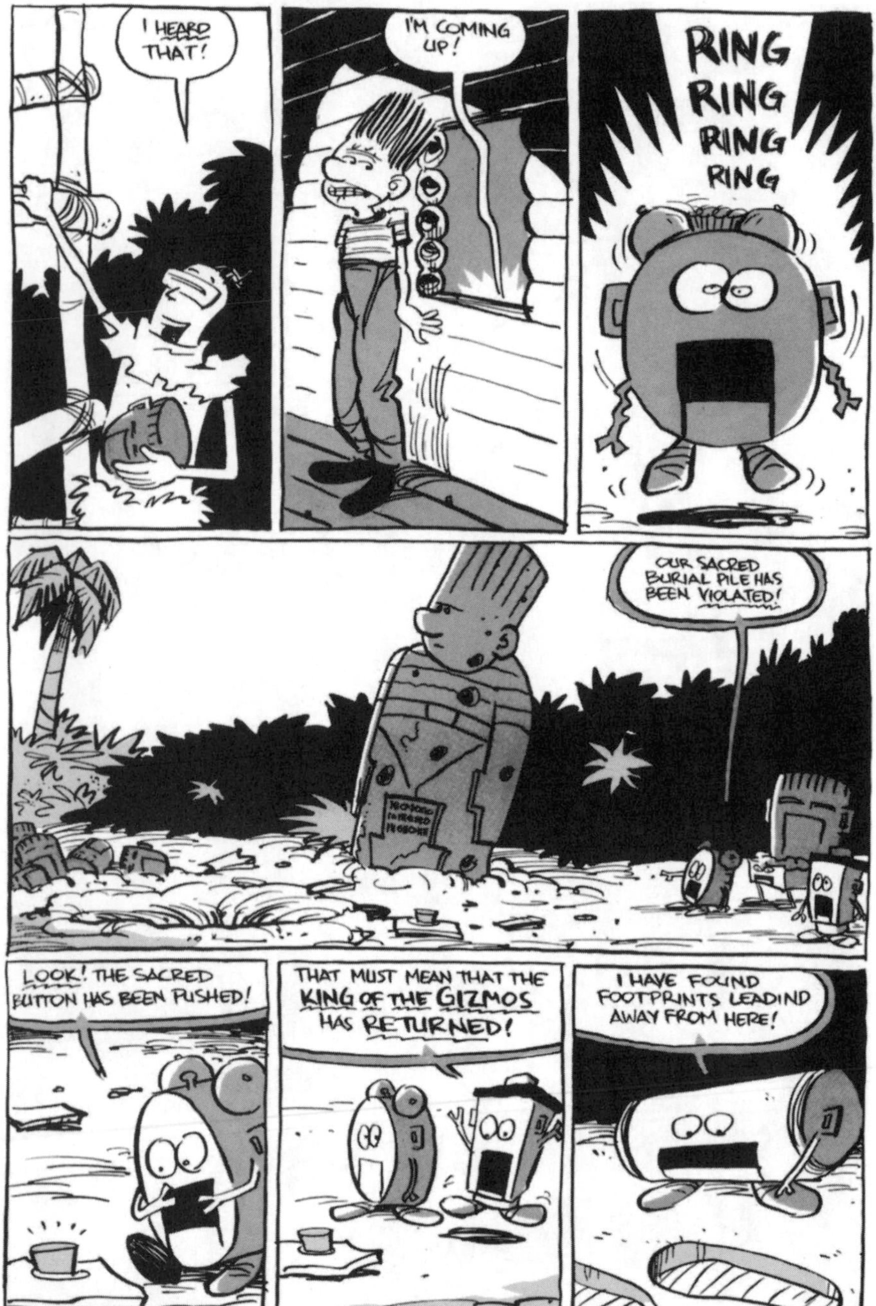

I HEARD THAT!
I'M COMING UP!
RING RING RING RING
OUR SACRED BURIAL PILE HAS BEEN VIOLATED!
LOOK! THE SACRED BUTTON HAS BEEN PUSHED!
THAT MUST MEAN THAT THE KING OF THE GIZMOS HAS RETURNED!
I HAVE FOUND FOOTPRINTS LEADIND AWAY FROM HERE!

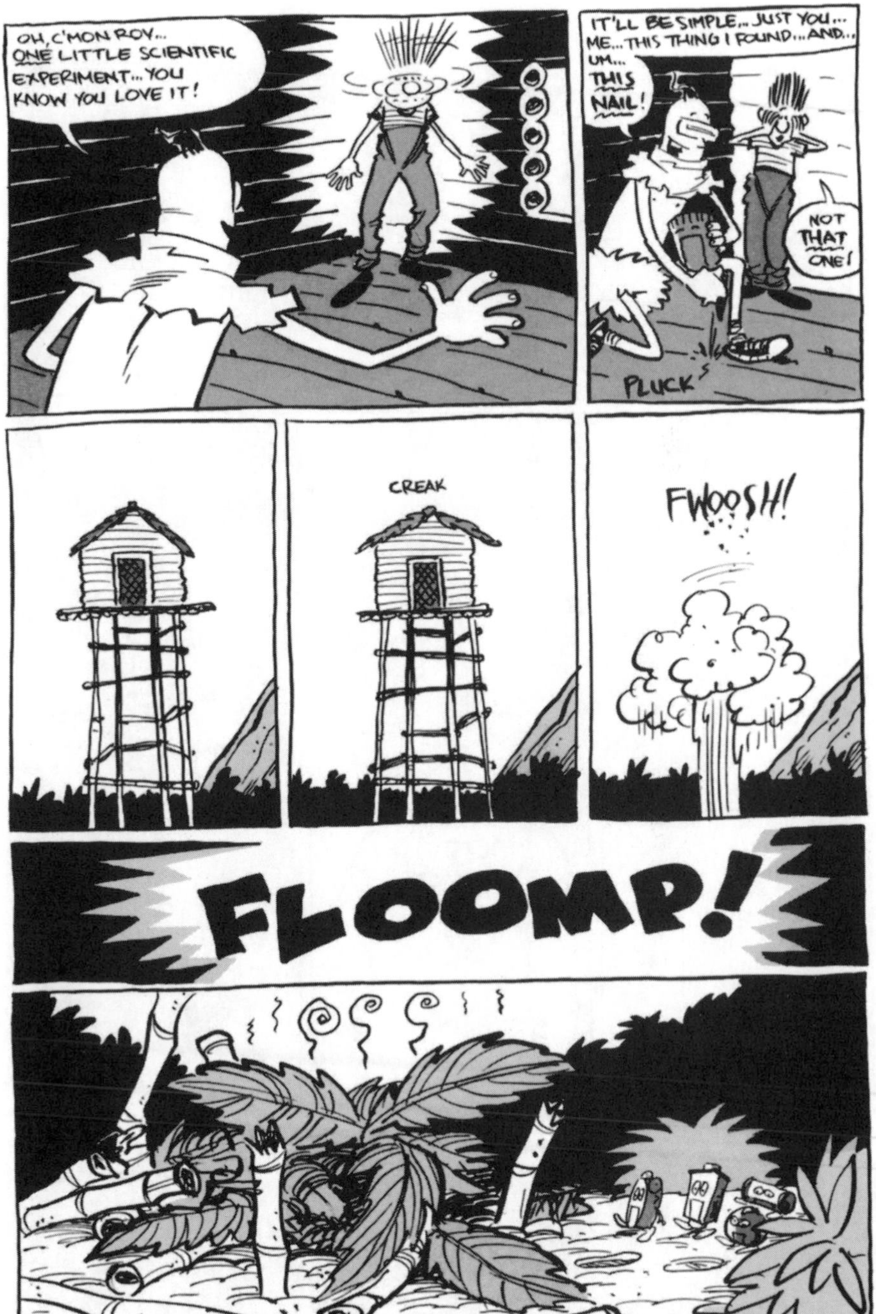

OH, C'MON ROY... ONE LITTLE SCIENTIFIC EXPERIMENT... YOU KNOW YOU LOVE IT!
IT'LL BE SIMPLE... JUST YOU... ME... THIS THING I FOUND... AND... UM... THIS NAIL!
NOT THAT ONE!
PLUCK
CREAK
FWOOSH!
FLOOMP!

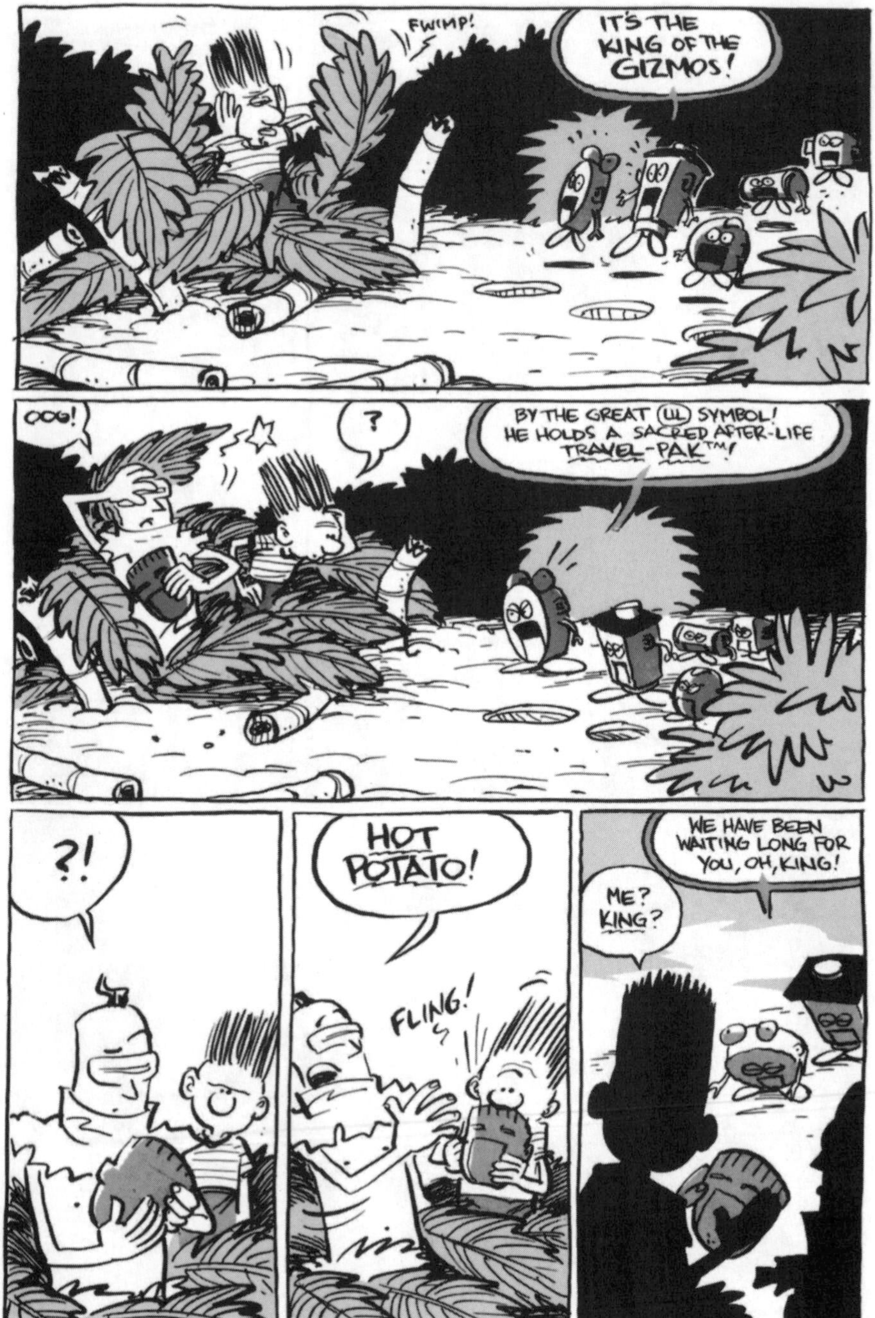
FWIMP!
IT'S THE KING OF THE GIZMOS!
OOG!
?
BY THE GREAT (LL) SYMBOL! HE HOLDS A SACRED AFTER-LIFE TRAVEL-PAK™!
?!
HOT POTATO!
FLING!
WE HAVE BEEN WAITING LONG FOR YOU, OH, KING!
ME? KING?

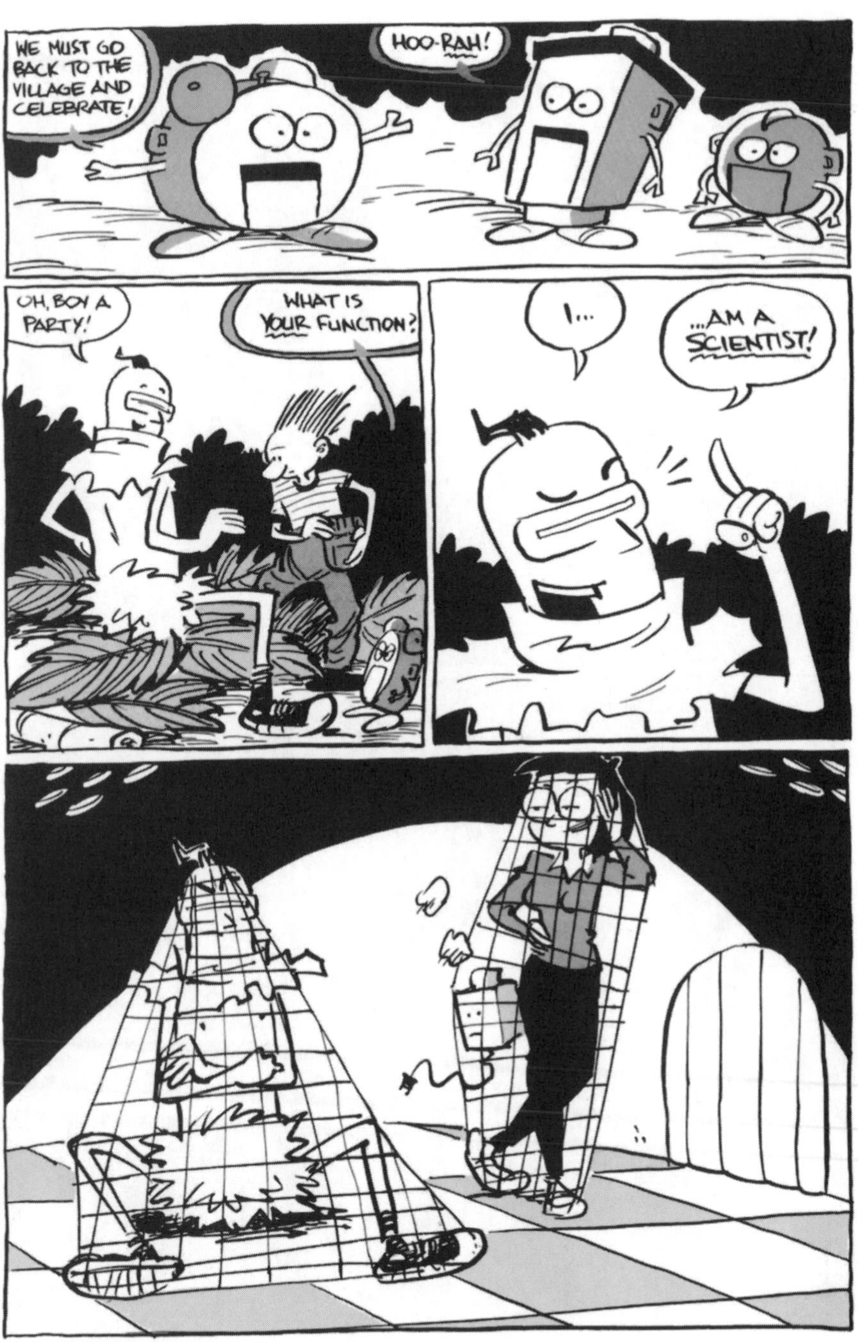
WE MUST GO BACK TO THE VILLAGE AND CELEBRATE!
HOO-RAH!
OH, BOY A PARTY!
WHAT IS YOUR FUNCTION?
I...
...AM A SCIENTIST!

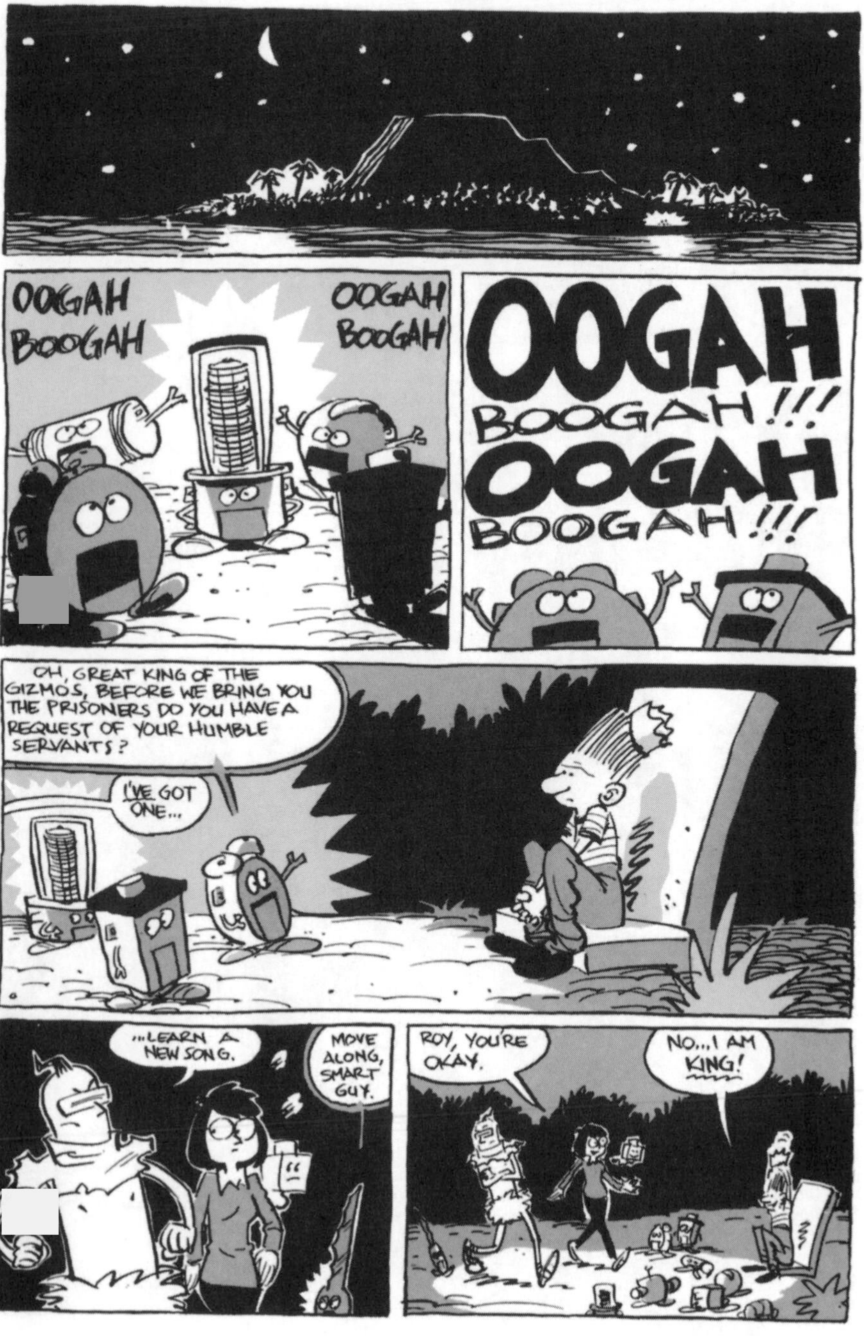
OOGAH BOOGAH
OOGAH BOOGAH
OOGAH BOOGAH!!! OOGAH BOOGAH!!!
OH, GREAT KING OF THE GIZMOS, BEFORE WE BRING YOU THE PRISONERS DO YOU HAVE A REQUEST OF YOUR HUMBLE SERVANTS?
I'VE GOT ONE...
...LEARN A NEW SONG.
MOVE ALONG, SMART GUY.
ROY, YOU'RE OKAY.
NO...I AM KING!

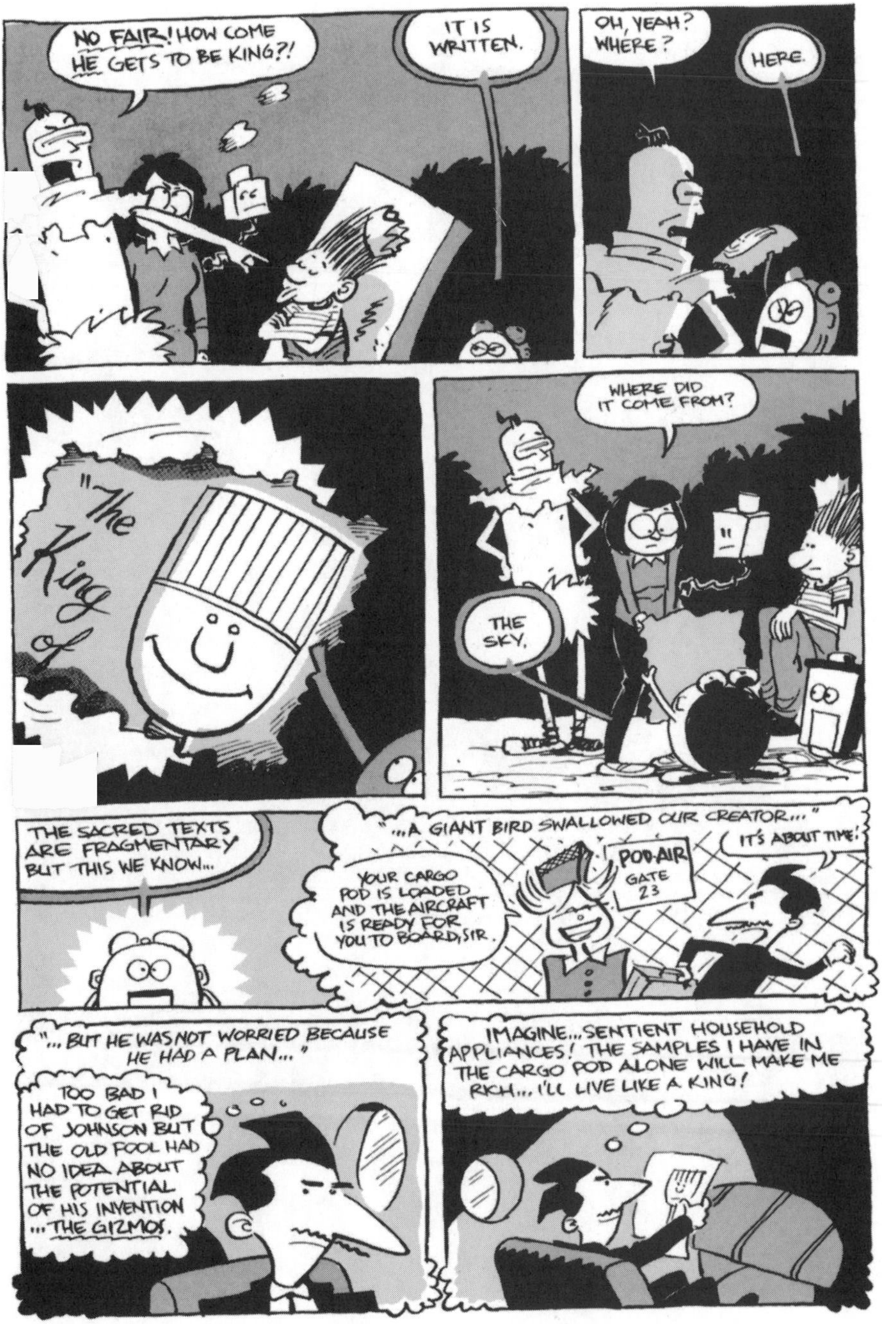
NO FAIR! HOW COME HE GETS TO BE KING?!
IT IS WRITTEN.
OH, YEAH? WHERE?
HERE.
"The King of
WHERE DID IT COME FROM?
THE SKY.
THE SACRED TEXTS ARE FRAGMENTARY BUT THIS WE KNOW...
"...A GIANT BIRD SWALLOWED OUR CREATOR..."
YOUR CARGO POD IS LOADED AND THE AIRCRAFT IS READY FOR YOU TO BOARD, SIR.
POD-AIR GATE 23
IT'S ABOUT TIME!
"...BUT HE WAS NOT WORRIED BECAUSE HE HAD A PLAN..."
TOO BAD I HAD TO GET RID OF JOHNSON BUT THE OLD FOOL HAD NO IDEA ABOUT THE POTENTIAL OF HIS INVENTION ...THE GIZMOS.
IMAGINE... SENTIENT HOUSEHOLD APPLIANCES! THE SAMPLES I HAVE IN THE CARGO POD ALONE WILL MAKE ME RICH... I'LL LIVE LIKE A KING!

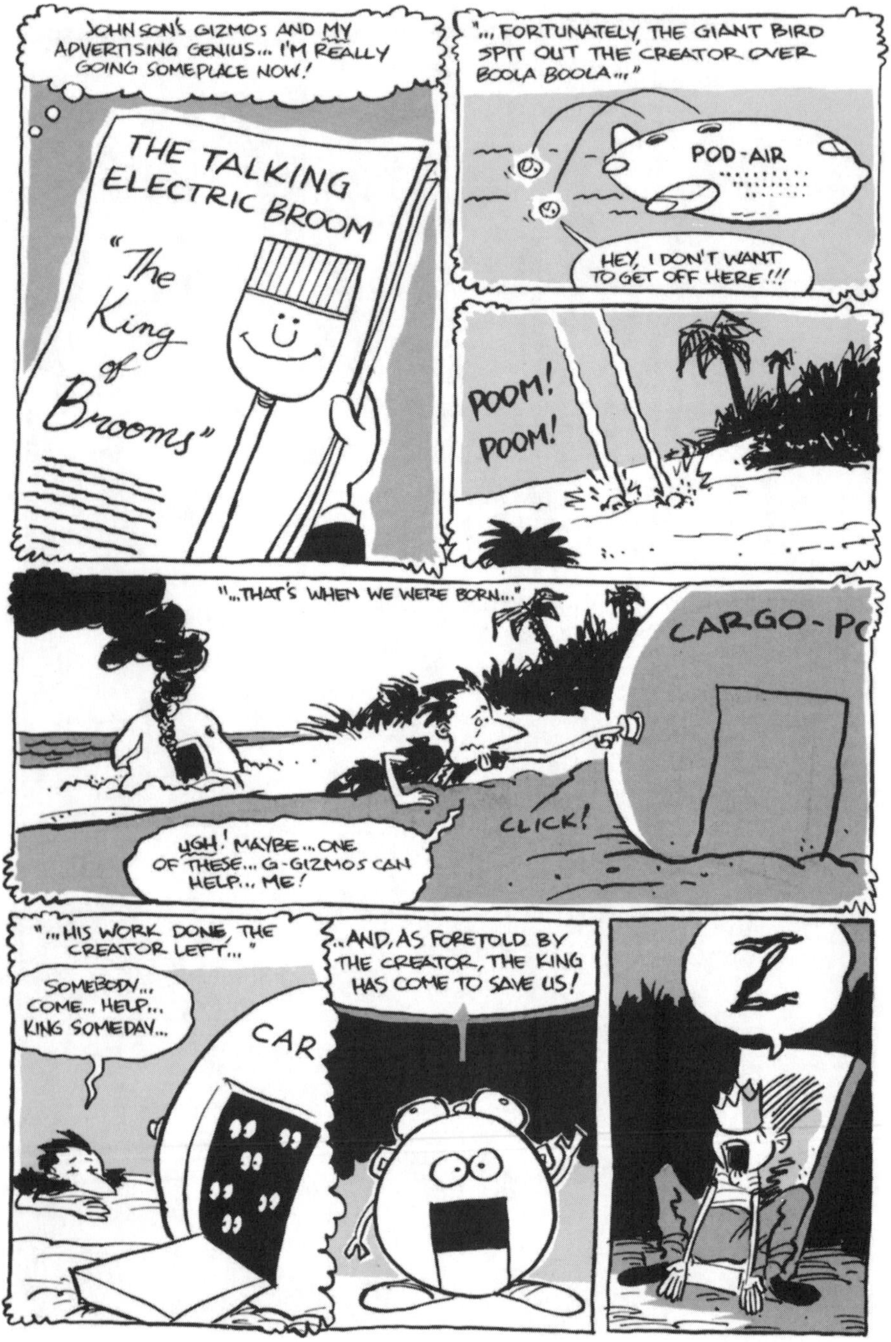
JOHNSON'S GIZMOS AND MY ADVERTISING GENIUS... I'M REALLY GOING SOMEPLACE NOW!
THE TALKING ELECTRIC BROOM
"The King of Brooms"
"... FORTUNATELY, THE GIANT BIRD SPIT OUT THE CREATOR OVER BOOLA BOOLA..."
POD-AIR
HEY, I DON'T WANT TO GET OFF HERE!!!
POOM! POOM!
"...THAT'S WHEN WE WERE BORN..."
CARGO-PO
CLICK!
UGH! MAYBE...ONE OF THESE... G-GIZMOS CAN HELP... ME!
"...HIS WORK DONE, THE CREATOR LEFT..."
SOMEBODY... COME... HELP... KING SOMEDAY...
CAR
..AND, AS FORETOLD BY THE CREATOR, THE KING HAS COME TO SAVE US!
Z

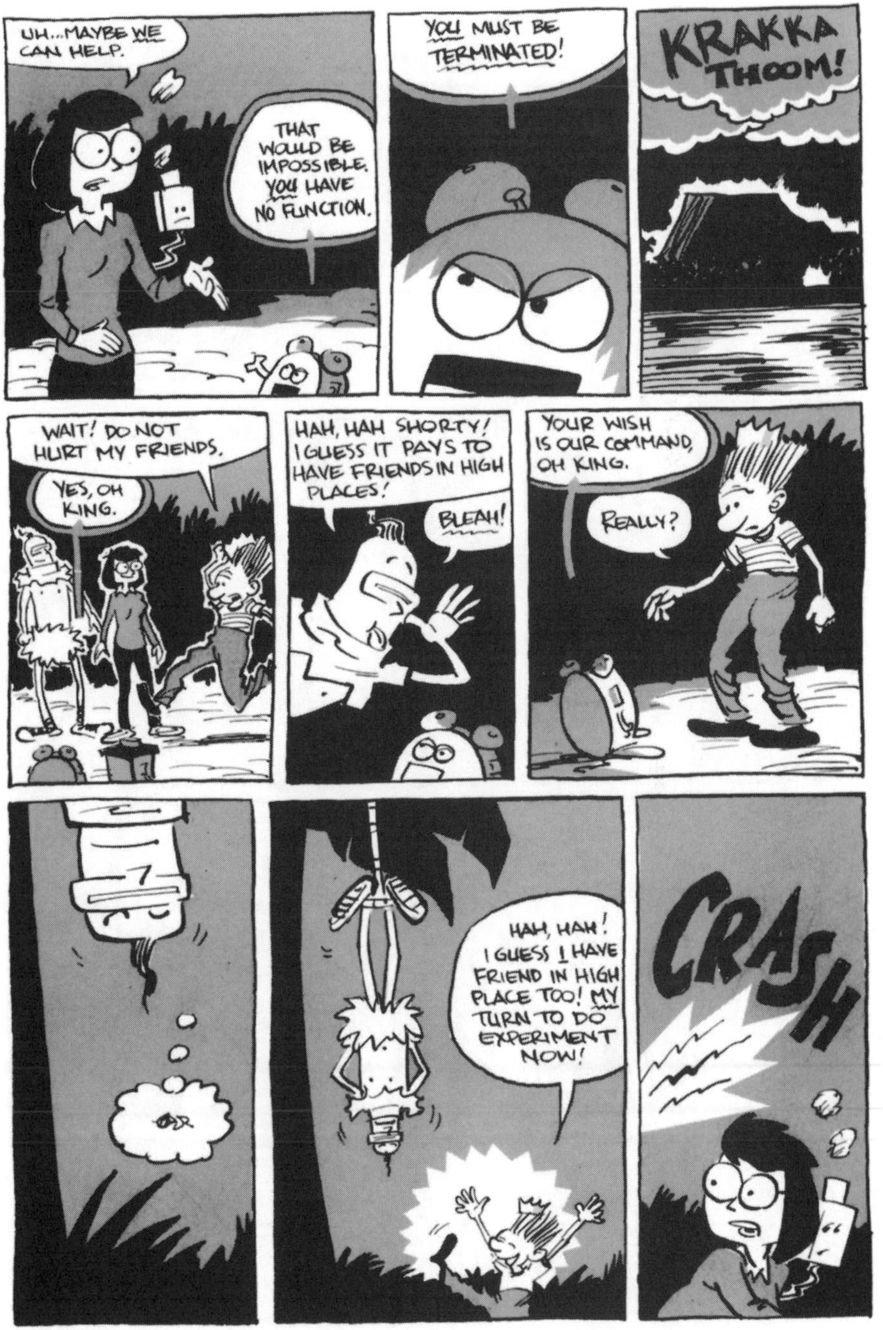
UH...MAYBE WE CAN HELP.
THAT WOULD BE IMPOSSIBLE. YOU HAVE NO FUNCTION.
YOU MUST BE TERMINATED!
KRAKKA THOOM!
WAIT! DO NOT HURT MY FRIENDS.
YES, OH KING.
HAH, HAH SHORTY! I GUESS IT PAYS TO HAVE FRIENDS IN HIGH PLACES!
BLEAH!
YOUR WISH IS OUR COMMAND, OH KING.
REALLY?
HAH, HAH! I GUESS I HAVE FRIEND IN HIGH PLACE TOO! MY TURN TO DO EXPERIMENT NOW!
CRASH

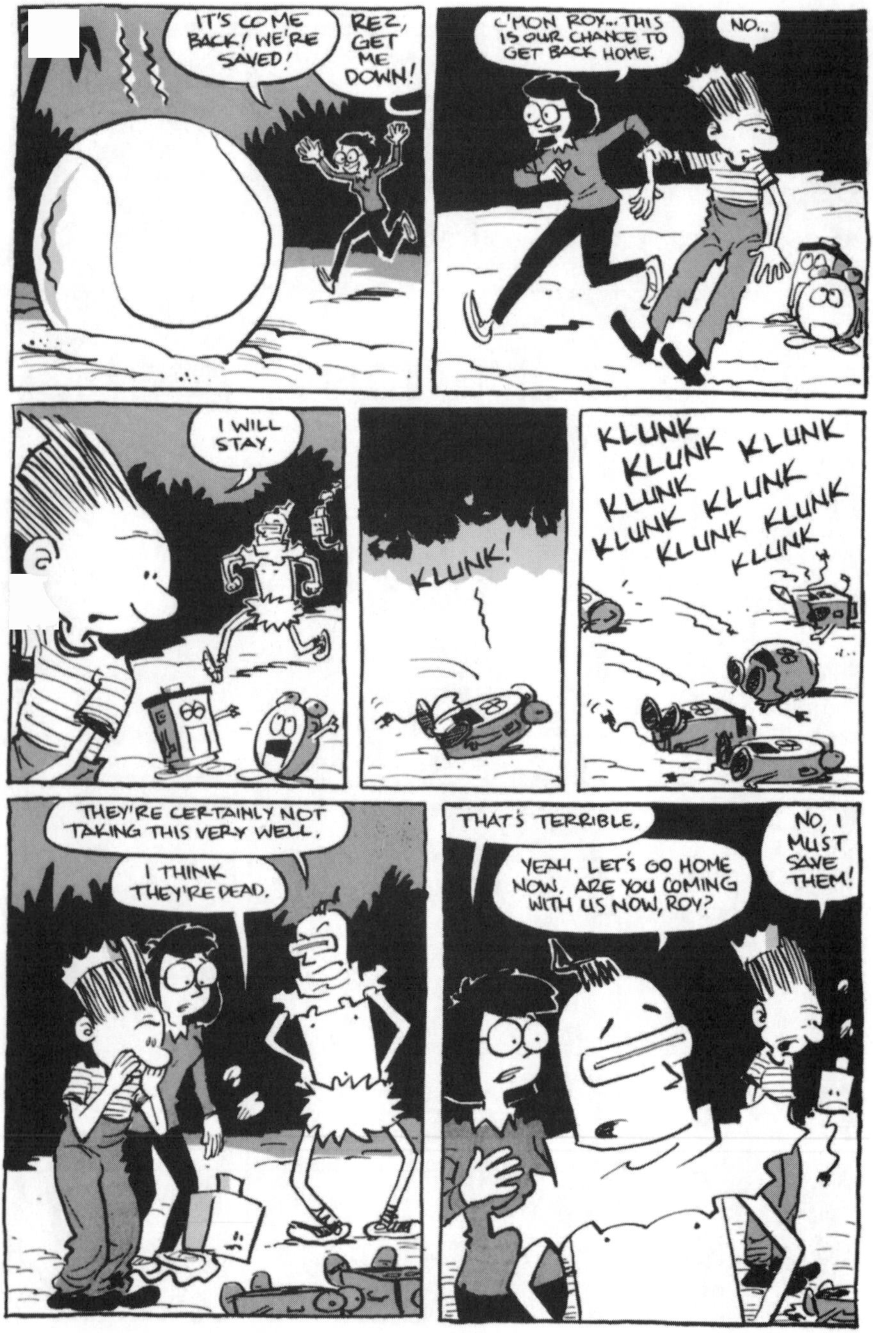
IT'S COME BACK! WE'RE SAVED!
REZ, GET ME DOWN!
C'MON ROY... THIS IS OUR CHANCE TO GET BACK HOME.
NO...
I WILL STAY.
KLUNK!
KLUNK KLUNK KLUNK KLUNK KLUNK KLUNK KLUNK KLUNK KLUNK KLUNK
THEY'RE CERTAINLY NOT TAKING THIS VERY WELL.
I THINK THEY'RE DEAD.
THAT'S TERRIBLE.
YEAH. LET'S GO HOME NOW. ARE YOU COMING WITH US NOW, ROY?
NO, I MUST SAVE THEM!

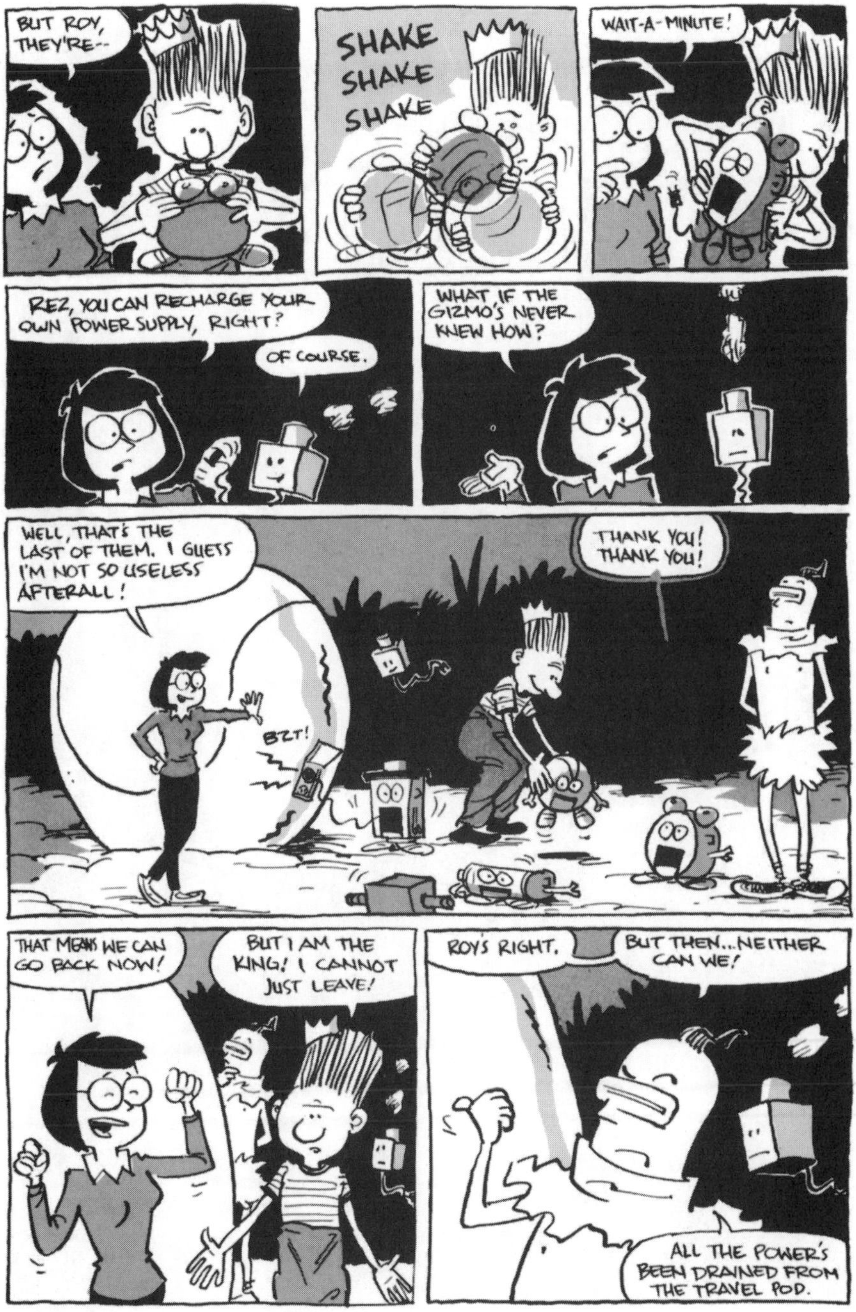
BUT ROY, THEY'RE--
SHAKE SHAKE SHAKE
WAIT-A-MINUTE!
REZ, YOU CAN RECHARGE YOUR OWN POWER SUPPLY, RIGHT?
OF COURSE.
WHAT IF THE GIZMO'S NEVER KNEW HOW?
WELL, THAT'S THE LAST OF THEM. I GUESS I'M NOT SO USELESS AFTERALL!
THANK YOU! THANK YOU!
BZZT!
THAT MEANS WE CAN GO BACK NOW!
BUT I AM THE KING! I CANNOT JUST LEAVE!
ROY'S RIGHT.
BUT THEN...NEITHER CAN WE!
ALL THE POWER'S BEEN DRAINED FROM THE TRAVEL POD.

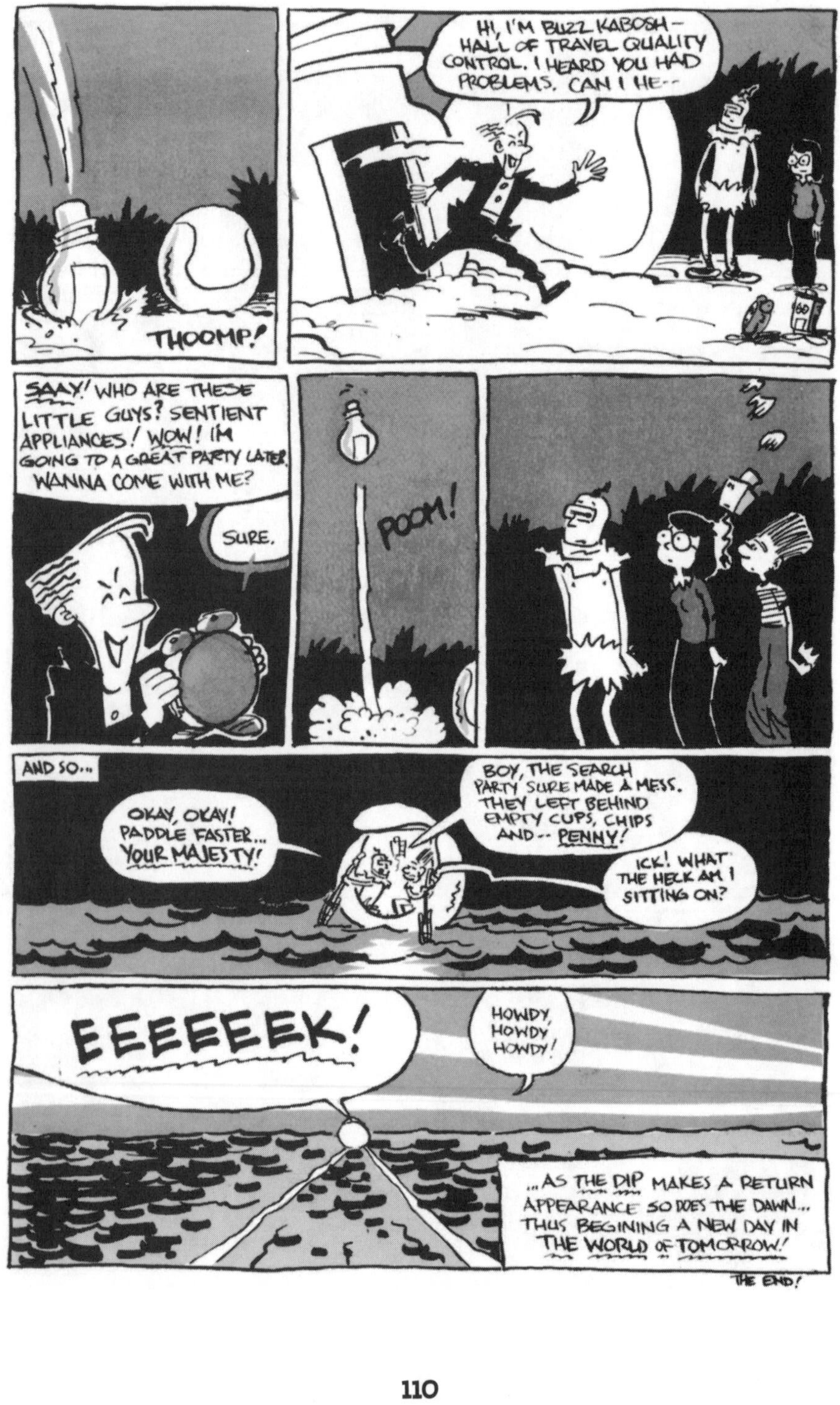
THOOMP!
HI, I'M BUZZ KABOSH - HALL OF TRAVEL QUALITY CONTROL. I HEARD YOU HAD PROBLEMS. CAN I HE--
SAAY! WHO ARE THESE LITTLE GUYS? SENTIENT APPLIANCES! WOW! I'M GOING TO A GREAT PARTY LATER. WANNA COME WITH ME?
SURE.
POOM!
AND SO...
OKAY, OKAY! PADDLE FASTER... YOUR MAJESTY!
BOY, THE SEARCH PARTY SURE MADE A MESS. THEY LEFT BEHIND EMPTY CUPS, CHIPS AND -- PENNY!
ICK! WHAT THE HECK AM I SITTING ON?
EEEEEEK!
HOWDY, HOWDY, HOWDY!
...AS THE DIP MAKES A RETURN APPEARANCE SO DOES THE DAWN... THUS BEGINING A NEW DAY IN THE WORLD OF TOMORROW!
THE END!

About the Author!

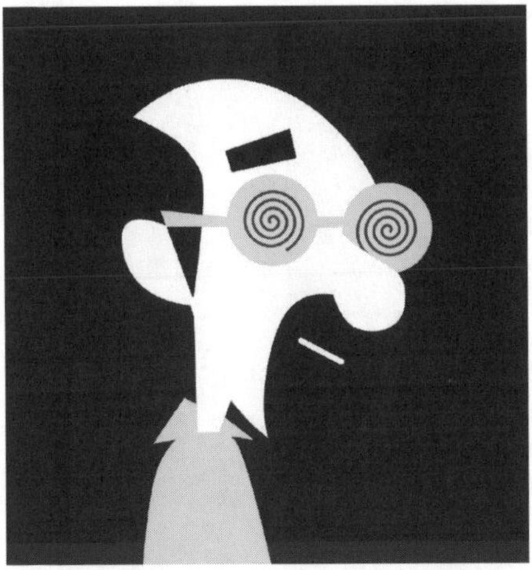

Scott Saavedra caught the Cartooning Bug early. His parents gave him plenty of liquids and saw to it that he had lots of rest but, alas, his condition remains as acute as it has ever been. Perhaps someday Science will find a cure. Until that time, he remains happily married to Ruth, a very nice lady copy editor (of Scientific Texts!). Their two kids, Edward and Kate, are so entertaining, scientifically speaking, that occasionally Scott's eyes exhibit a puzzling, rotating pattern. Curious.

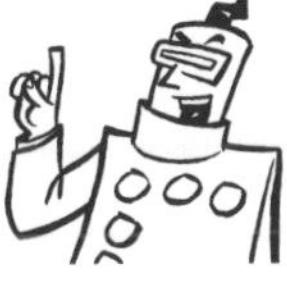

Coming Soon!

The Dr. Radium Collection Volume Three

For more information visit: **www.slavelabor.com** and **www.scottsaavedra.com**